P9-ARG-899

The Congressional Budget Process after Five Years

A Conference Sponsored by the American Enterprise Institute for Public Policy Research

The Congressional Budget Process after Five Years

Edited by Rudolph G. Penner

American Enterprise Institute for Public Policy Research
Washington and London

Library of Congress Cataloging in Publication Data
Main entry under title:

The Congressional budget process after five years.

(AEI symposia ; 81H)
Contents: Five years of congressional budgeting / Allen Schick — The CBO's policy analysis / Preston J. Miller and Arthur J. Rolnick — Commentary / Robert Hartman, William Beeman, John T. McEvoy — [etc.]
1. Budget — United States — Addresses, essays, lectures. I. Penner, Rudolph Gerhard, 1936– . II. American Enterprise Institute for Public Policy Research. III. Series.
HJ2051.C66 353.0072'2 81–8000
ISBN 0–8447–2219–7 AACR2
ISBN 0–8447–2218–9 (pbk.)

AEI Symposia 81H

Printed in the United States of America

The American Enterprise Institute for Public Policy Research, established in 1943, is a publicly supported, nonpartisan, research and educational organization. Its purpose is to assist policy makers, scholars, businessmen, the press, and the public by providing objective analysis of national and international issues. Views expressed in the institute's publications are those of the authors and do not necessarily reflect the views of the staff, advisory panels, officers, or trustees of AEI.

Contributors

Bruce Bartlett
Legislative Assistant, Office of Senator Roger Jepsen (Republican, Iowa)

William Beeman
Assistant Director, Fiscal Analysis, Congressional Budget Office

Edward Clarke
Management Analyst, Office of Management and Budget

Kenneth W. Dam
Harold J. and Marion F. Green Professor of Law and Director of the Law and Economic Program, University of Chicago

Bruce Davie
Chief Tax Economist, House Ways and Means Committee

Frank de Leeuw
Chief Statistician, Bureau of Economic Analysis

Steven Entin
Economist, Joint Economic Committee

Louis Fisher
Specialist, American National Government, Congressional Research Service

Robert Hartman
Senior Fellow, The Brookings Institution

Joel Havemann
Deputy Editor, *National Journal*

William Lilley III
Vice President, Government Affairs, American Express Inc.

John T. McEvoy
Staff Director, Senate Budget Committee

Preston J. Miller
Senior Economist, Federal Reserve Bank of Minneapolis

Donald G. Ogilvie
Associate Dean, School of Organization and Management, Yale University

Jan Olsen
Legislative Assistant, Office of Senator Orrin Hatch (Republican, Utah)

Attiat Ott
Professor of Economics, Clark University

Rudolph Penner
Director of Tax Policy Studies, American Enterprise Institute

Alice Rivlin
Director, Congressional Budget Office

Arthur J. Rolnick
Assistant Vice President for Regional and Banking Studies,
Federal Reserve Bank of Minneapolis

Allen Schick
Senior Specialist, American Government and Public Administration,
Congressional Research Service

David Sitrin
Deputy Associate Director, National Security,
Office of Management and Budget

Aaron Wildavsky
Professor of Political Science, University of California at Berkeley

Timothy E. Wirth
United States Congressman (Democrat, Colorado)

Contents

Foreword

Although the press and the public often focus on the budget recommendations of the president, budgets are made and unmade in Congress. It has always been thus, since our Constitution clearly requires a congressional appropriation before money can be spent by a president. A president has some negative power in that appropriations can be vetoed, but he has little positive power to initiate programs without the concurrence of a majority of the House and Senate.

In the past, presidents occasionally attempted to exert another sort of negative power. From time to time, they would refuse to spend money that Congress had appropriated. These "impoundments" reached an unusually high level during the Nixon administration, and Congress complained bitterly. President Nixon had an effective counterargument. Congress may have the constitutional power to tax and spend, but it had no orderly procedure for considering the budget as a whole. Revenues were considered separately from outlays; appropriations for individual programs were considered sequentially without anyone in Congress ever adding up the totals.

Congress responded with the Budget Impoundment and Control Act of 1974. It set up a procedure that can be used by presidents to gain congressional concurrence in impoundments of past appropriations, and it established a congressional budget process that requires Congress to vote explicitly on total budget authority, outlays, receipts, the deficit, and the appropriate public debt.

The papers in this volume were presented at an American Enterprise Institute conference in October 1979. They evaluate the process five years after enactment and consider alternative control mechanisms such as constitutional amendments to limit expenditures. The process has been a disappointment to many observers, and some participants in the conference believe that it should be disbanded. The budget process gives Congress the opportunity to get control of the budget, but ultimately its decisions are influenced more by external economic and political conditions than by internal procedures.

While this conference was sponsored by AEI's program of tax policy studies, it is clearly complementary with AEI's Congress Project. The Budget Act represents only one of many instances in which Congress, by modifying its formal rules, has altered both its internal distribution of power and its overall influence relative to that of the executive branch of government. Nowhere in Washington has Congress as an institution been the focus of sustained, scholarly investigation. AEI's Congress Project was initiated in 1979 to remedy that lack; this volume provides further evidence of the importance of that initiative.

William J. Baroody, Jr.
President
American Enterprise Institute

Preface

On October 22, 1979, the American Enterprise Institute held a conference to discuss the operation of the new congressional budget process approximately five years after the legislation establishing it had been passed. This book presents the papers delivered at that conference and summarizes the discussion following each session.

The new process was in some trouble at the time of the conference in that the second budget resolution for fiscal 1980 was stalled in conference and Congress was far behind its formal schedule that required that resolution to be passed by September 15. The resolution was eventually passed after Thanksgiving, just in time to begin debating the first budget resolution for fiscal 1981. While this is written, that resolution is mired in acrimonious controversy over the allocation of outlays between defense and nondefense spending. As a result, the budget process is in some jeopardy and could possibly become meaningless. It is tempting to add a supplement to this volume outlining the perils faced by the process since October 1979; since the outcome of the struggle is not yet known, that temptation was resisted. This volume confines itself to an analysis of the process as it existed during the debate on the second resolution for 1980.

Rudolph G. Penner

Part One

The First Five Years of Congressional Budgeting

Allen Schick

The Congressional Budget Act of 1974 created a budget process that is simple in design but complex in execution. The process centers on two concurrent budget resolutions, one scheduled for adoption by May 15 of each year, prior to floor consideration of appropriation bills and other budget-related legislation; the other by September 15, shortly before the start of the new fiscal year.[1] A budget resolution appears to be a simple measure, only a few pages long in printed form. Each resolution comprises the five fiscal aggregates specified by the Budget Act (revenues, new budget authority, outlays, the budget surplus or deficit, and the public debt). Each resolution also allocates total budget authority and outlays among nineteen budget functions, in accord with a uniform classification used for both executive and congressional budgeting.[2]

Yet, the making of a budget resolution can be a rather complex undertaking. Each resolution requires more than forty separate, but arithmetically consistent, decisions. The functional parts have to add up to the spending totals; the budget authority allocated to each function must dovetail with estimated outlays; the difference between total revenues and outlays must equal the budgeted deficit. The formulation of these resolutions is complicated by the fact that they are not the only budget decisions made by Congress. Claims on the budget also are decided when Congress makes appropriations, allocates tax burdens and benefits, and legislates entitlements into law. Because the budget resolutions do not have the force of law (as concurrent resolutions, they are not presented to the president for his signature), they cannot be used to levy taxes or appropriate money. Their sole purpose and effect

[1] At its discretion, Congress can adopt additional budget resolutions during the fiscal year. After President Carter took office in 1977, Congress adopted a "third" resolution for the fiscal year then in progress. Similarly, in 1979 Congress revised its final resolution for the fiscal year by attaching an amendment to the first resolution for fiscal 1980.

[2] The functional classifications predate the Budget Act, but, prior to 1975, they were used only as background information. The Budget Act gives these classifications decisional status.

is to guide Congress in its actions on revenue, spending, and debt legislation. This limited status makes the resolutions something less than full-fledged budgets but more than declarations of intent. Accordingly, Congress cannot be certain of what it is deciding when it adopts a budget resolution, nor can it make these decisions independent of its other processes for allocating federal resources.

The Uncertain Budget Act

There is another reason for uncertainty about the congressional budget process. The Budget Act was born in legislative conflict and was a product of legislative compromise. While the prevailing view is that the Budget Act was precipitated by conflict between President Nixon and Congress over the impoundment of funds, conflicts within Congress had a more direct and telling effect on the legislation. In the years before the Budget Act, Congress was buffeted by strife over spending limitations and committee jurisdictions. Spending demands were increasingly expressed through limited-term authorizations and satisfied through backdoor arrangements that circumvented the appropriations process.[3] The revenue and appropriations committees battled over responsibility for chronic budget deficits and over efforts to limit total federal expenditures. Five spending limitations were enacted between 1967 and 1973 but none succeeded in capping federal expenditures. The spending limits were futile because they could not withstand the spending pressures confronting Congress. Yet, at the same time that it was becoming more open and vulnerable to budgetary pressures, Congress was becoming more sensitive to budgetary scarcity.

Congress might have tried to extricate itself from these cross-pressures by erecting institutional barriers to the articulation or satisfaction of budgetary demands. It might, for example, have required balanced budgets or it might have made it more difficult for members to approve budget-increasing amendments to appropriation bills. These and other proposed restraints on its discretion, however, were rejected by Congress in the Budget Act. Congress elected instead for an open process. It encouraged legislative committees to press their views and wants, and it enabled the House and Senate to approve any budget satisfactory to their majorities. Rather than quashing budgetary conflict at the source, the Budget Act assured that it will bloom in the open. In deciding not to bottle up budgetary pressures but to allow a free fight over spending,

[3] The main types of backdoor spending are (1) authority to enter into obligations prior to appropriations (contract authority), (2) authority to borrow from the Treasury or the public (borrowing authority), and (3) provisions of law that mandate federal payments to eligible persons or groups (entitlements).

taxes, and the deficit, Congress institutionalized its own ambivalence over budget policy. Because it could not foreclose any substantive outcome in 1974, Congress left to each year's budget cycle a fight over what the decisions should be.

Unsurprisingly, therefore, there has been much budgetary conflict within Congress, and the budget process has experienced bruising defeats and glorious victories. All that Congress decided in 1974 was that the disputes are to be resolved through a process in which the majority rules. The budget committees win when they have the votes, not because they are armed with points of order and other procedural weapons. They lose when Congress brushes aside budget protests in order to advance some other interest, not because it wants to vitiate the budget process. These legislative ups and downs are unavoidable in any process that deals with competing values. Procedure is important in defining the terms of accommodation between the budget committees and other committees, but procedure itself will not block a willful congressional majority.

The congressional budget process operates on the principle of peer control. While the notion of hierarchical order in executive budgeting, with the president whipping agencies into line by use of his budget powers, betrays the great amount of bargaining that goes on throughout the process, nevertheless the president and his budget office are not merely the equals of the agencies they seek to control. In Congress, the budget committees stand on level ground with the committees subject to budgetary constraint. The budget committees cannot issue orders binding on peer committees, nor can they prevail when challenged by other committees unless they have more votes than the others. In these confrontations among peers, the outcome will depend on the particulars of each case, the lineup of legislative interests, and the mood within Congress. No peer structure can long survive if one side wins or loses all the time. So it is in Congress, with the budget committees winning some and losing some. In this respect, they are not different from executive branch budgeters. The president's Office of Management and Budget (OMB) loses dozens of big and small fights each year, but most of its defeats are hidden from public view, though original agency requests now are made public after the budget is submitted. OMB is sheltered by the president because it is to his advantage to foster the belief that he has a powerful budget office. Most of the congressional losses, however, are in public, thereby magnifying their importance as well as the import of the victories.

Conflict was ingrained into the congressional budget process because no legislative interest got all that it wanted in the Budget Act, nor was any interest completely thwarted. In the give and take of the legislative process, ambition checked ambition; the end product was an accommodation to the most salient interests of the affected parties. Conservatives who sought strong budget committees and a restrictive budget process had to settle for a process that does not prevent Congress from spending as it sees fit. Liberals who were apprehensive about the possible effect of any budget process on domestic programs had to accept new budget controls. Authorizing committees were able to shelter existing back doors, but not all new ones. They successfully resisted the imposition of deadlines on the enactment of authorizations but could not avert deadlines for the reporting of such legislation. The appropriation committees avoided the allocation of budget amounts among appropriations categories but had to accept allocations among budget functions. The tax committees blocked proposals to specify tax expenditures in the congressional budget, but they acceded to provisions that substantially increase attention to tax expenditures in the federal budget.

The Congressional Budget Act did not put an end to budgetary strife any more than the introduction of presidential budgeting brought perfect peace half a century ago. The Budget Act was a respite and a redirection. While it could not assure budgetary tranquility, it at least provided new conditions under which future battles would be fought.

Not the least of the reasons why Congress was able to accommodate diverse interests in the Budget Act was the ambiguous and permissive process that it established. While some matters such as scheduling were precisely decided, others were left to future implementation. The budget committees could turn into the strongest congressional committees, stamping their mark on all program and policy decisions that cost money to implement. Another possibility was for them to function as feeble participants, lacking genuine legislative jurisdiction of their own and dependent on other budget parties for support. The Budget Act ordained neither outcome. Nor did it spell out the impacts of the new process on the appropriating, authorizing, and taxing committees. No one can foretell the future by examining the Budget Act alone. It all depends on how the parties interact with one another in the congressional arena.

For this reason alone, the Budget Act promotes an augmentation of budgetary conflict. The act provides license and opportunities, threats and possibilities. Every party to the 1974 act has been compelled to jockey for advantage, assert its prerogatives, and ward off intrusion by others. The new process enlarges the potential for conflict within Congress because it expands the scope of participation and compels Congress to make more explicit budget choices than were required in the past. Priorities have to be decided; the parts must be consistent with the whole; Congress must go on record with regard to the size of the budget and the deficit; tax expenditures are displayed and can be challenged;

the cost of legislation and its impact on the congressional budget are identified.

The Budget Act has fueled conflict in yet another critical way. Prior to the act, the parts of the budget were cordoned off from one another. Tax policy was made via a single set of committees; appropriations went through their own process; authorizations had their own committee roots and routes. The Budget Act means that there is hardly a single financial decision that can be made via one set of committees alone. Revenue decisions involve both the tax and budget committees. The budget committees share spending power with the appropriations committees. The wills of all these committees have to be concerted in the development of the congressional budget.

Passing the Budget

Although the Budget Act institutionalized conflict within Congress, it also requires Congress to reach budgetary agreement each year. The first measure of budgetary performance, therefore, must be its ability to adopt the spring and fall resolutions. If these failed adoption, the Budget Act would quickly become a dead letter. On the surface, this does not appear to be a difficult task. Budgets and appropriations regularly are adopted, no matter how difficult the choices or deep the cleavages, because they are essential for the continuation of government. American governments approve tens of thousands of budgets each year, even though the parties to them rarely get all that they want.

In Congress, appropriations rank high on the list of "must" legislation. Even the most intractable positions bend to the necessity of providing funds to federal agencies. Congressmen know that some divisive matters must be deferred as the price for obtaining agreement on appropriations. If the level of conflict is too high or too intense to permit enactment of the regular bills, Congress manages to paper over its disagreement with continuing appropriations, stopgap measures that provide funds until the regular appropriations are passed. Thus, the great chasm between pro- and antiabortion forces has been bridged in continuing appropriations. The combating parties have been willing to lay aside their passions and ideologies in order to permit the uninterrupted operation of major departments.

Nothing has to stop if Congress fails to adopt a budget resolution. The Budget Act bars Congress from considering tax or appropriation measures until it has passed the first resolution or from adjourning sine die until it has approved the second resolution. These procedural roadblocks would be swiftly discarded if Congress were to decide that it would rather make do without a budget process. The budget resolutions can be "must" legislation only as a state of mind, not as a matter of fact. As long as congressmen feel that they have no option other than to adopt the resolution, they will be able to devise numbers on which a majority can agree. If they were to feel that a budget is worthwhile only to the extent that it satisfies their substantive interests, the process certainly would break down. This happened after World War II, when Congress first tried to produce a legislative budget but abandoned the enterprise after several abortive attempts.[4]

Thus far, Congress has succeeded in adopting all the required resolutions. Legislators have been willing to subordinate policy goals to budgetary peace. Several of the "close calls" demonstrate that, while congressmen may be willing to carry budgetary conflict to the brink, they are not yet willing to risk destruction of their process. After voting *no*, two Republicans supplied the necessary votes to report the first 1976 resolution out of the House Budget Committee (HBC). Two years later, many congressmen switched to support a revised resolution after the first version was defeated in the House. HBC's Congresswoman Marjorie Holt (Republican, Maryland) explained that "when the resolution was defeated, everybody in the House who wanted to have the process succeed reevaluated what we were doing."[5] In May 1979, after the House had rejected its first version, the Budget Committee immediately produced a revised resolution that won majority support. In September of the same year, after another House rejection (this time, the second resolution for fiscal 1980), HBC again worked out a version that was able to pass the House.

The fact that all the required resolutions have been passed does not mean that the road to adoption has been easy. Members sometimes are willing to threaten failure of the budget process as a means of extracting more favorable terms. Pete Domenici (Republican, New Mexico), member of the Senate Budget Committee, insisted that he would rather have no budget than one that did not provide the allocation that he wanted for defense:

> . . . if this is the time to bust the budget process, there is no better one. If we need time to say "It just won't work," then I think this is as good a one as any . . . .
>
> If there ever is an issue when this Senator will opt out of the budget process, it is this situation. I would not vote for a House figure that they have submitted to us for military preparedness

[4] On the 1946 effort to establish a legislative budget, see Avery Leiserson, "Coordination of Federal Budgetary and Appropriations Procedures under the Legislative Reorganization Act of 1946," *National Tax Journal*, vol. 1 (June 1948).

[5] U.S., Congress, *Transcript of Conference on First Concurrent Resolution for Fiscal Year 1978*, 95th Congress, 2nd Session, 1978, p. 1971.

> and use as a defense that I am trying to preserve the budget process.[6]

Domenici fired this broadside during a stalemate in the conference on the first resolution for 1978. After the deadlock was broken and he had voted for the compromise, his tune changed. He then insisted that there is no process

> more important to our institutions, to the House of Representatives and the Senate, and to the prosperity of America, than the budget process . . . . Because of that, I felt that the stalemate in the conference was probably going to end up with the real probability of no Budget Act at all . . . if we had come back without resolving it, then I think the Budget Reform Act and its tremendously important qualities for credibility in this democratic process could very well have gone by the board.[7]

One cannot be certain that congressmen will always be willing to relent for the sake of the budget process. Sooner or later, this argument will lose force; the process will survive only if it satisfies the expectations of a congressional majority.

In the House. In five years of congressional budgeting, passage was much more easily achieved in the Senate than in the House. In the House, steadfast Republican opposition combined with Democratic factionalism to endanger the budget process. As shown in table 1, some resolutions squeaked through with only a few votes to spare, while three were approved only after prior rejection. Voting *no* was a budgetary habit for all but a few House Republicans. On the average, only one of twenty Republicans voted for a budget resolution. After the Democrats took control of the White House in 1977, House Republicans became even more united in opposition to the resolutions produced by the majority party. Clearly, the sizable budget deficits were the main sticking point for most of the Republicans. Republicans have become even more determined in their demands for balanced budgets. Thus, Congressman John Rousselot's (Republican, California) perennial balanced budget proposal attracted 75 Republican votes in its first try (for fiscal 1976) and 128 Republican votes in the budget resolution for fiscal 1980.

House Republicans view the budget resolutions as the great divide between the two parties, as one of the few contemporary issues on which there ought to be a clear-cut demarcation between Republican and Democratic positions. They regard the budget as a political statement

[6] Ibid., pp. 155–156.

[7] U.S., Congress, Senate, *Congressional Record*, 95th Congress, 1st session, May 13, 1977, p. 7541.

TABLE 1

REPUBLICAN AND DEMOCRATIC VOTES ON HOUSE BUDGET RESOLUTIONS, FISCAL YEARS 1976–1980

	Vote		*Democrats*		*Republicans*	
Resolutions	Yes	No	Yes	No	Yes	No
Fiscal year 1976						
First resolution	230	193	225	55	5	138
Second resolution	225	191	214	67	11	124
Fiscal year 1977						
First resolution	221	155	208	44	13	111
Second resolution	227	151	215	38	12	113
Third resolution	239	169	225	50	14	119
Fiscal year 1978						
First resolution (First round)	84	320	82	185	2	135
First resolution (Second round)	213	179	206	58	7	121
Second resolution	199	188	195	59	4	129
Fiscal year 1979						
First resolution	201	197	198	61	3	136
Second resolution	217	178	215	42	2	136
Fiscal year 1980						
First resolution	220	184	211	50	9	134
Second resolution (First round)	192	213	188	67	4	146
Second resolution (Second round)	212	206	212	52	0	154

NOTE: These votes are on passage of the resolution in the House, not on adoption of the conference report.

about the reach and purpose of the federal government, its economic role, and the national priorities of the United States. For House Republicans, the budget resolutions sum up the essential differences between the two parties; the dollar disputes, accordingly, do not merely reflect conflicts over money but go to the heart of the American political process. This Republican conception of the budget resolutions has been clearly articulated by Congressman Barber Conable (Republican, New York), a leading member of both the Ways and Means and the Budget Committees. After the House rejected the first resolution for fiscal 1978, Republicans were pressed to supply some of the votes needed to win majority support for the new version. Most Republicans, however, persisted in their negativism; Conable took the floor to defend his party against charges that it would be responsible should the budget process fail. Reminding the Democrats that they had a 2-to-1 lead in the House, he admonished, "You are the ones who control the legislative program for the next 2 years, and you are the ones who should properly be held accountable to the people for the overall performance of the Congress."[8] The budget, he contended, was too basic an issue for the Republicans to submerge their differences just for the sake of reaching legislative agreement:

> On many issues Republicans and Democrats agree: we all understand the wide areas of consensus which are possible and appropriate in the moderate climate of American politics. But the more basic the issue—and what issue is more basic than the setting of the year's priorities?—the greater the obligation on those charged with the decisions of government to consider a range of options rather than to try to force a consensus.[9]

In line with their conviction that the two parties should diverge on budget policy, Republicans have regularly offered an across-the-board cut (sometimes with selected functions excluded) as an alternative to HBC's resolution, but they have never been able to overcome the Democratic majority. The first of these—Congressman Delbert Latta's (Republican, Ohio) substitute for the fiscal 1976 resolution—lost by almost 90 votes (159 to 248), a margin that was exceeded in voting on the first resolution for fiscal 1978. The Republicans modified their strategy for the 1979 budget, coupling tax and spending reductions in a single amendment. This effort to attract Democratic votes carried the Republicans to the brink of success. All but one of the voting Republicans supported the substitute for the first 1979 resolution, along with 60 Democrats. When the fifteen-minute voting period had expired, the electronic scoreboard in the House showed the substitute in the lead. However, the speaker prolonged the roll call, giving party whips additional time to persuade recalcitrant Democrats to change their votes. The final count was 197 to 203 against the substitute, after which only three Republicans voted for the resolution. The Republican alternative for fiscal 1980 concentrated on a reduction in the size of the deficit, but it too went down to defeat, by a 191-to-228 vote.

Since the Republicans as a group have not tried for piecemeal revisions in the resolutions, the defeat of their all-or-nothing substitute leaves them without significant voice in congressional budget policy. This is perhaps their strongest incentive for opposing the resolutions.

[8] U.S., Congress, House, *Congressional Record*, 95th Congress, 1st session, May 5, 1977, p. 4066.

[9] Ibid.

From the start of markup in HBC through the completion of floor action, House Republicans have been outsiders, neither courted nor consulted by the Democratic majority. Whether self-imposed or dictated by the majority, this alienation of House Republicans from the budgetary process has been as formidable a barrier to support of the resolutions as the ideological distance between the two parties. Because they have not been able to point to anything in the resolutions that was truly their own, Republicans have not voted for them.

If this explanation is correct, the price for Republican support need not be radical concessions such as a balanced budget or even the cuts called for in the substitute resolutions. While most Republicans would persist in opposition, modest concessions (for example, more money for defense, less for social programs) might secure sufficient additional votes to assure passage of the resolutions in the House. This happened in the fiscal 1978 budget when twenty-nine Republicans voted for the conference report on the first resolution. In conference, Republican Marjorie Holt repeatedly suggested that her party would supply the necessary votes if defense spending (the principal issue in dispute between the House and Senate) were set at a higher level than House Democrats wanted. Her offer was reluctantly accepted by the Democrats only after they were unable to reach agreement among themselves. Holt then appealed to fellow Republicans to live up to the bargain, even though

> many minority Members of the House are appalled at the idea of voting for a budget with a $65 billion deficit.
>
> I think if we are going to be part of setting the priorities of this country, we have got to get in here and be active in it. We cannot sit back and vote "no"; that is easy, that is beautiful, but we have got to participate if we are going to have any effectiveness in it at all.[10]

The 1978 budget proved to be a special case. The Democrats offered concessions for Republican support because they had no alternative. In previous and subsequent resolutions, the Democrats went it alone and most Republicans were content to vote *no*.

The Democrats' Dilemma. With the Republicans lined up in opposition, the main variable has been the number of Democratic defections. The closeness of the vote turns on this consideration. The first resolution for 1976 made it through with only four votes to spare because sixty-eight Democrats joined the opposition; the second resolution for 1978, however, enjoyed a seventy-six vote margin because only thirty-eight Democrats defected. This voting pattern has compelled Democratic leaders

[10] Ibid., p. 4560.

to take an active role in moving the resolutions through the House. They cannot afford to sit back and rely on the Budget Committee because defeat of a resolution might be interpreted as a rejection of Democratic budget policy. The leadership's involvement has extended beyond the customary whip counts to ascertain how rank-and-file Democrats expect to vote. Democratic leaders have effectively superseded the HBC chairman as floor managers of the budget resolutions.

Democratic rejectors have come from both the conservative and liberal wings of the party. The more conservative or liberal a Democratic member of the House is, the greater the likelihood that he will be dissatisfied with the results. Alienated conservatives have outnumbered the liberals by about 2 to 1, a ratio due to the decision of Democratic leaders to tilt toward the liberals. Because of the polarization of House Democrats, party leaders know that they cannot woo both factions nor can they tilt so markedly to one side as to risk further loss of support from the other. Although a move to the right might win back some conservatives and also pick up some Republicans, the Democratic leadership has deliberately avoided this course. It has not wanted to be dependent upon Republican votes to pass the resolutions, nor has it wanted to aggravate liberal disaffection with the budget process. The Democratic strategy has been to hold down liberal desertions while appealing to the large number of "swing" Democrats in the House.

The Democrats want to pass their own resolution. They have been as willing as the Republicans to cast the budget as a contest between the two parties. This approach was enunciated by Majority Leader Jim Wright (Democrat, Texas) in a "Dear Democratic Colleague" letter after the House had rejected the initial 1978 budget resolution:

> The majority party has the responsibility to act—to ratify this document and proceed with the important business of the Congress. We can expect *no help from the Republicans*. They have the luxury of criticizing without assuming responsibility.
>
> So it is up to us. We must produce enough *Democratic* votes for the resolution to pass it—just as we have done in each of the last two years. This is the only way Congress can fulfill its constitutional responsibility to control and direct spending. And that's what it means to be the majority party.[11]

In accord with this view, Democratic leaders have tried to make the resolutions more palatable to party liberals, thereby writing off the possibility of attracting Republicans or conservative Democrats. At first, the leadership relied on floor amendments. Majority Leader Thomas

[11] U.S., Congress, House, letter from Congressman Jim Wright to Democratic members of the House, May 4, 1977.

P. O'Neill (Democrat, Massachusetts) sponsored successful spending increases to the first and second resolutions for 1976. This strategy had an obvious drawback; it put House Democrats in the position of openly promoting higher spending and large deficits. Accordingly, in subsequent years Democratic leaders concentrated on working their will in HBC. Thus, during markup of the first resolution for 1977, Majority Leader O'Neill headed a move to add funds for job programs and for startup of national health insurance and the Humphrey-Hawkins full employment legislation. Moreover, HBC's Democratic contingent was liberalized (by a change in its membership) at the start of the ninty-fifth Congress, making it easier for the leadership to influence the budget resolutions through behind-the-scenes consultations with the HBC chairman and Democratic members of the committee. When the House rejected the first attempt to pass a resolution for fiscal 1978, Congressman Wright, who became majority leader after O'Neill moved to the speaker's position, drafted the HBC compromise that finally won House approval.

In seeking support for the resolutions, party leaders have appealed to rank-and-file Democrats to "vote the process, not the numbers." Lukewarm Democrats have been whipped into line by the argument that they would be held culpable for the failure of the budget process and that they must therefore vote for the resolution even if they are unhappy with its priorities. The leadership's repertoire includes old-fashioned arm twisting as well as intensive lobbying during the weeks prior to floor action. In 1978, the speaker set up a twenty-five-member task force (headed by Butler Derrick [Democrat, South Carolina], a second-term congressman on the Budget Committee) to round up Democratic votes.

The "vote for budget process" theme becomes explicit during floor debate on the budget resolutions. "Today, once more," Majority Leader Wright told the House as it neared a final vote on the first resolution for 1979, "I am asking Members of this body to set aside what may be their own personal preferences and predilections and cast a yea vote for this resolution."[12] Democrats have been asked to vote for the process because the numbers are the best that they can get without losing majority support. In the 1978 debate, Wright used this argument: "I plead with my colleagues to look at his budget resolution on balance and recognize that it is the best that we collectively have been able to do."[13]

[12] U.S., Congress, House, *Congressional Record,* 95th Congress, 2nd session, May 2, 1978, p. 3439.

[13] U.S., Congress, House, *Congressional Record,* 95th Congress, 2nd session, May 10, 1978, p. 3735.

Voting for the process also means voting against floor amendments, even attractive ones, that might lose votes for the final resolution:

> Members should not be vying with one another, each attempting to make this entire budget over in his own individual image. We must recognize that the task of the Committee on the Budget and the task of Congress in this resolution is not to try to imprint the stamp and stain of each individual personality upon the budget.[14]

Most House Democrats vote for the budget process. "I am going to vote for the budget resolution," Appropriations Chairman George Mahon (Democrat, Texas) announced in 1978. "It is important that we support the budget process."[15] Mahon provided a penetrating clue as to why congressmen can vote for a budget resolution even if they are not quite satisfied with its contents: "Fortunately, this resolution only sets a target and does not actually provide the spending itself. That will be done in later actions through various appropriations and other spending bills."[16]

Evidently, not all Democrats have been persuaded by the "vote for the budget process" argument. Some cannot vote for numbers out of line with their own budget priorities. This position was well stated by liberal John Conyers (Democrat, Michigan), who has voted against most of the budget resolutions:

> I will say this to all of the Members who think that we cannot support the budget process if we vote against the budget resolution . . . . There are only two things we can do with a budget resolution. We can vote it up or we can vote it down. If we vote it down, it does not mean that we are against the budgetary process in the Congress. It means that we do not like what went into the budget.[17]

The House has managed to pass budget resolutions because most Democrats (including most of the liberals) have been willing to vote for the process even when they have not liked everything in the budget. It would seem that "vote the process" is an appeal that loses force in repetition. One cannot expect congressmen to forgo their substantive interests endlessly, just to keep the budget process alive. As budgeting

[14] U.S., Congress, House, *Congressional Record,* 95th Congress, 2nd session, May 3, 1978, p. 3485.

[15] U.S., Congress, House, 95th Congress, 2nd session, *Congressional Record,* May 10, 1978, p. 3721.

[16] U.S., Congress, House, *Congressional Record,* 94th Congress, 2nd session, April 29, 1976, p. 3652.

[17] U.S., Congress, House, *Congressional Record,* 94th Congress, 2nd session, April 28, 1976, p. 3521.

becomes more commonplace on Capitol Hill, members might become less willing to vote for resolutions that do not reflect their budget priorities. The long-term health of the congressional budget process cannot be secured by frantic appeals to vote against one's interests or instincts.

In the Senate. The formulation of a budget resolution has followed a markedly different course in the Senate. There has been little of the strident partisanship that has characterized House action, nor heated opposition to the Senate Budget Committee's (SBC) recommendations. Many issues provoke controversy, some in committee, a few on the floor. At no time has a Senate resolution been in danger of defeat. Most of the resolutions have passed the Senate by better than a 2-to-1 margin, with many Republicans joining in support. (See table 2 for the voting patterns in the Senate.)

On the basis of traditional differences between the two chambers, one might have expected the Senate's budget to be consistently higher and more liberal than the House's. Such has not been the case, however. The budget resolutions emerging from the SBC have had less of a Democratic tint than those advanced by the House committee. The SBC has usually provided more for defense, while the HBC has usually allocated more for social programs. The SBC usually has recommended lower outlays and a smaller deficit than its House counterpart. The SBC's resolution has not been built along party lines; as a result, its Republicans have had a significant voice in shaping budget policies and priorities. Moreover, most SBC members have tended to band together in bipartisan support of their committee's recommendations even when they are on the losing side during markup. This pattern was cast the first time SBC produced a resolution, in the spring of 1975. As the markup neared a conclusion, many members expressed dissatisfaction with one or another outcome. Many indicated that although they would vote to report the resolution, they might oppose it on the floor. Senator Edmund Muskie (Democrat, Maine) perceived that, if this were to occur, the SBC's overall budget influence would be weakened. He therefore urged SBC colleagues to back the resolution even though it did not contain everything they wanted.

> There is no point in sending something that is fruitless to the Floor. If we send something to the Floor and end up with 15 members of the Committee for one reason or another deciding that they can't support it, we are really going to be in a tough box.[18]

[18] U.S., Congress, Senate, Committee on the Budget, *Transcript of Senate Markup of the First Budget Resolution for Fiscal Year 1976,* 94th Congress, 1st session, 1975, p. 743.

TABLE 2

REPUBLICAN AND DEMOCRATIC VOTES ON SENATE BUDGET RESOLUTIONS, FISCAL YEARS 1976–1980

	Senate		*Democrats*		*Republicans*	
Resolutions	Yeas	Nays	Yeas	Nays	Yeas	Nays
Fiscal year 1976						
First resolution	69	22	50	4	19	18
Second resolution	69	23	50	8	19	15
Fiscal year 1977						
First resolution	62	22	45	6	17	16
Second resolution	55	23	41	5	14	18
Third resolution	72	20	55	3	17	17
Fiscal year 1978						
First resolution	56	31	41	14	15	17
Second resolution	63	21	46	8	17	13
Fiscal year 1979						
First resolution	64	27	48	8	16	19
Second resolution	56	18	42	6	14	12
Fiscal year 1980						
First resolution	64	20	44	5	20	15
Second resolution	90	6	55	1	35	5

Senator Henry Bellmon (Republican, Oklahoma) took the same position for the Republicans. He cautioned against "this Committee going in 15 different directions on the Floor. I don't think anyone here has gotten what he really wanted."[19] Most SBC members fell into line, subordinating their substantive interests to the needs of the budget process. By taking this posture, the SBC was able to muster a broad coalition for its budget decision. In that precedent-making case, all of the Democrats were joined by three Republicans in a lopsided 13-to-2 vote to report the resolution. Subsequent resolutions have been approved by similar margins in committee.

Most SBC members fight over the numbers but manage to lay aside their differences when all is done. One popular explanation why SBC members agree on the numbers is that they are not compelled to agree on the line items. Other explanations warrant consideration. Nobody is a total loser on the SBC; everyone comes away from the battle with important wins in the process. SBC members apparently see their res-

[19] Ibid., p. 745.

olutions as mixed bags that give them some matters of importance but deny them others. Few are provoked to opposition by the feeling that they have lost all the important fights. The budget outcomes in the SBC thus resemble much Senate legislation in which the final product is fashioned through give and take by collegial bargainers rather than by complete victory for one side and defeat for the other.

The Senate budget resolution is not rutted in the standard schisms of American politics. It is not a Democratic or a Republican budget; nor is it a liberal or a conservative budget. In fact, the ideologues on both sides tend to be among the least successful voters in committee. Since it is not stamped with an unacceptable label, most SBC members can comfortably band together in support of the resolution.

Controversy within the SBC is constrained rather than passionate. With few exceptions, Democrats and Republicans do not speak with the sense of urgency that affects HBC deliberations. Within the SBC, one rarely hears the impassioned pleas for the cities, the poor, or unemployed youth. Nor do most of the conservatives speak in doomsday tones about the sins of deficit spending. For most of the Democrats and Republicans, voting is more an outgrowth of each member's program interests than of conformity to an ideological position or to the party line. Republicans and Democrats alike happen to vote with their respective majorities most of the time because party cohorts usually share the same policy orientations. A member's defection from the party is not regarded as a breach of loyalty or as abandonment of an ideological commitment.

Various institutional differences between the House and Senate contribute to an understanding of the SBC's harmony at the end of markup. The wider electoral compass of Senators moderates political passions by giving them more heterogeneous constituencies than House members have. Their relative electoral longevity shelters them from the political opprobrium of high deficits. Senators are accustomed to operating under unanimous consent, a practice that depends on a good deal of bipartisan cooperation. SBC members leave markup in concord because they entered it disposed to reach agreement. In between, they fight for the best deal they can get, but most do not let roll-call defeats sway them from endorsing the committee's budget.

Senate action on the budget resolutions has mirrored the relative calm within the Senate Budget Committee. SBC Chairman Muskie and Bellmon, the ranking Republican, recognized that the surest way to prevail on the floor was to present a united front. They hoped that, with the committee solidly behind its product, the Senate would see the resolution as a rational and fair budget policy, not just as a bundle of compromises or as the personal preferences of those who happened to be on the committee. Their strategy has been successful; as noted earlier, the budget resolutions have consistently rolled up big majorities in the Senate.

Accommodating Congress

Passing the budget resolutions is much more than markups, roll calls, and voting patterns. In order to produce defensible resolutions, the budget committees must be informed concerning the intentions and expectations of other congressional committees. In the hectic months preceding the markup of the first resolution, the members and staffs of the budget committees must concentrate on knowing Congress, its interests and concerns, the status of and prospects for legislation, and the legislative lineup on critical issues.

The need for knowledge about Congress goes far beyond the obvious fact that Congress has the final say on budget resolutions. Rather, the budget committees must know Congress because their resolutions touch on the interests and jurisdiction of virtually every legislative committee. The budget committees cannot make substantive judgments about programs without knowing what the relevant committees think or want.

No matter how much the budget committees know about federal programs, they cannot establish themselves as program experts on Capitol Hill. They can strive for special recognition with respect to fiscal policy and the budget's aggregates, but they cannot attain recognition as specialists concerning the budget's parts. To the committees of jurisdiction, the budget committees cannot escape being viewed as dilettantes and meddlers, not as the legitimate program specialists. For this reason, the budget committees are always vulnerable to having their numbers and competence challenged by the committees of jurisdiction. The committees that make the "real" decisions also are the claimants in the process; the budget committees can ignore these claims only at the risk of having their resolutions rejected or disregarded.

In formulating their resolutions, the budget committees cannot operate ex parte, as if they were the only ones in Congress with a legitimate interest in what is decided. At all stages of congressional budgeting, the House and Senate committees must be sensitive to the wants and expectations of other committees. Much of the pre-markup activity of the budget committees is aimed at improving their understanding of congressional intentions. Each committee begins with a "quick and dirty" analysis of the president's budget. This staff exercise orients the budget committees to prospective issues, identifies the programs that have been cut or added, and examines the extent to which programs have been adjusted for inflation. The purpose of this exercise is not to acquire program knowledge; it is much too superficial for that. Rather, the budget committees are seeking clues to the likely concerns and reactions of other committees. By the time markup starts, the budget committees have a good idea of what can be expected in their respective houses. Discussions in markup are peppered with queries and comments about what the affected committees want. Members prefer to accommodate those interests rather than fight. When Muskie urged a reduction in defense spending for fiscal 1976 to "send the Appropriations Committee a message," Senator Ernest Hollings (Democrat, South Carolina) shot back:

> Why don't we send them a different message that we are sort of going along with them? This damn Budget Committee, it is like bone fishing. You have to get the Senate and Congress unbolted first. By gosh, now is the time to get established and get support and get this thing going.[20]

The two budget committees accommodate in different ways. The HBC conducts a line-item review to assure that the allocation for each function has sufficient room to provide for all wanted programs. The HBC knows exactly which programs are assumed in its resolutions, the program initiatives it expects, and any proposed cutbacks. These expectations are "tested" in consultations with affected committees and Democratic leaders.

The SBC's accommodations are linked to the current policy (or law) estimates, which enable the committee to be confident about funding levels without undertaking a line-by-line review of the budget. When it deviates from current policy, the SBC is aware of the prospective impact on Senate committees and federal programs.

Budget committeemen define their committee's role in terms of congressional expectations. "Our function," Muskie advised the Senate, "is to try to reflect a consensus of the Senate on issues insofar as evidence of a consensus is available to us."[21] Senator Robert Dole (Republican, Kansas) put forth a similar view:

> The Budget Committee should not pass spending targets that force the adoption of program changes that have not been contemplated. It has been and should continue to be the Budget Committee's practice to reflect in its spending targets and its

[20] U.S., Congress, Senate, Committee on the Budget, *Transcript of Markup of the Second Budget Resolution for Fiscal Year 1976,* 94th Congress, 1st session, 1975, p. 628.

[21] U.S., Congress, Senate, *Congressional Record,* 94th Congress, 2nd session, September 9, 1976, p. 15490.

> scorekeeping the budget effects of pending legislation that appears to have some possibility of enactment.[22]

Despite the best of preparations, budget numbers are changing all the time. Fresh requests from the White House, reestimates of spending rates, changes in economic conditions, shifts in committee sentiments—all can produce last-minute adjustments that were unforeseen when markup began. The budget committees are willing to accommodate these adjustments until the end; in some years, for example, the budget committee chairman has offered floor amendments to account for items that were unknown when the resolution was reported. Accommodations also are made at the conference stage, as late news can sway the bargain in favor of one of the budget committees. Congressman Robert Giaimo (Democrat, Connecticut) interrupted a conference on the third resolution for fiscal 1977: "I am told the Appropriations Committee has just marked up some numbers that might be of interest here."[23] He proposed a level consistent with the appropriations action. Pete Domenici, one of the Senate conferees, was not convinced: "What are we doing here marking up these functions if we are just waiting for appropriations to give us the figures?"[24] Yet, when all the talking was over, the conference accepted the numbers implied by the appropriations decision.

In an accommodating environment, a "tight" budget is one that provides only the amounts reasonably expected to be required by Congress. Although the budget committees want to exert downward pressure on the budget, the better part of discretion is to hedge a bit in the first resolution, with claims that, if the funds are not needed later in the year, they can be excised from the second resolution. When SBC debated the international affairs function for fiscal 1978, Senator Bennett Johnston (Democrat, Louisiana)—who wanted a lower allocation for that function—urged a delay on the ground that the authorizing committee had not completed hearings on related legislation. Muskie acknowledged in response that

> it is just not possible for all of the authorizing committees to have in-depth hearings prior to March 15.
>
> But what we are about here is setting targets. Those targets are adjustable between May 15 and September 15. By that time, hopefully, we will have had the hearings. . . . In the meantime, we have to set targets which give committees of the

[22] U.S., Congress, Senate, *Congressional Record,* 94th Congress, 1st session, November 19, 1975, p. 20494.

[23] U.S., Congress, *Transcript of Conference Committee on Third Concurrent Resolution for the 1978 Fiscal Year,* 95th Congress, 1st session, 1977, p. 78.

[24] Ibid., p. 79.

> Congress room to operate, which give the administration room to operate.[25]

"Giving room" is an essential feature of budget accommodation. It means not cutting to the bone or below the amount that Congress is expected to spend. The following exchange was occasioned by Senator Orrin Hatch's (Republican, Utah) effort to use the budget process to pressure Congress for a reduction in food stamp expenditures:

> I do not think the Budget Committee is just an adding machine. It has the ability to put pressure on these committees. . . . I think it is a very powerful committee and if it exerts its pressure and power, it can do an awful lot. . . .

The SBC's Bellmon, however, was unwilling to take up the gauntlet.

> . . . at the present time, the mood in Congress is not to cut back in food stamps. But now the Budget Committee has to take this into account. We cannot come in with a budget that flies in the face of the votes of the Senate and the laws that are on the books. . . . All the Budget Committee and budget process can do is make room for the entitlement programs that are on the books.[26]

In almost 100 interviews with congressmen and staff, no one expressed the view that the budget allocations were knowingly set below legislative expectations. "We got all that we needed," one committee's staff director exulted. The chief clerk of an appropriations subcommittee complained that the budget target was too permissive: "We were faced with pressure to spend up to the full budget allocation. It's almost as if the budget committee bent over backwards to give Appropriations all that it wanted and then some."

For the budget committees, a restrictive budget is one that does not exceed congressional needs. This is Muskie's version of the SBC's role: "One way that we try as a committee to exert pressure upon tendencies to expand spending is to try to hold these total numbers down to what we reasonably believe is going to happen."[27]

Although they understand the need for accommodation, once in a while budget committee members yearn for a more independent posture, one that does not merely go along with the tide of congressional

[25] U.S., Congress, Senate, Committee on the Budget, *Transcript of Markup of the First Concurrent Resolution for the 1978 Fiscal Year,* 95th Congress, 1st session, 1977, pp. 525–526.

[26] U.S., Congress, Senate, *Congressional Record,* 95th Congress, 1st session, September 9, 1977, p. 14509.

[27] U.S., Congress, Senate, *Congressional Record,* 94th Congress, 2nd session, September 9, 1976, p. 15489.

developments. This excerpt from the SBC's markup of the first 1978 resolution was Muskie's reaction to a suggestion that more money be set aside for the Postal Service.

> I am getting quite a deal of frustration allowing all these programs and agencies leeway to cover what they might or might not do later on in the year. What is wrong with forcing them to prove their case later in the year? . . . Why should we allow everybody this leeway and swallow the deficit here without having a case made?[28]

The budget committees usually opt for accommodation because they cannot choose the forum in which disgruntled claimants "make their case." If shortchanged committees were willing to wait until the second resolution to show the budget committee that they needed increased allocations, there would be no pressure for early accommodations. The more likely course for such committees, however, is to take their case directly to the House or Senate when the first resolution is debated. Once this is done, the issue is transformed from a matter of budget allocation into a challenge to the competence of the budget committee. Here is one such challenge, from HBC Member Omar Burleson (Democrat, Texas), who persuaded the House to add billions of dollars to the 1978 budget for defense programs:

> The Defense Task Force of the Committee on the Budget, on which I serve, held only three formal hearings of about 6 hours in all. It made no recommendation to the chairman nor to the Committee on the Budget. It had absolutely no input, and there was no discussion with respect to this matter.
>
> On the basis of the chairman's recommendation and only his recommendation, really, the level of $116 billion is included in this resolution for national defense. You will search in vain for any valid rationale for this action because there is none. The recommendation of the Committee on the Budget is totally inconsistent with recommendations of the congressional committees of the Congress which bear the primary responsibility for national defense. Without exception the House and the Senate Committees on Appropriations and the Committees on Armed Services of both Houses, recommended increases, not decreases in the defense budget, after extensive hearings. These conclusions were reached covering days of study, line-by-line items. There was no such action in the Committee on the Budget.[29]

[28] U.S., Congress, Senate, *Transcript of Markup of First Concurrent Resolution, 1978*, 95th Congress, 2nd session, 1978, pp. 347–348.

[29] U.S., Congress, House, *Congressional Record*, 95th Congress, 1st session, April 27, 1977, p. 3627.

The fact that committee chairmen are among the most consistent supporters of budget resolutions attests to the accommodating role of the budget committees. Moreover, chairmen rarely complain about the allocations made to their committees or offer amendments to raise the budget levels for the functions in which they are interested. Budgetary accommodation cannot be accomplished, however, merely by deferring to the legislative interests of other committees. To do so might require outlay totals and deficits in excess of congressional preferences. Budget accommodation involves reading the mood of Congress, not just sizing up the prospects for particular legislative proposals.

The budget committees must sense whether Congress is in an expansive or parsimonious mood, whether it is bent on program expansion or reluctant to endorse initiatives that would add to the deficit. When Congress is in an expansive mood, it is hard for the budget committees to hold the line or cut corners in accommodating the legislative interests of other committees. Under these circumstances, one can expect some slack in the spending allocations. During the first four years of the budget process, Congress was in an incremental mood, willing to authorize some initiatives and hesitant to curb existing programs. The fifth congressional budget (for fiscal 1980) was constructed under a different set of congressional expectations, however. Congress was in an economy mood spurred by the Proposition Thirteen tax cut in California and by petitions from more than twenty-five states for a national convention to place a balanced budget requirement in the Constitution. During the four months between the convening of the Ninety-sixth Congress and adoption of the first resolution for fiscal 1980, more than 100 measures were introduced in the House and Senate, calling for restrictions on the deficit or on federal expenditures. This mood change affected the terms of accommodation, strengthening the position of the budget committees vis-à-vis claimant committees.

This mood change helped both the budget committees in defending their fiscal 1980 recommendations. The HBC produced a first resolution that assumed $6 billion in legislative savings from changes in existing law. Moreover, many domestic categories were held to below-inflation increases. Nevertheless, the committee was more successful in warding off floor amendments than it had been in earlier years, when its resolutions were more favorably disposed toward the spending plans of other committees. In fact, the only significant floor change was an across-the-board amendment pruning another $2.5 billion from the budget. The SBC tried to use concern about the deficit and spending to its advantage in the second resolution for fiscal 1980. This resolution contained a "reconciliation" instruction for various Senate committees to report legislation cutting more than $4 billion from existing programs. The reconciliation was directed at some of the most powerful committees including finance, appropriations, agriculture, and veterans' affairs. The size of the reconciliation was scaled down in closed-door negotiations convened by Senate Democratic leaders. Although the "consensus" reconciliation was approved by a wide margin in the Senate, it was subsequently deleted in conference after protracted disagreement between the two chambers. House Democrats refused to accept the rollback of expenditures; the conference settled for some hortatory language concerning legislative savings.

Setting Congressional Priorities

When the Budget Act was being written, many reformers hoped that the new process would occasion an annual priorities debate within Congress. The various budget functions would compete for limited resources, with more for one category portending less for the others. The House Rules Committee endorsed this concept in its version of the budget reform legislation; Congress, it argued,

> should have the opportunity to determine spending priorities by comparing the relative value of each program area within a comprehensive budget process. Because the present system is fragmented, with decisions stretching over many months, Congress has no real opportunity to decide spending priorities. It would be given this opportunity if the initial budget resolution set forth the appropriate target for each category.[30]

Despite these expectations, the budget process has not triggered a fresh examination of national priorities. In fact, Congress did more reordering of budget priorities when it lacked a budget process than it did in the five years it had one. Table 3 reveals that, during the 1972–1975 period, there was a massive shift in the relative shares of national defense and income security, the largest categories in the budget. Defense lost its lead as the biggest function and dropped from about one-half to one-quarter of total outlays. Income security took over first place, growing to fully one-third of the budget and accounting for almost one-half of total outlay increase in the 1972–1975 years.

The post-1975 shifts were on a much smaller scale. Energy doubled its budget share, but it was still one of the smaller functions. The portion going to agriculture also climbed, but its zigzagging fortunes did not bring it up to its 1972 share. Fiscal assistance (revenue sharing) and international aid declined, although the actual spending for each of these

[30] U.S., Congress, House, Committee on Rules, 93rd Congress, 1st session, H. Rept. No. 93–658, November 20, 1973, p. 33.

TABLE 3: DISTRIBUTION OF BUDGET OUTLAYS BY FUNCTION, SELECTED YEARS, 1969–1979
(in millions of dollars)

	Actual Budget Outlays						*Second Resolution*	
Function	1969	% Total	1972	% Total	1975	% Total	1979	% Total
National defense	79,418	43.0	76,550	33.0	85,550	26.2	112,400	23.1
International affairs	4,573	2.5	4,674	2.0	6,861	2.1	7,100	1.5
General science	5,016	2.7	4,174	1.8	3,989	1.2	5,000	1.0
Energy	1,001	0.5	1,270	0.5	2,179	0.7	8,100	1.7
Natural resources	2,848	1.5	4,195	1.8	7,329	2.2	11,500	2.4
Agriculture	5,779	3.1	5,279	2.3	1,660	0.5	7,500	1.5
Commerce and housing	553	0.3	2,206	0.9	5,604	1.7	2,800	0.6
Transportation	6,531	3.5	8,395	3.6	10,392	3.2	17,300	3.5
Community development	1,545	0.8	3,413	1.5	3,692	1.1	9,600	2.0
Education, training, employment, and social services	7,538	4.1	12,519	5.4	15,870	4.9	30,300	6.2
Health	11,758	6.4	17,471	7.5	27,647	8.5	48,100	9.9
Income security	37,281	20.2	63,911	27.5	108,605	33.3	159,300	32.7
Veterans benefits	7,640	4.1	10,730	4.6	16,597	5.1	20,700	4.2
Administration of justice	761	0.4	1,650	0.7	2,942	0.9	4,200	0.9
General government	1,649	0.9	2,466	1.0	3,089	0.9	4,000	0.8
Fiscal assistance	430	0.2	673	0.3	7,187	2.2	8,800	1.8
Interest	15,793	8.6	20,582	8.9	30,974	9.5	48,000	9.8
Allowances	—	—	—	—	—	—	800	0.2
Offsetting receipts	−5,545	−3.0	−8,137	−3.5	−14,075	−4.3	−18,000	−3.7
Total budget outlays	184,548		232,021		326,092		489,500	

NOTE: Percentages may not total 100 because of rounding.

categories was relatively stable. The slippage in commerce and housing was due more to accounting practices than legislative policy.[31] Defense's share of the budget stabilized, though the Pentagon received big dollar increases in its allocation.

Those who wanted the congressional budget to be a contest over national priorities have been greatly disappointed. Accommodating budgets avoid explicit trade-offs among the functions, preferring instead to treat each as a discrete policy choice. Spending decisions are compartmentalized by the budget committees as each works through the roster of functions until it has completed the list. At no time in the first five years of budgeting did either committee explicitly vote to take from one function in order to give more to another. Although they began with an overview of economic conditions and have a sense of what they expect the totals to be, the committees do not decide the aggregates until they have made the functional allocations. Senator Muskie explained the SBC's markup procedure in resisting a floor move to shift funds from defense to domestic programs. The committee goes

> through each of the 19 functions of the budget carefully, without carrying any total target for spending. . . . Each function's total and, indeed, the missions within each function, are addressed in that fashion. There is no arbitrary ceiling imposed on domestic spending. There is an honest attempt to address legitimate needs in each function.[32]

A similar procedure was outlined by the HBC's Robert Giaimo in responding to Republican proposals to make functional decisions only after the budget's totals have been determined:

> . . . if we attempt to set overall budget limits without going into the specific functional categories and taking into account programs and activities which may be funded, we will be proceeding in a factual vacuum . . . there is no way for us to know what the implications of such a procedure would be for various programs.[33]

Members of the budget committees were careful to avoid structuring their decisions in ways that might be construed as shifting funds among the functions. Thus, when Senator Glenn Beall (Republican, Maryland) suggested adding funds for social programs after the SBC had cut funds

[31] Receipts from the scale of participation certificates and mortgages by the Government National Mortgage Association fluctuate substantially from year to year, for example. Since these receipts are treated as negative expenditures, they cause wide wings in budgeted outlays, even when program levels are stable.

[32] U.S., Congress, House, *Congressional Record*, 95th Congress, 2nd session, April 25, 1978, p. 6243.

[33] U.S., Congress, House, *Congressional Record*, 95th Congress, 2nd session, May 2, 1978, p. 3418.

for defense, he took pains to divorce his proposal from the previous action:

> I am not doing this with the idea we are making a trade-off between defense and other parts of the budget. I think that that is very dangerous . . . I do not want to associate this increase with any cut in the defense budget.[34]

Accommodating budgets are made piecemeal because Congress does not have a single or homogeneous interest that it seeks to maximize in the budget process. Congress itself is a coming together of diverse interests; the budget committees satisfy Congress by satisfying particular interests. They accommodate by breaking the budget into its parts and deciding how much to allocate to each. While the piecemeal approach progresses with an eye on the totals and concern as to how the partial decisions add up to the budget, claims are not openly pitted against one another. The competition is ever-present but usually muted.

The budget process is neatly structured to facilitate this accommodation to the parts. Each function covers a portion of the interests at work in Congress. Some of the functions (defense, agriculture, and veterans, for example) correspond to distinct interests; some (such as income security and the education, training, employment, and social services category) are groupings for a number of interests, each of which must be watchful that the allocation covers its wants. A few important national interests—housing is the leading case—are submerged in the categories; affected parties have to sift through various parts of the budget to assure that they are tended. When they address the question of how much priority should be accorded to a function, members do not refer to the function's relative value but to its particular needs, the programs budgeted within it. They want to know whether an allocation will cover existing programs or force cutbacks, whether it will allow real growth or only an adjustment for inflation. They make priority decisions by comparing the allocation for a function with the allocation made to the same function in the previous year. Their most important calculations are within, not between, functions.

This does not mean, however, that Congress considers itself inactive with respect to budgetary priorities. It defines priorities in terms of giving each function its due, more or less than it got last year, more or less than the president wants, more or less than current policy. Priority setting is usually at the margins, a little more versus a little less for each function. Members who seek to reorder budget priorities tend to be impatient with marginal changes, but marginal change is the pace at

[34] U.S., Congress, Senate, Committee on the Budget, *Markup of First Concurrent Resolution for Fiscal Year 1976*, 94th Congress, 2nd session, 1976, p. 538.

which conflicts can be contained by accommodating to past decisions while responding to new claims.

The House and Senate have rebuffed all proposals to reorder the budget's priorities by taking from one function and giving to another. The first of these "transfer" amendments was proposed by a HBC liberal member, Elizabeth Holtzman (Democrat, New York), for the 1977 budget. "I am deeply disturbed," she protested to the House, "that the budget we are presented with this time fails to carry out the essential promise of the Budget Act—to set congressional priorities and to address the serious problems facing this country."[35] Another House liberal, Richard Ottinger (Democrat, New York), exulted

> I believe for the first time in the history of this body, we have an opportunity to present this body with a choice of real priorities, in one motion. We have a chance to weigh in this amendment a cut in the fat and waste in the Defense Department against badly needed social programs at home. . . .
>
> Many of us have talked for years about reordering priorities; this is our chance to do it.[36]

The House did not take the bait. It gave the transfer amendment fewer votes than any other floor amendment to that year's budget. The 85-to-317 rejection had all but one Republican and a majority of the Democrats lined up in opposition. This outcome was repeated in subsequent years. HBC's Parren Mitchell (Democrat, Maryland) carried the ball for the transfer amendment in 1978: "I wanted to get on the Budget Committee—I was anxious to serve on it . . . [but] this Budget Committee has produced a first budget resolution which does not establish priorities."[37]

This time the transfer scheme was rejected by a 102-to-306 margin, with the voting pattern similar to the previous year's. The House had an additional opportunity in the 1979 budget, but again (by a 98-to-313 vote) it decided against shifting funds from defense to domestic programs. For fiscal 1980, Mitchell abandoned the transfer route and sought more funds for domestic programs through increased revenues, but the House rejected his proposal in a 130-to-277 vote.

Transfer fared no better in the Senate. George McGovern (Democrat, South Dakota) attempted to redistribute $4.6 billion in the 1979 budget from defense to several domestic functions: $2 billion for edu-

[35] U.S., Congress, House, *Congressional Record*, 94th Congress, 2nd session, April 27, 1976, p. 3455.

[36] U.S., Congress, House, *Congressional Record*, 94th Congress, 2nd session, April 29, 1976, p. 3558.

[37] U.S., Congress, House, *Congressional Record*, 95th Congress, 1st session, April 26, 1977, p. 3558.

cation, employment, and social services; $1.9 billion for energy; and lesser amounts for transportation and community development. His ploy was quite obvious; by voting for the transfer, senators would be able to add funds for cherished projects without increasing the deficit. The plan did not work; McGovern was overwhelmed, 14-to-77, receiving fewer votes than any other Senate amendment to the 1979 budget. He tried a different approach in the first resolution for fiscal 1980. He sought to allocate half of the funds that would be cut from defense to various domestic functions (energy, transportation, and education) and the other half to a reduction in the budget deficit. This was rebuffed by a wide margin, 24 to 69.

Congress has no tolerance for conflict that would be generated by open competition among functions. Precisely because the budget process sensitizes Congress to the fact that more for one function can mean less for another, Congress prefers to decide each function in turn, thereby playing down the inevitable tensions of budgeting. The budget that emerges from this process is nobody's ordering of preferences. It does not conform in all its particulars to any member's comparative preferences, let alone to those of a congressional majority. It does not have to be anyone's budget because most congressmen have strong feelings about only a few of the items in it. If they are satisfied about these, and not deeply disturbed by the total spending and deficit levels, they can be persuaded to vote for the budget resolutions.

Consensual priorities are acceptable to members who have favorable views about some parts of the budget and are indifferent about the others. Their price for agreeing with the budget is to have their priorities satisfied, leaving others to take care of the matters on which they are indifferent. It was on this basis that Muskie prodded the stalled House-Senate conference on the 1978 budget to resolve its disagreements:

> I have learned in this key spot of chairing the Senate Budget Committee that if I want to advance those budgetary objectives in which I am interested, I have got to recognize the budget priorities that others entertain, and I have got to be willing to support the final product.[38]

When the conferees finally reached agreement on the 1978 budget, Muskie rallied support for it as a "careful and delicate balance of priorities . . . the budget process is built upon the balancing of needs, upon flexibility and compromise."[39] It was a consensual budget in which no

[38] U.S., Congress, *Transcript of Conference Committee on First Concurrent Resolution for Fiscal Year 1978*, 95th Congress, 1st session, 1977, p. 151.

[39] U.S., Congress, Senate, *Congressional Record*, 95th Congress, 1st session, May 13, 1977, p. 7537.

side got all that it wanted and there was no announced reordering of national objectives.

Consensual budgets, however, do not appeal to congressmen who have strong feelings *against* parts of the budgets. Those who would take from defense do not only want more for domestic needs but want less for the military. They make accommodation difficult because the programs they would cut have strong advocates within Congress.

Toward a Realistic View of the Congressional Budget Process

Budget watchers on Capitol Hill keep score of congressional budget actions as if the survival of the process turns on each outcome. They tally the victories and defeats and switch moods in accord with the latest results. In the throes of defeat, members denigrate the budget process as just a bookkeeping exercise, an "adding machine" that does not make much of a difference. In triumph, the process is exalted as the means by which Congress has recaptured the power of the purse, set the economy on a stable and productive course, and established the priorities of the United States.

These vicissitudes of congressional budgeting grow from uncertainty concerning its purpose, impact, and durability. Congress is not quite sure of what it wrought in 1974, nor of the extent to which it can abide the new discipline. Past failures of legislative budgeting are etched into the institutional memory of Congress, inflating the importance of each victory or defeat. Each major confrontation is seen as a test of the staying power and potency of budget reform, and, because the conflicts are fought in the open, the outcomes assume an importance far beyond their real meaning.

Moodiness about the budget process also arises from a tendency to test the process in terms of expectations that were not inscribed in the 1974 act. Those who seek stern budgetary discipline have been annoyed by the continuing deficits and spiraling expenditures, disregarding the plain fact that the Budget Act permits Congress to adopt any budget policy it deems appropriate. Those who want a revamping of national priorities have been disappointed by the slow pace of change, as if a budget process alone could uproot interest-group politics in the United States or change the basic workings of Congress.

An understanding of congressional budgeting must be grounded on realistic expectations. Congress does not have an all-purpose budget process that meets the conflicting and exaggerated expectations of those who have promoted it. The budget is only one of the decisional processes available to Congress, and not always the most powerful one. The budget is only one of a number of interests that Congress has to take into account. As much as it might want to control spending or curb the deficit, there are other things on the mind of Congress. The full range of program interests competes with the budget for congressional attention. The peer controls on which the budget process is grounded cannot permit use of the budget as a checkpoint through which all other legislation must be reviewed. The budget cannot be the sole yardstick for measuring the worth of the bills produced by legislative committees.

The competition between budget and other values is affected by the mood of the moment. Congress is not always equally solicitous of the views of its budgeters. Sometimes it is eager to push ahead with spending plans, and expansionist fever surmounts the budget controls. Moods change. When Congress is more concerned about stock taking and retrenching, it might favor strict budget control over competing interests. Congressional budgeters cannot expect to be equally powerful or listened to each year. Sometimes there will be a strong congressional market for their point of view; at other times, a weak one. The appropriations committees have lived with these swings in congressional sentiment for 110 years; the budget committees also will have to ride out the ups and downs in their legislative esteem.

It is a mistake to regard the budget as the arena for making more than $500 billion of program decisions each year. A task of this magnitude—or even a fraction of this size—would overburden the executive branch's and Congress's capacity for bridging political differences. Yet, the congressional budget process often is measured in terms of how it makes (or unmakes) the totality of program decisions for the United States. Consider the expectations shown for the budget process in the following remarks by Senator Muskie on the occasion of the Senate's inaugural debate on a budget resolution:

> The Budget and Impoundment Control Act of 1974 is not a bookkeeping tool. It is a policy instrument that gives us new control over the direction America takes.
>
> It enables us to say indeed, it requires us to say—how America's resources will be used.
>
> How much shall we spend? How much can we afford?
>
> How much shall we tax? How big will the public sector be?
>
> Will the transition from energy plenty to energy scarcity be smooth or rough?
>
> How and where shall we invest today to meet the energy needs of tomorrow?
>
> Who will bear the heaviest burden?
>
> What challenges does the world hold for us after Vietnam? How much shall we invest in arms? How much in trade development? How much in intelligence? How much in diplomacy?

> Where shall we encourage Americans to live; in cities or in suburbs, or in rural America?
> How much for education?
> How much for health; for research; or disease prevention; or hospitals; or doctor training; or clean water and clean air?
> Shall we do all of these things, knowing that it will mean not doing something else?
> How can we insure 200 million Americans a better life tomorrow, and next year, and for generations?[40]

Even discounting its verbal excesses, this is an extraordinary statement. A Congress that tried to do these things would never work its way through its first budget resolution. So many discordant interests would have to be reconciled that the process surely would collapse in disarray. Moreover, it would be astonishing for the United States to practice pluralist politics along with monolithic budgeting. If the budget process were the all-reaching, consistent, critical decision process it often is credited with being, command over the budget would bring control over the political system as well. If the budget committees exercised dominion over foreign policy, energy resources, and all the other policy matters encompassed in Muskie's sweeping statement, they would have extraordinary leverage over all the other participants and committees in the legislative process.

The budget must be seen as only one—and not always the most important or decisive—arena for public choice. Congressional committees make budget decisions when they develop legislation; administrators make budget decisions when they promulgate regulations; the president influences the budget when he hits the campaign trail. It might be said that the federal government has two budget processes or that the budget process serves two rather different functions. It is at once the process by which decisions are made and the process by which decisions are costed out and recorded. Some program decisions are made in the budget; others are merely translated into dollar terms when the budget is assembled. For a good part of the federal budget—much more than half—the budget is the document in which decisions are recorded, not where they are made. Legislation mandating the payment of black lung benefits is accounted for in each year's budget, but the decision is made at the legislative stage, when the entitlement is conferred. Because the budget comprehensively accounts for all financial transactions, it is easy to be deceived into thinking that the budget is the place where the critical choices are made.

[40] U.S., Congress, Senate, *Congressional Record*, 94th Congress, 1st session, April 29, 1975, p. 7067.

Congress has been told again and again during its years of budgetary experience that it must choose between a budget process that is merely a bookkeeping device or—to return to Muskie's words—one that is "a policy instrument." These two conceptions of budgeting are posited as opposites; Congress cannot have it both ways. Congress is urged to use its budget for making policy; otherwise, the process would become only an accounting tool. Both types of budgets, however, will coexist as long as Congress has its own budget process.

The operation of the budget process will be heavily influenced by the fiscal condition of the country. But one cannot be certain of how Congress would respond to fiscal scarcity. One possibility would be for Congress to tilt the balance of power toward its budget specialists, away from its program advocates. Without changing the rules or procedures in the 1974 act, Congress might vote more stringent resolutions and insist on holding the line when appropriations and other spending measures reach the floor. It might impose tough reconciliation requirements on committees and compel them to scale down laws mandating higher levels of expenditures than those set in its budget resolutions. Congress might even do something about entitlements that consume a rising share of the federal budget. These moves, if implemented, would embolden the budget committees vis-à-vis other legislative powerholders.

Fiscal scarcity could lead to a different outcome, escapist budgeting in which Congress turns to unrealistic budget levels as a way out of its problem. It might adopt resolutions with "acceptable" deficits in full expectation that the amount would be raised later in the year, when the revenue and/or spending targets prove unattainable. Congress could then claim that it acted prudently but its budget was overtaken by events beyond its control. Both responses might coexist in the same budget cycle. Thus, the first budget resolution for fiscal 1981 purported to be in balance, though it was widely expected on Capitol Hill that the federal government would incur a large deficit. But that first resolution also contained a reconciliation instruction which led to multibillion dollar savings in entitlements and other programs. The future effectiveness of congressional budgeting might depend on whether it tilts more to escapism or to realistic attempts to deal with the nation's fiscal condition.

The CBO's Policy Analysis: An Unquestionable Misuse of a Questionable Theory

Preston J. Miller
and
Arthur J. Rolnick

The Congressional Budget Office (CBO) is in an unenviable position. It is called upon, upon short notice, to produce objective, quantitative studies of the economic effects of alternative government policies. This is a most difficult task under the best of conditions. It then is not too surprising, given the time and political constraints within which the CBO staff must work, that one can find fault with its procedure.

Our main criticism of the CBO's analysis, though, is that many of its faults are not neutral: they tend to have bias that encourages active stabilization policies. The CBO's virtual neglect of economic uncertainties and its emphasis on short time horizons make active policies appear much more attractive than even its own macroeconometric model would suggest.

It would not be enough, however, for the CBO to make better use of its existing model. The CBO's model, like all existing macroeconometric models, is useless for policy analysis; it allows neither reliable prediction of the economic effects of alternative policies nor proper evaluation of alternative economic outcomes. The CBO should adopt a rational expectations, equilibrium approach in order to overcome these difficulties.

In part 1 of this paper, we describe the control-theoretic framework that has been adopted by most macro analysts and examine its implication for policy analysis. We next describe the CBO's approach and indicate how it misuses this framework. In part 2, we criticize the tra-

---

This paper first appeared in the *Journal of Monetary Economics* 6 (April 1980), pp. 171–198. The views expressed are solely those of the authors and do not necessarily represent the views of the Federal Reserve Bank of Minneapolis or the Federal Reserve System. The authors would like to thank Tom Sargent and Neil Wallace for their comments.

ditional macroeconometric approach to policy analysis and conclude by recommending the rational expectations, equilibrium approach.

How the CBO Misuses the Traditional Macroeconometric Approach

To help us evaluate the CBO's analysis, we first describe the control-theoretic framework that many macroeconometric analysts have adopted for policy evaluation.[1] This framework imposes important criteria that must be met for an analysis to be valid. We argue that the CBO falls considerably short of meeting these criteria.

The Macroeconometric Approach. The control-theoretic framework consists of the following three elements:

1. a model that describes the effects of changes in the variables that the decision makers control (instruments) on the rest of the variables in the system
2. an objective function that assigns values to alternative paths of the variables important to decision makers (goals)
3. a technique for finding the settings of the instruments that maximize the objective function.

This framework is quite general and has been readily adapted to macro policy analysis. The typical macroeconometric model, objective function, and techniques used to compute the best values of the instruments are described next.

[1] See, for example, G. C. Chow, "Effect of Uncertainty on Optimal Control Policies," *International Economic Review*, vol. 14 (October 1973), pp. 632–645; idem, "A Solution to Optimal Control of Linear Systems with Unknown Parameters," Econometric Research Program, Research Memorandum, no. 157 (Princeton: Princeton University, December 1973); idem, *Analysis and Control of Dynamic Economic Systems* (New York: J. Wiley and Sons, 1975); idem, "An Approach to the Feedback Control of Nonlinear Econometric Systems," *Annals of Economic and Social Measurement*, vol. 5 (Summer 1976), pp. 297–309; idem, "The Control of Nonlinear Econometric Systems with Unknown Parameters," *Econometrica*, vol. 44 (July 1976), pp. 685–695; R. Craine and A. Havenner, "Optimal Control in a Linear Macroeconomic Model with Random Coefficients," in *IEEE Conference on Decision and Control* (San Diego, December 1973); idem, "A Stochastic Optimal Control Technique for Models with Estimated Coefficients," *Econometrica*, vol. 45 (May 1977), pp. 1013–1021; J. Kareken, T. Muench, and N. Wallace, "Optimal Open Market Strategy: The Use of Information Variables," *American Economic Review*, vol. 63 (March 1973), pp. 156–172; D. Kendrick, "Adaptive Control of Macroeconomic Models with Measurement Error," in *5th NBER Conference on Stochastic Control in Economics* (New Haven: National Bureau of Economic Research, May 1977); William Poole, "Optimal Choice of Monetary Policy Instruments in a Simple Stochastic Macro Model, *Quarterly Journal of Economics*, vol. 84 (May 1970), pp. 197–216; and H. Theil, *Economic Forecasts and Policy* (Amsterdam: North-Holland, 1965).

The typical macroeconometric model is a large system of equations describing the dynamic interactions of many economic variables. The variables involved consist of those determined within the model (the endogenous variables) and those affecting the endogenous variables but determined outside the model (the exogenous variables), such as weather and policy instruments.

Because of its mathematical tractability, macro analysts usually use a linear model or a linear approximation to a nonlinear model in their analysis. It will be useful for our discussion to represent a linear macroeconometric system by

$$A_0 y_t + \ldots + A_m y_{t-m} = B_0 x_t + \ldots + B_n x_{t-n} + \varepsilon_t \quad (1)$$

and

$$x_t = C_1 x_{t-1} + \ldots + C_p x_{t-p} + u_t. \quad (2)$$

Here y_t is an $L \times 1$ vector of endogenous variables, x_t is a $K \times 1$ vector of exogenous variables, and ε_t is an $L \times 1$ and u_t a $K \times 1$ vector of random disturbances. The A_j's are $L \times L$ matrices, and the B_j's are $L \times K$ matrices of system coefficients. The C_j's are $K \times K$ matrices of coefficients that define the exogenous processes. Equation (1) represents the structural relationships in the economy, including both behavioral equations and accounting and balance sheet identities. Equation (2) contains, among other exogenous relationships, the rule followed by policy makers.[2] For simplicity, we assume that equation (2) contains only the policy rule.

Also because of its mathematical tractability, economists usually have employed a quadratic objective function. G. C. Chow, for example, postulates for a T-horizon control problem the function

$$W = \sum_{t=1}^{T} (z_t - \hat{z}_t)' J_t (z_t - \hat{z}_t), \quad (3)$$

where the z_t's are $Q \times 1$ vectors of exogenous and endogenous variables ($Q \leq K + L$), the $\hat{z}_t$'s are $Q \times 1$ vectors of given targets, and the J_t's are known symmetric, positive, semidefinite $Q \times Q$ matrices.[3] The quadratic functional form is one of the simplest mathematical forms that satisfies the assumption of decreasing marginal rates of substitution and is commonly used in many fields of applied econometrics.[4]

[2] For simplicity, we assume that the rule depends only on exogenous variables. If the rule depends on both exogenous and lagged endogenous variables, it is contained in equation (1), though the arguments that follow are not affected.

[3] Chow, "Approach to Feedback Control."

[4] For a general discussion of the use of quadratic preferences, see H. Theil, *Optimal Decision Rules for Government and Industry* (Amsterdam: North-Holland, 1964), pp. 2–5.

Given a macroeconometric model and an explicit objective function, the problem of finding the optimal rule is technical and, because of coefficient uncertainty, usually quite difficult. One has to find the settings of the policy instruments over the planning horizon ($t=1,\ldots,T$) that maximizes W subject to equation (1). The solution is a rule that describes how to set policy instruments in each period based on available information. Assuming that current information includes last period's realizations, the optimal rule will be of the form

$$x_t = D_1\begin{bmatrix} x_{t-1} \\ y_{t-1} \end{bmatrix} + \ldots + D_h\begin{bmatrix} x_{t-h} \\ y_{t-h} \end{bmatrix}$$

which in general is different from equation (2). [The D_j's are $K \times (K+L)$ matrices.] In the case of linear models as represented in equation (1), with known coefficients, the method of dynamic programming has been successfully used to find the optimal rule. Even in the case of linear models, with unknown coefficients but known distributions of coefficients, optimal rules have been found.[5] Little progress, however, has been made in the case where the uncertainty about coefficients is due to estimation.[6]

At least in theory, though, the control-theoretic approach can produce—for a given model and objective function—a policy rule that yields the highest level of welfare over the policy horizon. Nevertheless, because in practice policy analysts are not policy makers, they cannot compute this rule. Seldom, if ever, are they given enough information about the objective function. They are usually told which variables are important, but they do not know how to evaluate alternative outcomes for these variables or how far to extend the analysis. Policy analysts, in practice, have never been able to calculate the optimal rule.

Many macro analysts, however, have adopted an alternative procedure that, under certain conditions, is equivalent to following the best policy. Roughly stated, the procedure is as follows. In the initial decision period, the model's residuals are set to zero; the model is then used to estimate the impact over the whole horizon of alternative sequences of

[5] For examples of both cases, see Chow, *Analysis and Control*, chaps. 8, 10.

[6] Suggested approximations to this problem can be found in ibid., chap. 10; D. Kendrick and B. H. Kang, "An Economist's Guide to Wide Sense Dual Control," Project on Control in Economics, Department of Economics (Austin: University of Texas, January 1975); E. C. MacRae, "Optimal Estimation and Control: A Structural Approximation," Special Studies Paper, no. 27 (Washington, D.C.: Board of Governors of the Federal Reserve System, July 1972); E. C. Prescott, "The Multi-period Control Problem under Uncertainty," *Econometrica*, vol. 40 (November 1972), pp. 1043–1058; E. Tse and Y. Bar-Shalom, "An Actively Adaptive Control for Linear Systems with Random Parameters," in *IEEE Transactions on Automatic Control*, AC–18 (April 1973), pp. 109–117; and A. Zellner, *An Introduction to Bayesian Inference in Econometrics* (New York: J. Wiley and Sons, 1971), chap. 11.

policy instrument values. Policy makers choose the most preferred outcome, and policy instruments in the first period are set at the values in the sequence associated with that outcome. When new information becomes available, forecasts, conditional on alternative sequences of policy instrument values, are again generated over the entire forecast horizon; again, the policy makers' choice of the most preferred outcome determines the settings of policy instruments, until new information is available. H. Theil has shown that this procedure is equivalent to following the best rule if the world (and hence the model) is linear and the coefficients are known.[7] This is the well-known certainty-equivalence theorem. The period-by-period approach it implies is well suited to the actual problems faced by policy analysts since no explicit objective function is required.

The period-by-period approach only yields an approximation to the best rule. Coefficients, as well as residuals, have to be treated as stochastic; most are unknown and must be estimated from a fairly limited data set. It immediately follows that the certainty-equivalence approximation to the best rule will only be as good as the precision of the estimates of the model's coefficients; the less known about the coefficients of the model, the further the approximation is from the best policy. The approximation, moreover, will probably not deviate in a neutral way; it will likely be biased toward policy activism. When there is coefficient uncertainty, the certainty-equivalence rule generally will call for a larger response to current information (that is, a larger change in the policy instruments) than the optimal rule response.[8]

Macroeconometric practitioners, therefore, should be cautious in their policy analysis. They are clearly handicapped by the lack of a well-defined objective function. To compensate, they must estimate the consequences of alternative policies over a reasonably long period so that it covers the likely policy horizon. To avoid seriously biasing their analysis toward activism, they must present not only their mean forecast of the impact of alternative policies but the rest of the distribution as well.

The CBO's Approach

Even though the CBO works directly for policy makers, it faces the same handicaps as other macroeconometric analysts. Congress does not provide it with an objective function, yet it is required to analyze al-

[7] Theil, *Economic Forecasts,* pp. 423–424.

[8] If variability in policy instruments is used to generate information about coefficients, the certainty-equivalence approach could imply a smaller response to current information than the optimal rule. For other conditions under which the responses could be smaller, see Chow, *Analysis and Control,* pp. 249–250.

ternative congressional policies. Like many other practitioners, it has adopted the period-by-period approach and presents Congress with forecasts of the impact of alternative policies.

To generate these forecasts, the CBO uses a hybrid macroeconometric model. It forecasts macro goal variables, such as the rate of inflation and the unemployment rate, typically over one to two years. Each forecast is conditioned on a sequence of policy actions. The Social Security Tax Reform Act of 1977 and the fiscal 1979 congressional budget are two recent policies examined by the CBO in this way.[9]

The CBO's Analysis of Two Recent Congressional Policies. The 1977 social security amendments were an attempt to make the social security system solvent for at least the next four decades. They imposed a substantial increase in payroll taxes, beginning with $6.6 billion in 1979 and increasing to $24.9 billion by 1982. The tax increase included both an increase in the taxable income level and an increase in tax rates. (The amendments called for some benefit cuts, but they were relatively minor.)

This change in the system's tax structure appears to be a significant step toward keeping the system solvent on a cash-flow basis; but it could also have significant side effects on employment, output, and inflation. The CBO focused mainly on the policy's short-run impact on these macro variables. It compared a no-tax-increase policy to the 1979 tax increase. The CBO's analysis indicated that the reduction in aggregate demand caused by immediately higher taxes would translate into lower real GNP. In ensuing periods, inflation would increase. Specifically, the CBO found that by 1982 this tax increase would reduce real gross national product (GNP) by almost 1 percent and employment by 0.5 million, while increasing the GNP deflator around one half percentage point. These effects were expected to build up gradually prior to 1982.[10]

Another issue that the CBO recently examined with the macroeconometric approach was the inflation-unemployment trade-off facing policy makers in the summer of 1978. What would be the likely outcome for the economy under the proposed 1979 fiscal budget? Would inflation continue at a high rate? If so, what would be the cost of reducing inflation in terms of lost output and employment?

The CBO's analysis of the economy indicated that the policy makers were in a dilemma. While inflation was to continue at high rates, at least through 1979, the economy was to experience only a moderate rate of

[9] U.S., Congress, Congressional Budget Office, "Aggregate Economic Effects of Changes in Social Security Taxes," August 1978; idem, "Inflation and Growth: The Economic Policy Dilemma," July 1978.

[10] Congressional Budget Office, "Aggregate Effects," p. 30.

growth. Any tightening of monetary or fiscal policy to fight inflation, therefore, could easily push the economy into a recession. Specifically, under the fiscal 1979 budget, which included a $15 billion tax cut, and under an assumed moderate course for monetary policy (the treasury bill rate not rising much above 7 percent), real GNP was expected to grow in the 3.5 to 4.5 percent range in 1978, slowing to between 2.7 and 4.2 percent in 1979; the unemployment rate was expected to be within a 5.2 to 6 percent range by the fourth quarter of 1979. Inflation, meanwhile, could go as high as 7.8 percent in 1978 and slow little in 1979.[11]

The CBO estimated that to lower inflation even modestly would cause a recession. Under the same fiscal budget assumptions but assuming a significantly tighter monetary policy (the treasury bill rate rising to 8.5 percent by early 1979), it estimated that real output would begin to decline by early 1979, leading eventually to a recession and 7 percent unemployment by the end of 1979. The CBO found that this significant loss in output and jobs would lead only to a one half percentage point reduction in the 1979 inflation rate.

The CBO concluded that traditional fiscal and monetary policies, at least in the short run, would be an expensive way to fight inflation. It instead suggested the use of a different mix of monetary and fiscal policies and new structural programs that eventually would improve the inflation-unemployment trade-off. The CBO recommended that the government take a closer look at its own actions and regulations that raise the private sector's costs, that it intervene directly in the wage-price determination process with some form of incomes policy, and that it promote measures to increase the supply of goods and services.[12]

The CBO's Macroeconometric Model. The CBO's analysis follows the standard macroeconometric approach. The model it employs to generate estimates of the impact of alternative policies, however, is a departure from the usual macroeconometric model.[13]

Several prominent econometric models are specifically designed to address macroeconomic policy issues; here the CBO has a problem. While generally appealing to the same Keynesian theory, these models

[11] Congressional Budget Office, "Inflation," p. 26.

[12] Congressional Budget Office, "Aggregate Effects," pp. 60–65.

[13] The CBO's model discussed here is presented in its Multipliers Project; see U.S., Congress, Congressional Budget Office, "A Methodology for Analyzing the Effects of Alternative Economic Policies," August 1977. The model is explicitly referenced in the CBO's social security tax study; see Congressional Budget Office, "Aggregate Effects," p. 26. No specific model is mentioned in the fiscal 1979 budget analysis (Congressional Budget Office, "Inflation"), but some version of such a model was presumably used.

differ considerably in detail and structure.[14] As a result, they produce a wide range of policy impacts. Experimenting with five such models—Data Resources, Inc. (DRI); Wharton; Chase; MIT-Penn-SSRC (MPS); and Fair—the CBO found, for example, that a $10 billion annual increase in government expenditures caused some increase in prices in one model, while causing virtually no change in another. Which model should it believe?

The CBO decided to believe partly in them all. To "make sense out of the diverse estimates," the CBO constructed its own model by averaging these five macroeconometric models.[15] The averaging procedure is reported in CBO's Multipliers Project.[16] The procedure is to take a weighted average of certain so-called key ratios of endogenous variables (the consumption-to-income and investment-to-income ratios, for example) across models. The CBO averaged this way, instead of, say, averaging reduced-form policy multipliers, because it claimed to have some prior information about such ratios and virtually none about policy multipliers. This information determined the weights the CBO used in its averaging scheme.

The CBO constructed the first version of its model to answer the question, What happens to GNP, consumption, fixed investment, other GNP components, transfer payments, tax revenues, and wages, when there is a change in federal expenditures? Monetary policy and corporate tax versions were also constructed. The following simplified version of the CBO's fiscal expenditure model will help explain its procedure:

$$\Delta Y_{t+i} = \Delta C_{t+i} + \Delta I_{t+i} + \Delta G_{t+i}$$

$$\Delta C_{t+i} = a_i \Delta Y_{t+i}$$

$$\Delta I_{t+i} = b_i \Delta Y_{t+i}$$

$$\Delta G_{t+i} = \Delta \overline{G} \qquad i=1, \ldots, 10$$

[14] The consumption equations of two prominent models help to illustrate how large these differences can be. (See Board of Governors of the Federal Reserve System, "Equations in the MIT-Penn-SSRC Econometric Model of the United States," unpublished staff paper [Washington, D.C., January 1975] and M. D. McCarthy, *The Wharton Quarterly Econometric Forecasting Model Mark III,* Studies in Quantitative Economics, no. 6 [Philadelphia: University of Pennsylvania, 1972].) To explain consumption expenditures, the MPS model builders estimated a single aggregate equation with essentially three explanatory variables: disposable personal income, wealth, and inflation. The Wharton model builders estimated a disaggregated equation dividing consumption into autos, other durables, nondurables, and services. As in the MPS model, disposable personal income and wealth are explanatory variables, but the Wharton model also includes the unemployment rate and an interest rate differential. MPS explanatory variables enter as constrained distributed lags; Wharton's are mostly contemporaneous, with no distributed lags.

[15] Congressional Budget Office, "Methodology for Analyzing," p. 1.

[16] Ibid., entire report.

where ΔY, ΔC, and ΔI denote the change in income, consumption, and investment, respectively, in period $t+i$ due to exogenous changes in government spending, $\Delta\overline{G}$, initiated at $t+1$. The ten values of a_i and b_i are the parameters the CBO derives.

The a_i's and b_i's are constructed by simulation for given G's. The CBO first simulates each model for some given level of government expenditures and other exogenous variables. The models are then simulated again with the same exogenous variables but with new levels of G that reflect a once-and-for-all jump of $\Delta\overline{G}$ vis-à-vis the original path. For each model, ten quarters of key ratios are computed. The CBO would compute the ten quarters of a_i's and b_i's for our illustrative model by averaging these ratios across models and incorporating (in some unspecified way) its prior information about the a_i's and b_i's (see table 1). The accompanying table contains the consumption-income ratios (a_i's) that the CBO computed for the five models and the averaged coefficients that it used in its fiscal expenditure model.[17] These coefficients were based on a sustained $10 billion increase in government expenditures.

The Multipliers Project is the CBO's attempt to construct a consensus model to forecast the impact of a particular change in policy. It clearly cannot be used to study policy changes in general. Except for policy changes that are simply multiples of the one that the CBO used to generate its key ratios, different policies generally yield different ratios.[18] Since any specific CBO model has limited use, the CBO produced different versions of its model for different policies. Thus, there is a monetary policy version and a corporate tax rate version.[19]

While limited to particular policies only, a CBO model can be used to forecast policy effects on all the endogenous variables in the system. Yet the CBO uses the model only to predict nominal income. The impact on real GNP, inflation, and unemployment are derived from other equations that the CBO estimates directly. The specific equations are reported in an unpublished study[20] and described in the following way:

> . . . employment and unemployment changes resulting from a policy change are derived from an Okun's law type of relationship between unemployment and the real GNP gap, lagged one quarter. . . . A two-equation, wage-price model and a CPI–GNP deflator relationship are then used to derive a GNP deflator consistent with the unemployment rate. The deflator,

[17] Ibid., p. 6.

[18] Ibid., p. 18.

[19] Ibid., pp. 15, 20.

[20] U.S., Congress, Congressional Budget Office, "A Simplified Wage-Price Model," unpublished, 1975.

TABLE 1

QUARTERLY VALUES OF a_i

	Models					*Basic Multipliers Model*
Quarter	DRI	Wharton	Chase	MPS	Fair	
1	.41	.26	.55	.25	.68	.35
2	.63	.26	.47	.37	.80	.45
3	.68	.28	.56	.44	.95	.51
4	.71	.30	.65	.51	.97	.55
5	.73	.39	.68	.58	1.02	.60
6	.73	.49	.67	.62	.96	.62
7	.73	.69	.69	.65	.97	.67
8	.71	.83	.70	.70	.98	.70
9	.71	.75	.70	.72	.95	.71
10	.71	.67	.70	.76	.90	.71

together with the level of nominal GNP, determines real GNP. The new real GNP gap determines the next period's unemployment.[21]

The logic of this model implies that the inflationary effects of aggregate demand policies stem entirely from changes in the unemployment rate acting through the Phillips curve. In the current period, unemployment is predetermined, so that a change in aggregate demand policies affects real GNP but not prices. (Thus, if the Federal Reserve System announced that it intended to double or triple the money supply and then actually carried out its plan, the CBO model would predict that initially output would increase but prices would not be affected.) In subsequent periods, the changes in real GNP alter the real GNP gap, thereby causing changes in unemployment that work through the Phillips curve to changes in prices.

The CBO's Analysis: Flawed and Biased toward Activism

How seriously should Congress take the CBO's model and its policy forecasts? Should it abandon fiscal and monetary policy restraint because it is an expensive way to fight inflation and instead adopt wage-and-price controls? Should it also reconsider the social security tax increase because it will permanently lower real GNP? We think not. Even if macroeconometric models were useful for policy analysis (and there are

[21] Congressional Budget Office, "Methodology for Analyzing," p. 25.

good reasons to think they are not, as we discuss in part 2), the CBO's analysis is seriously flawed.

The most obvious problems with the CBO's approach stem from its model. To construct an average forecast, it chose five of the dozen or so existing macroeconometric models, but it never provides a rationale for its selections. Did it pick models based on ex-post or ex-ante forecasting properties or some other criteria? The CBO never describes the prior information that it used to weight coefficients across models. One must wonder how good this information is and whether or not it was ignored by all other model builders. Without it being reported, we can neither assess its quality nor reproduce the CBO's analysis. Another criticism is the model's potential lack of consistency. One of the major advantages of a macroeconometric model is that it can impose balance sheet and income constraints. One never has to worry about agents spending more than they receive because the model automatically enforces this constraint. It is not obvious that this holds for the CBO's model because it goes outside the averaged model to predict unemployment and inflation. Furthermore, we are again not provided with a rationale for its procedure. Although the CBO reports real GNP and inflation forecasts from its averaged model, no explanation is given as to why the CBO replaces these forecasts with those generated by its own forecasting equations.[22]

These shortcomings of the CBO's model raise serious doubts about its results but do not bias them in any obvious way. However, when the CBO forecasts policy effects for only one to two years and when it virtually ignores the uncertainty implicit in its model, it does bias its results.

Horizon Too Short. Earlier in this paper, we suggested that a careful analysis of alternative economic policies must include outcomes over the entire policy horizon. If policy analysts instead forecast the impact of alternative policies for only one or two years and then repeat the analysis two years later (because policy makers really do care about more than just the immediate future), they in effect are solving for the optimal rule over the wrong policy horizon. It can readily be shown that a better policy would result by extending the initial analysis over a longer period.

Cutting the horizon short in this case also is not neutral. Most standard macroeconometric models—and the CBO's does not appear to be an exception—predict that a move to an expansionary policy will stimulate output and have little effect on inflation over a period of one to two years. Subsequently, the real output effect will die out, while the

[22] Ibid., p. 24.

inflationary effect will grow. By truncating the forecasts at less than two years, therefore, the CBO gives the misleading picture that changes in policy will have major effects on real output and negligible effects on inflation. The accompanying chart demonstrates these effects using an older version of the MPS model described by F. de Leeuw and E.M. Gramlich.[23]

Uncertainty Ignored. Earlier in this paper, we argued that a careful policy analysis must incorporate uncertainty. Yet here again the CBO fails, and again it biases its results toward activism. The theory of decision making generally suggests that the less we know, the less we should do.[24] For economic policy, this means that the more uncertainty about the impact of economic policies, the less responsive policy actions should be to current conditions. Thus, ignoring or just understating uncertainty will generally imply a more activist policy than is warranted. The CBO has done exactly that, by virtually ignoring the forecasting differences among macroeconometric models as well as ignoring the stochastic properties of the models themselves.

The CBO obviously recognizes that there is some uncertainty about policy forecasts. In fact, incorporating this uncertainty into its model was the purpose of the CBO's Multipliers Project. Nevertheless, simply averaging forecasts across models does not accomplish this purpose. The extent of this diversity, moreover, appears to be substantial. Consider, for example, its estimates of the consumption-to-income ratio (see table 1). The range of this coefficient across models in the first quarter is .25 to .68. The range decreases in later quarters and is .67 to .90 in the tenth quarter. The investment-to-income ratio varies from .02 to .08 in the first quarter and increases in range to .01 to .24 by the tenth.[25]

The stochastic properties of the individual models are another major source of uncertainty that is not incorporated into the CBO's analysis. The available evidence suggests that these models generate fairly large forecasting errors and are not stable over time. Yet no reference to this problem is found in any of the CBO studies.

There are two substantive ways to describe the accuracy of an econometric model. The first is a model's implied forecasting properties, that is, the distribution of forecasting errors implied by the estimation procedure and the sample period data and commonly summarized by the standard error of forecast statistic. The second is the actual fore-

[23] F. de Leeuw and E. M. Gramlich, "The Channels of Monetary Policy," *Federal Reserve Bulletin,* June 1969, pp. 472–491.

[24] This is not necessarily true if we allow policy makers to experiment with variability in policy instruments in order to learn more about the structure.

[25] Congressional Budget Office, "Methodology for Analyzing," p. 10.

FIGURE 1

THE OUTCOME OF A TAX CUT*

Short Term: What Congress Sees

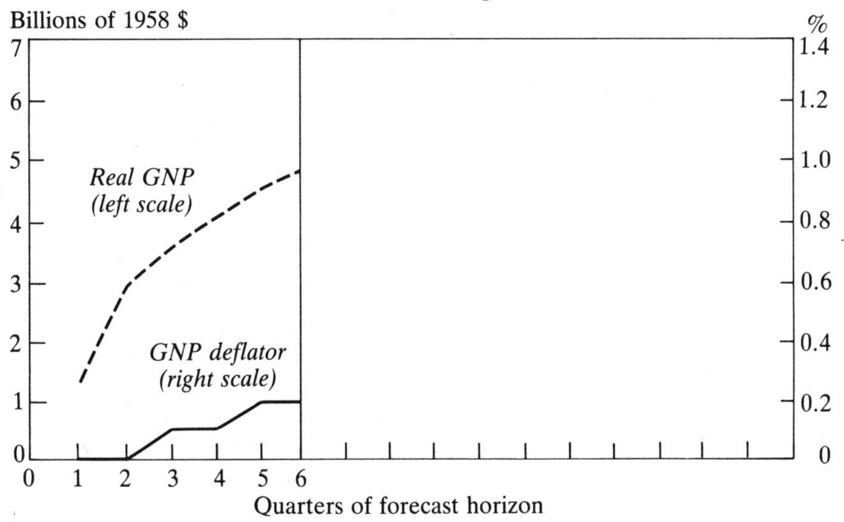

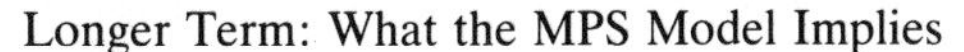

Longer Term: What the MPS Model Implies

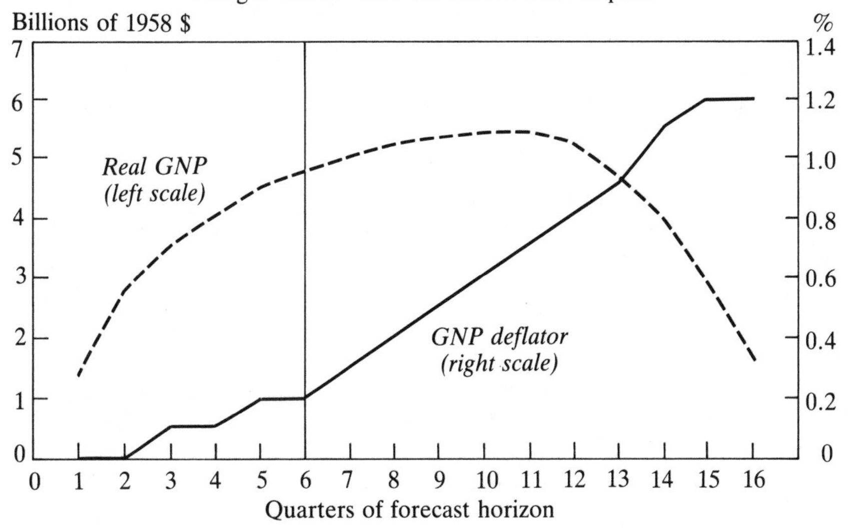

*Effects of a 0.02 decrease in the personal income tax rate, initial conditions of 1964, Q1 (see de Leeuw and Gramlich, "Channels of Monetary Policy," p. 489).

casting record of the model outside the sample period, which is usually summarized by the average of actual forecasting errors.

Both statistics are needed to judge the accuracy and usefulness of a model. The standard error of forecast measures the expected accuracy of a model, the degree of accuracy that we can expect a model to produce over a long period of time if the model is correct. The actual forecast errors then provide a test of a model. If they are, say, two or more times greater than the standard error of forecast, we can reject the model at a high level of confidence. Either it never captured the true coefficients or the true coefficients have changed. In either case, the model is not a reliable forecasting tool. A minimum forecasting criterion for a credible model, therefore, is passing a test of stability. That is, the model (the estimated parameters) must be stable over time.[26]

Clearly, this is a necessary but not a sufficient criterion. We can always build a model with large enough standard errors of forecast so that it easily passes a test of stability. For sufficiency, then, models should have relatively small standard errors of forecast so that they provide some information to policy makers.

Although we do not have forecasting statistics for the specific models the CBO used in its Multipliers Project, the evidence we do have suggests that these models are suspect. Macro models have generally done poorly on both forecasting criteria. Standard errors of forecast are usually quite large, well outside the range policy makers would find useful; actual forecast errors are even larger, raising doubts about the reliability of these models.

The frequent use of intercept adjustments provides some casual evidence that macroeconometric models do not hold up over time. In practice, macroeconometric models are hardly ever used with their originally estimated coefficients. Intercept adjustments might be justified as an efficient technique for reestimating a model as current information becomes available. Yet no systematic or testable procedure has been used. Instead, we observe ad hoc adjustments that are rarely explained or defended. Either macro analysts have simply not done a careful job of describing their reestimation techniques, or their models really do not capture fixed economic relationships.

Formal testing of macroeconometric models, while limited, strongly confirms the latter proposition. Since the structure of most macro models is rather complex, the only practical way to calculate their forcasting properties is by simulation. The only study we know of that simulated the distribution of forecasting errors for several macroeconometric

[26] This test corresponds to the single-equation test devised by G. C. Chow in "Tests for Equality Between Sets of Coefficients in Two Linear Regressions," *Econometrica,* vol. 78 (July 1960), pp. 591–605.

models and tested for stability (a study by T. Muench and others) raises serious doubts about the credibility of such models.[27] The standard errors of forecast (estimated with pre-1970 data) were quite large for several key goal variables, and the models dramatically failed stability tests.

The distribution of forecasting errors for real GNP growth estimated in the Muench study illustrates the questionable value of macro-econometric models. The standard error of forecast for real growth was estimated at 2.5 percentage points for a four-quarter prediction and 3 percentage points for a six-quarter prediction. Since the CBO's model is based on models similar to the ones analyzed in this study, the fore-casting properties are likely to be about the same. If this is true, it would imply that the CBO's 3 percent real GNP forecast for 1979 has a one-standard-error confidence band of 0.5 to 5.5 percent and a two-standard-error confidence band of −2.0 to 8.0 percent. It is likely that this margin of error would be considered large by most policy makers and would give them little confidence in the CBO's ability to forecast the future course of the economy.

Consumption, residential construction, business inventories, and short-term interest rates were other variables that the Muench study found to have rather large standard errors of forecast. Yet this was not true of all variables; the price level, for example, had a small confidence band. Nevertheless, here the models broke down the most. Actual fore-cast errors for the GNP deflator were quite large, significantly greater than three times the standard error of forecast, and probably caused these models to fail on the multivariate test.[28]

The evidence suggests that the macroeconometric models used by the CBO have generally large forecasting errors and are not stable over time. Could the averaged model be stable and have relatively small forecast errors even though the underlying models lack these properties? We doubt it. Although we have no formal statistics, it is likely that an ad hoc average of unstable models will also be unstable. Besides the within-model errors, the diversity that the CBO found across models suggests rather large standard errors of forecast.

The Phillips curve in the CBO's model, which is not an average constructed from other models, also is unlikely to meet the minimum forecasting criteria. Both casual observations and formal tests suggest that the Phillips curve has not been stable. As late as the early 1970s, the estimated relationship between inflation and unemployment sug-

[27] T. Muench, A. Rolnick, N. Wallace, and W. Weiler, "Tests for Structural Change and Prediction Intervals for the Reduced Forms of Two Structural Models of the U.S.: The FRB-MIT and Michigan Quarterly Models," *Annals of Economic and Social Measurement*, vol. 3 (July 1974), pp. 491–519.

[28] Ibid., pp. 502, 511.

gested that the economy would experience as little as 4 percent inflation with an unemployment rate of 4 percent.[29] In recent years, there have been a number of tests on the stability of Phillips curve relationships as posed by the CBO; they have uniformly rejected the hypothesis that the relationships remained invariant over the 1970s.[30] So this crucial equation in the CBO model is also suspect.

There is obviously much evidence at least to question the stability and accuracy of macroeconometric models, yet the CBO hardly mentions the problem. It sometimes reports ranges for real GNP growth and inflation, but it does not tell what these ranges represent. Based on the available evidence, the inflation range may be a one-standard-error confidence band; the real growth range, however, is significantly smaller than that. The CBO's words also suggest much more certainty than is warranted:

> The first concurrent resolution provided for a $15 billion cut in taxes for fiscal year 1979 . . . as compared with revenues from currrent policies. According to CBO estimates, if the entire tax cut were dropped, real growth from the fourth quarter of 1978 to the fourth quarter of 1979 would be about 0.5 percentage point lower and the unemployment rate would be 0.2 percentage point higher than the baseline forecast. . . . The price level, as measured by the Consumer Price Index, would be only around 0.2 percent lower by the end of 1980.[31]

Thus, by ignoring the uncertainty implicit in its own model and by overstating the accuracy of its forecasts in this way, the CBO misleads policy makers into having too much confidence in macro analysts' ability to predict the impact of a change in policy. It therefore encourages more policy change than is warranted.

What's Wrong with the Macroeconometric Approach and What's the Best Alternative

We have argued that the CBO has not made good use of the macroeconometric approach to policy making. In particular, it has neglected uncertainty and long-run effects of policies—omissions that tend to encourage activist policies. Even if these misuses of the macroeconometric

[29] R. E. Lucas, Jr., "Understanding Business Cycles," in K. Brunner and A. H. Meltzer, eds., *Stabilization of the Domestic and International Economy*, Carnegie-Rochester Conference Series on Public Policy, vol. 5 (Amsterdam: North-Holland, 1977), pp. 7–29.

[30] For examples of such tests, see S. K. McNees, "An Empirical Assessment of 'New Theories' of Inflation and Unemployment," in *After the Phillips Curve: Persistence of High Inflation and High Unemployment* (Boston: Federal Reserve Bank of Boston, June 1978), pp. 37–40.

[31] Congressional Budget Office, "Inflation," p. 56

approach were corrected, however, the CBO's analysis would still be objectionable. The macroeconometric approach itself is deficient.

The macroeconometric approach to policy making suffers two fundamental deficiencies:

1. The behavioral relationships in macroeconometric models do not remain invariant to changes in monetary or fiscal policy rules. Those relationships are estimated under the assumption of fixed policy rules over the sample period. The models logically cannot be manipulated to analyze the effects of alternative policies because deviations in policy from the historical rules cause the decision rules of individuals to change. Since the macroeconometric behavioral relationships are aggregations of individual decision rules, they too must change when policy rules change.

2. Macroeconometric models are mute on the implications of alternative policies for efficiency and income distribution. Without the capability to relate policy outcomes to economic welfare, macroeconometric policy evaluation has been carried out in terms of proxy variables, such as the level of real GNP, the unemployment rate, and the inflation rate. These proxy variables can give very misleading signals, however, about the desirability of alternative policies.

In this section, we discuss in more detail these fundamental deficiencies of the macroeconometric approach and argue that they have important policy implications. The rational expectations, equilibrium approach, the alternative to the macroeconometric policy approach, overcomes these deficiencies and implies that less activist and less inflationary policies are desirable. The CBO's choice of the macroeconometric approach to policy making and its failure to acknowledge the alternative rational expectations approach is thus another source of bias in its advice. We describe a rational expectations theory of the business cycle and then indicate how such a theory is incorporated into the policy-making framework.

Instability of Macroeconometric Models

In discussing the uncertainty about macroeconometric model forecasts, we cited evidence that these models do not remain invariant over time. This empirical finding of model instability over time prompted economists to search for theoretical explanations. The most plausible explanation was advanced by R.E. Lucas, Jr.;[32] his explanation serves as a severe criticism of the macroeconometric approach to policy making.

[32] R. E. Lucas, Jr., "Econometric Policy Evaluation: A Critique," in K. Brunner and A. H. Meltzer, eds., *The Phillips Curve and Labor Markets*, Carnegie-Rochester Conference Series on Public Policy, vol. 1 (Amsterdam: North-Holland, 1976), pp. 19–46.

Lucas's explanation for the instability of macroeconometric models rests on the dependence of individual decisions to the government's policy rules. His point can be made simply with game theory. Suppose we consider policy making to be an economic game between the government on the one hand and private agents on the other. The question then arises, Which player makes the last move? Lucas points out that in macroeconometric policy analysis it is assumed that the government makes the last move. Individual decision rules, implicit in macroeconometric models, are estimated over a historical period; in predicting the effects of alternative policies, it is assumed that these decision rules are fixed. Thus, the search for optimal policies in macroeconometric models consists of allowing government policy rules to vary, while holding individual decision rules fixed.

Although we can construct more general examples by allowing for differences in utility functions, longer planning horizons, and some degree of uncertainty, the main point still holds. To predict accurately the impact of economic policies, a useful model must not only identify decision rules [the *A*'s and *B*'s in (1)], but it must also identify how they change under alternative policies (changes in the *C*'s).[33]

This criticism of macroeconometric models is not just theoretical nitpicking; it has a major impact on policy analysis. In some standard macroeconometric models, the real impact of aggregate demand policies can literally disappear once individuals are allowed to respond rationally to changes in government policies.[34] In these simple models, nonactive policies are optimal, and the inflation-unemployment tradeoff proves to be illusory.

Macroeconometric Policy Evaluation

The unemployment rate and inflation rate are not, however, the ultimate concerns of policy. The ultimate concerns are the levels of welfare of the individuals in the society. Yet, macroeconometric models force the

[33] For an elaboration of this view, see, for example, J. Marschak, "Economic Measurements for Policy and Prediction," in William C. Hood and T. C. Koopmans, eds., *Studies in Econometric Method,* Cowles Foundation Monograph, no. 14 (New Haven: Yale University Press, 1953); Lucas, "Econometric Evaluation"; and R. E. Lucas, Jr., and T. Sargent, "After Keynesian Macroeconomics," *Federal Reserve Bank of Minneapolis Quarterly Review* (Spring 1979), pp. 1–16.

[34] See T. Sargent and N. Wallace, " 'Rational' Expectations, the Optimal Monetary Instrument, and the Optimal Money Supply Rule," *Journal of Political Economy,* vol. 83 (April 1975), pp. 241–254; B. T. McCallum, "Price Level Adjustments and the Rational Expectations Approach to Macroeconomic Stabilization Policy," *Journal of Money, Credit, and Banking,* vol. 10 (November 1978), pp. 418–436; and B. T. McCallum and J. K. Whitaker, "The Effectiveness of Fiscal Feedback Rules and Automatic Stabilizers under Rational Expectations," *Journal of Monetary Economics,* vol. 5 (1979), pp. 171–186.

desirability of alternative policies to be judged in terms of macroeconomic variables, and they provide no clues on the link between these variables and economic welfare. As T. Sargent states, "The models themselves can't be used to tell who is hurt by inflation (anticipated or unanticipated?), why inflation is bad, or why a larger variance in the unemployment rate is bad."[35] Moreover, recent advances in economic theory clearly indicate that any link between macro variables and economic welfare is extremely tenuous.

Search theories of the labor market suggest that there are policies (such as elimination of unemployment insurance) that would lower the unemployment rate (at a given inflation rate) and yet could reduce welfare. Such policies can result in too much of individuals' time being allocated to labor and too little to leisure and, thus, can make them worse off.

The theory of optimal tax structure implies that some amount of taxation by inflation could be optimal.[36] In this case, policies that reduce inflation below its efficient rate (at a given unemployment rate) would be welfare reducing, since they result in too little government revenues being raised by the inflation tax.

Even policies that dampen the business cycle need not be desirable. Sargent devised a tax policy rule in a rational expectations model of the business cycle that effectively stabilizes output.[37] That rule, however, is Pareto dominated by a purely passive rule for which policy actions do not respond at all to current conditions. In Sargent's model, output fluctuations result from optimal adjustments in the private sector to unavoidable random shocks. Efforts by the government to smooth the output fluctuations, then, just interfere with the adjustments being made in the private sector and increase the total costs of adjustment.

Replacement by the Rational Expectations, Equilibrium Approach

Since the macroeconometric approach as used by the CBO does not allow us reliably to predict the outcomes associated with different policies nor to rank policy outcomes in terms of welfare, a different approach to policy making is required. We argue that a rational expec-

[35] T. Sargent, "Comments on the Shiller and Kalchbrenner and Tinsley Papers" (Paper delivered at Conference on the Monetary Mechanism in Open Economics, Helsinki, Finland, August 4–9, 1975), p. 2.

[36] See, for example, A. Drazen, "The Optimal Rate of Inflation Revisited," *Journal of Monetary Economics,* vol. 5 (June 1979), pp. 231–248; E.S. Phelps, "Inflation in the Theory of Public Finance," *Swedish Journal of Economics,* vol. 75 (March 1973), pp. 67–82; and J. Siegel, "Notes on Optimal Taxation and the Optimal Rate of Inflation," *Journal of Monetary Economics,* vol. 4 (April 1978), pp. 297–305.

[37] T. Sargent, *Macroeconomic Theory* (New York: Academic Press, 1979).

tations, equilibrium approach is needed. This approach is nothing more than classical economics applied in a dynamic, stochastic setting.

Keynesian theory, which underlies the macroeconometric approach, at one time filled a void. It was developed as a separate branch of economics because of classical theory's inability to explain certain business cycle phenomena. In particular, the classical neutrality propositions seemed to be contradicted by observed positive correlations persisting from one business cycle to another between real variables, such as output and employment, and nominal variables, such as the price level and money supply.

Keynes correctly attributed these correlations to "sticky" wages. In an economy where wages and prices adjust instantaneously to new market conditions, such correlations would not be observed. Shifts in nominal demand would result in fluctuating wages and prices, but they would leave the real wage, and hence output and employment, unchanged. The question is, What makes nominal wages sticky?

Keynesian economists have explained sticky wages by assuming either nonoptimizing agents or nonclearing markets.[38] Either of these assumptions generally is enough to overturn the classical neutrality propositions.

Due to the pathbreaking work of Lucas, there is no longer a void to be filled.[39] Lucas succeeded in reconciling the observed business-cycle correlations with the classical neutrality propositions. He was able to construct rational expectations models of the business cycle that do not violate the classical postulates of optimizing agents and clearing markets. The major contribution of Lucas's work is the return of business-cycle analysis to the fold of classical economics.

If business-cycle phenomena are subject to classical economic analysis, it then follows that government stabilization policies are subject to classical analysis and evaluation. That is, they can be analyzed and evaluated—as are all other government economic policies—in the traditional framework of public finance and welfare economics.

In the following sections, we discuss the rational expectations theory of the business cycle and its incorporation into the policy-making frame-

[38] On nonoptimizing agents, see J. Tobin, "Money Wage Rates and Employment," in S. Harris, ed., *The New Economics: Keynes' Influence on Theory and Public Policy* (New York: A. A. Knopf, 1947), pp. 572–587; on nonclearing markets, see R. E. Hall, "The Rigidity of Wages and the Persistence of Unemployment," in A. M. Okun and G. L. Perry, eds., *Brookings Papers on Economic Activity,* no. 2 (Washington, D.C.: Brookings Institution, 1975), pp. 301–335; and J. B. Taylor, "Aggregate Dynamics and Staggered Contracts," *Journal of Political Economy,* vol. 88 (February 1980), pp. 1–23.

[39] R. E. Lucas, Jr., "Expectations and the Neutrality of Money," *Journal of Economic Theory,* vol. 4 (April 1972), pp. 103–124.

work. We conclude by suggesting that this approach will lead economists to ask better questions.

Foundations of the Rational Expectations Theory of the Business Cycle. The rational expectations theory of the business cycle has its roots in the work of Lucas.[40] Lucas extended classical macroeconomic theory by explicitly considering uncertainties faced by economic agents and costs incurred in gathering information. He was able to show that sticky wages, and thus output fluctuations, can occur as the result of actions of optimizing agents in markets that clear.

In order to illustrate the principles of Lucas's theory, we offer the following simple story.[41] Agents enter into contracts that specify wages and prices over a number of periods into the future. The length of the contract is struck as a balance. The shorter the contract, the less agents are vulnerable to unanticipated inflation but the more they must pay in terms of information-gathering and contracting costs. Agents in this story are assumed to form forecasts of future prices rationally; that is, their forecasts are equal to the true mathematical expectations conditional on the set of information they have on hand. Rational forecasts of prices, thus, are unbiased; rational agents cannot be systematically fooled by aggregate demand policies.[42]

All uncertainty is assumed to stem from two sources: random changes in government aggregate demand policies and random shifts in consumer preferences. When agents observe a price change for a single good, they cannot determine whether it is due to

1. a change in aggregate demand policies that can be expected to cause proportionate changes in prices of other goods
2. a shift in preferences that can be expected to cause relative price changes
3. some combination of the two

Thus, agents cannot infer with certainty the behavior of average prices from the behavior of any single price.

Prices are more flexible than wages in this story because firms only have to know parameters of the demand and cost curves for their own

[40] Ibid.

[41] Our story essentially extends the model in Lucas, "Expectations," by incorporating a theory of endogenous contracting. An explicit model along the lines of our story, however, has not been fully worked out.

[42] This proposition holds as long as agents' information sets contain past prices. For a proof, see T. Sargent, "Rational Expectations, the Real Rate of Interest, and the Natural Rate of Unemployment," in A. M. Okun and G. L. Perry, eds., *Brookings Papers on Economic Activity,* no. 2 (Washington, D.C.: Brookings Institution, 1973), pp. 429–472.

product to set prices, while workers must consider the prices of all goods when they enter contracts to determine wages. Thus, with smaller information costs, the contracting period for prices is shorter than that for wages. To simplify our story, we assume that prices adjust instantaneously.

According to our story, a government aggregate demand policy action that is essentially neutral—such as money transfers proportional to individuals' initial holdings and funded by money creation—has different effects depending on whether or not it is correctly anticipated. Anticipated policy actions will be incorporated into workers' price expectations and reflected in long-term contracts. They will affect wages as well as prices but leave the real wage, and hence output, unchanged.

Unanticipated policy actions, in contrast, will have real effects. An unanticipated increase in money holdings, for example, will act to raise prices more than agents had previously expected. Firms then have the incentive to hire more workers at fixed dollar wages and at lower real wages, while workers are bound to offer their services for wages that exchange for smaller quantities of consumption goods. Thus, in this case, output and employment will increase, and firms will benefit at the expense of workers.

The distinction between anticipated and unanticipated policy changes provides an explanation for observed correlations between aggregate demand variables and measures of real output, for example, observed Phillips curves. Unanticipated policy changes, as we have seen, result in positively correlated movements in prices and output and, hence, can explain an observed negative Phillips curve relationship between the rate of inflation and the unemployment rate. However, anticipated changes in an essentially neutral policy will affect prices but not real variables. Anticipated changes to more stimulative policies, then, might explain why the observed Phillips curve has shifted up since the early 1960s.

Our story produces not only an explanation for sticky wages and fluctuations in output but also an explanation for regular cycles in output, that is, "persistence." The impulses that cause output to fluctuate in our story are the price-expectational errors of the workers. Since workers enter into multiperiod contracts, price-expectational errors in one period get carried over into future periods—such as in J.B. Taylor's model.[43] In Taylor's model, contract lengths are fixed exogenously, however; that introduces a role for active government stabilization policy. In our story, the lengths will depend on the government's policy

[43] Taylor, "Aggregate Dynamics."

rule, since the choice of policy rule will have an impact on the inflation process. In our story, there is no role for active stabilization policy.[44]

If individual agents are rational, Lucas argues that they will attempt to make the last move. Under different government policy rules, individual decision rules will be different. Thus, when government changes policy, individual decision rules and macro relations, which are the sums of these rules, will change in response. Lucas attributes this failure to account for the response of individual decision rules to changes in policy—the failure to allow individuals the last move—as a major cause for the instability of macroeconometric models over time.

Lucas's point can be expressed in terms of our earlier notation. In our representation of a macroeconometric model as

$$A_0 y_t + \ldots + A_m y_{t-m} = B_0 x_t + \ldots + B_n x_{t-n} + \varepsilon_t \qquad (1)$$

$$x_t = C_1 x_{t-1} + \ldots + C_p x_{t-p} + u_t, \qquad (2)$$

his point is that a change in the government's rule, represented by a change in the C's, is also going to change the A's and B's. A simple consumption example illustrates why.

Let disposable income be exogenously generated by the process

$$DI_t = c_1 DI_{t-1} + c_2 DI_{t-2} \qquad \text{(i)}$$

where DI_t (an element of the x_t vectors) is period t disposable income and c_1 and c_2 are parameters that are directly affected by government tax policies.

For simplicity, we assume that all agents are identical, plan one period ahead, and consume CON_t (an element of the y_t vector), a constant portion (β) of their "permanent" disposable income (DI_t^p) at time t. Thus, we have

$$CON_t = \beta DI_t^p \qquad \text{(ii)}$$

and

$$DI_t^p = (1-\alpha)E_t(DI_t) + \alpha E_t(DI_{t+1}) \qquad 0 \le \alpha < 1, \qquad \text{(iii)}$$

where $E_t(DI_t)$ and $E_t(DI_{t+1})$ are forecasts of current and future dispos-

[44] Keynesian economists have objected to two basic assumptions in rational expectations models of the business cycle: that agents' expectations are rational and that markets clear. For a defense of the rational expectations assumption, see Sargent, "Comments on Papers," and R. Townsend, "Market Anticipations, Rational Expectations, and Bayesian Analysis," *International Economic Review*, vol. 19 (June 1978), pp. 481–494. For a defense of the market-clearing assumption, see R. J. Barro, "Second Thoughts on Keynesian Economics," *American Economic Review*, vol. 69 (May 1979), pp. 54–59; and Lucas and Sargent, "After Keynesian Macroeconomics."

able income based on information available at time t and where α reflects preferences between present and future consumption.

Now assuming agents know current and past income and use information efficiently, it follows that

$$E_t(DI_t) = DI_t \text{ and } E_t(DI_{t+1}) = c_1DI_t + c_2DI_{t-1}. \qquad \text{(iv)}$$

Substituting (iv) into (iii) and then (iii) into (ii) yields

$$CON_t = \gamma_1DI_t + \gamma_2DI_{t+1} \qquad \text{(v)}$$

where $\gamma_1 = \beta[(1-\alpha)+\alpha c_1]$ and $\gamma_2 = \beta\alpha c_1$.

Equation (v) is the consumption-to-income decision rule that holds under the income-generating process (i). The parameters γ_1 and γ_2 are quite easy to estimate, and the equation will do a good job predicting consumption, if tax policies do not change. But what if they do? Equation (v) cannot accurately predict the effect on consumption. Any change in policy, that is, any change in c_1 and/or c_2, affects the coefficients γ_1 and/or γ_2. Thus, if taxes were lowered in period $t+1$, equation (v) would predict no change in period t consumption, yet in fact consumption would change. Notice that this problem only disappears if agents do not care about their future ($\alpha=0$). Equation (v) then reduces to

$$CON_t = \gamma_1DI_t \qquad \text{(vi)}$$

where $\gamma_1 = \beta$ and the impact of changes in either current or future taxes will not affect γ_1.

The Rational Expectations Theory in the Policy-Making Framework. The object of policy is to maximize social welfare; with rational expectations models, this objective can be stated in terms of individual utilities. There then is no need to use aggregate proxy variables. Each individual in the economy is assumed to maximize the expected discounted flow of utility over time, where each period's utility depends on contemporaneous consumption and leisure. Policy evaluation in rational expectations models generally takes the determination of income distribution to be outside the scope of the analysis. The set of Pareto efficient policies, together with the implied income distributions, is described; no attempt is made to select one policy from this set.

Explicit general-equilibrium, microeconomic models are used for rational expectations policy analysis. These models specify the economic environment of their hypothesized agents: initial endowments, utility functions, production processes, information technologies, and sources of random disturbances. They then specify the rules of the game, which include the permissible strategies of agents and the trading technology.

A solution, or equilibrium, exists when

1. Each agent follows a maximizing strategy subject to
   a. the economic environment
   b. the rules of the game
   c. the strategies of other agents;
2. Aggregates add up, such as total sources equal total uses.

The solution describes how resources are allocated in equilibrium.

In a Debreu-type, nonstochastic, general-equilibrium model, for example, the economic environment consists of many agents and firms—agents with given endowments of goods and concave utility functions, firms with nonincreasing returns-to-scale production functions, and information sets of all agents composed of prices of individual goods. The rules of the game are that agents maximize utility and firms maximize profits, all by determining how many goods to buy and sell on the market at prices called out by a Walrasian auctioneer. A solution is a set of prices such that each individual maximizes utility subject to her or his budget constraint, each firm maximizes profits, and demand equals supply in each market.

In rational expectations models, it is necessary to specify the information that accrues over time to individuals as well as to the government. The solutions to the models depend crucially on assumptions about information costs and availability. For each assumed government policy, there is a corresponding solution to the rational expectations model that describes equilibrium allocations of goods, and hence utilities, across individuals. Policy analysis consists of determining the set of Pareto optimal policies and the properties of the policies in that set.

The rational expectations, equilibrium approach not only allows proper evaluation of alternative outcomes, it conceivably can overcome the invariance problem inherent in macro modeling. Because rational expectations models are based explicitly on theories of individual optimizing behavior, they offer some hope of discovering how individual decision functions will change when government policies change. Earlier we discussed how a change in tax policy can lead to a change in individual consumption functions. Later, in our simple rational expectations business-cycle story, we saw that individuals' labor supply depends on predictions of future prices and that these predictions incorporate the systematic part of government policy. A change in the government policy rule changes expectations of future prices conditioned on a given set of data. This change in the way expectations are formed causes a change in the relationship of the amount of labor individuals supply to current and past conditioning variables. In general, only the economic environment (for example, utility and production functions) can be expected to remain invariant to a change in the policy rule.

Because rational expectations models are based on explicit theories of individual optimizing behavior, they conceivably make it possible to identify parameters of individual objective functions. This knowledge allows us to solve agents' optimization problems anew each time there is a change in policy rules in order to determine how individual decision functions change.

Implications for Policy Making. The rational expectations approach emphasizes that policies must be considered as rules. Individuals' actions today in response to a tax cut, for example, will be different, depending on whether they expect no future tax cuts or whether they expect future tax cuts every time real GNP declines. In order to determine the impact of a policy action, it is necessary to specify how individuals believe policy will respond in given situations in the future.

Not only are we restricted to evaluating policy rules; we can consider only those rules well understood by the economic agents. Anticipated and unanticipated policy actions can be expected to have different effects. Our theories explain individual behavior under a set of anticipated, or understood, policies. We do not know how to predict the effects of an unanticipated change to a new policy rule. Presumably, individuals initially expect the old policy to remain in place, and then they learn about the policy change over time. How fast do they learn, and what type of behavior do they display over this learning period? Existing theory does not supply answers to these questions.

Although we can only evaluate well-understood rules, the question remains whether these policy rules should be active, in the sense that policy actions respond to current economic conditions, or passive. We argue that passive rules are preferable.

First, theoretical justification for active rules is not strong. In some simple rational expectations models, for instance, active policy rules do not outperform passive rules.[45]

Second, the econometric requirements for adopting beneficial, quantitative active rules are staggering. In order to determine a good active policy rule, it is necessary to determine how different policy rules affect economic outcomes. As we have argued, this requires the identification of parameters in individual objective functions so that we can determine how agents' decision functions depend on the policy rule. This is no easy task. Moreover, a model where such identification is

[45] See Sargent and Wallace, "Rational Expectations"; McCallum, "Price Level Adjustments"; and McCallum and Whitaker, "Effectiveness of Fiscal Feedback."

possible involves complicated cross-equation, cross-time restrictions, which make estimation extremely difficult. Estimation subject to these constraints is at the frontier of current knowledge.[46]

Given the present limitations to knowledge, we make some modest proposals. First, we should aim for stable and neutral fiscal and monetary policies. We should avoid sharp changes in federal expenditures and tax rates, balance the federal budget on average over the business cycle, and keep the ratio of high-powered money to total government debt approximately fixed.[47] Second, we should concentrate on improving economic institutions. Rational expectations theory makes it clear that the economic structure matters. Automatic tax stabilizers and transfer program rules affect the way the economy adjusts following shocks.[48] The financial system—how it is set up and regulated—also can have important effects on how the economy adjusts.[49] Third, we should concentrate on some classical issues: How much public goods should the government provide? How should it finance these goods, by taxation or debt issue? How should a given amount of revenue be collected through different taxes? We believe that the payoff to applying sound economic analysis to these classical issues is currently greater than the payoff to searching for quantitative, active stabilization policy rules.

Conclusion

We have argued that a rational expectations, equilibrium approach to policy-making yields two basic advantages over a macroeconomic approach:

1. It allows us to determine, at least conceptually, how individual decision functions change when policy rules change.
2. It allows us to evaluate policies in terms of social welfare.

We also believe economists are led to ask better questions when working in a general equilibrium framework. We list a few examples:

[46] L. Hansen and T. Sargent, "Formulating and Estimating Dynamic Linear Rational Expectations Models: I," Research Department Working Paper, no. 127 (Minneapolis: Federal Reserve Bank of Minneapolis, 1979).

[47] For defenses of these proposals, see R. E. Lucas, Jr., "Rules, Discretion, and the Role of the Economic Advisor" (Paper delivered at National Bureau of Economic Research Conference on Rational Expectations and Economic Policy, Bald Peak, Melvin Village, New Hampshire, October 13–14, 1978); and J. Bryant and N. Wallace, "Open Market Operations in a Model of Regulated, Insured Intermediaries," *Journal of Political Economy,* vol. 88 (February 1980), pp. 146–173.

[48] See McCallum and Whitaker, "Effectiveness of Fiscal Feedback."

[49] See J. Bryant, "The Political Economy of Overlapping Generations," Research Department Staff Report, no. 43 (Minneapolis: Federal Reserve Bank of Minneapolis, 1979).

• The CBO staff asked whether a tax cut is needed to spur employment. A more relevant question is, What is the efficient rate of inflation in the optimal tax structure of our monetary economy?

• The CBO staff asked how changes in social security taxes will affect inflation. More relevant questions are, What is the role of social security in an economy with fiat money, and what are minimally distorting tax and payment schedules?

• The CBO staff asked whether high interest rates cause inflation. A more relevant question is, What is the optimal mix of fiat money and fiat bonds in an economy with a risky bank sector?

Some will protest that we have presented too difficult a program for economists to follow. They will say that we at least have some chance of getting answers to the types of questions asked by the CBO staff, that we have no chance of coming to grips with the more difficult—albeit more relevant—questions we posed. They are wrong. Economists have made significant progress in answering our questions.[50] It is time that government economists apply the economics of the 1970s to contemporary policy problems.

References

Barro, R.J. "Unanticipated Money Growth and Unemployment in the United States." *American Economic Review* 67 (March 1977): 101–105.

———. "Second Thoughts on Keynesian Economics." *American Economic Review* 69 (May 1979): 54–59.

Board of Governors of the Federal Reserve System. "Equations in the MIT-Penn-SSRC Econometric Model of the United States." Unpublished staff paper, Washington, D.C., January 1975.

Brainard, W. "Uncertainty and the Effectiveness of Policy." *American Economic Review* 57 no. 2 (May 1967): 411–425.

Bryant, J. "The Political Economy of Overlapping Generations." Research Department Staff Report, no. 43. Minneapolis: Federal Reserve Bank of Minneapolis, 1979.

Bryant, J., and Wallace, N. "Open Market Operations in a Model of Regulated, Insured Intermediaries." *Journal of Political Economy* 88 (February 1980): 146–173.

Chow, G.C. "Tests for Equality between Sets of Coefficients in Two Linear Regressions." *Econometrica* 78 (July 1960): 591–605.

[50] On inflation as a tax, see N. Wallace, "The Overlapping Generations Model of Fiat Money," in J. Kareken and N. Wallace, eds., *Models of Monetary Economies* (Minneapolis: Federal Reserve Bank of Minneapolis, 1980); on social security taxation, see P. A. Diamond and J. A. Mirrlees, "A Model of Social Insurance with Variable Retirement," *Journal of Public Economics,* vol. 10 (December 1978), pp. 295–336; and on the optimal mix of fiat money and fiat bonds, see Bryant and Wallace, "Open Market Operations."

———. "Effect of Uncertainty on Optimal Control Policies." *International Economic Review* 14 (October 1973): 632–645.
———. "A Solution to Optimal Control of Linear Systems with Unknown Parameters." Econometric Research Program, Research Memorandum, no. 157. Princeton: Princeton University, December 1973.
———. *Analysis and Control of Dynamic Economic Systems.* New York: J. Wiley and Sons, 1975.
———."An Approach to the Feedback Control of Nonlinear Econometric Systems." *Annals of Economic and Social Measurement* 5 (Summer 1976): 297–309.
———. "The Control of Nonlinear Econometric Systems with Unknown Parameters." *Econometrica* 44 (July 1976):685–695.
Craine, R., and Havenner, A. "Optimal Control in a Linear Macroeconomic Model with Random Coefficients." In *IEEE Conference on Decision and Control.* San Diego, December 1973.
———. "A Stochastic Optimal Control Technique for Models with Estimated Coefficients." *Econometrica* 45 (May 1977): 1013–1021.
de Leeuw, F., and Gramlich, E. M. "The Channels of Monetary Policy." *Federal Reserve Bulletin* (June 1969): 472–491.
Diamond, P. A., and Mirrlees, J. A. "A Model of Social Insurance with Variable Retirement." *Journal of Public Economics* 10 (December 1978): 295–336.
Drazen, A. "The Optimal Rate of Inflation Revisited." *Journal of Monetary Economics* 5 (June 1979): 231–248.
Hall, R. E. "The Rigidity of Wages and the Persistence of Unemployment." In *Brookings Papers on Economic Activity,* edited by A.M. Okun and G.L. Perry, no. 2, pp. 301–335. Washington, D.C.: Brookings Institution, 1975.
Hansen, L., and Sargent, T. "Formulating and Estimating Dynamic Linear Rational Expectations Models: I." Research Department Working Paper, no. 127. Minneapolis: Federal Reserve Bank of Minneapolis, 1979.
Kareken, J.; Muench, T.; and Wallace, N. "Optimal Open Market Strategy: The Use of Information Variables." *American Economic Review* 63 (March 1973): 156–172.
Kendrick, D. "Adaptive Control of Macroeconomic Models with Measurement Error." In *5th NBER Conference on Stochastic Control in Economics.* New Haven: National Bureau of Economic Research, May 1977.
Kendrick, D., and Kang, B. H. "An Economist's Guide to Wide Sense Dual Control." Project on Control in Economics, Department of Economics. Austin: University of Texas, January 1975.
Lucas, R. E., Jr. "Expectations and the Neutrality of Money." *Journal of Economic Theory* 4 (April 1972): 103–124.
———. "An Equilibrium Model of the Business Cycle." *Journal of Political Economy* 83 (December 1975): 1113–1144.
———. "Econometric Policy Evaluation: A Critique." In *The Phillips Curve and Labor Markets,* edited by K. Brunner and A. H. Meltzer, Carnegie-Rochester Conference Series on Public Policy, vol. 1, pp. 19–46. Amsterdam: North-Holland, 1976.
———. "Understanding Business Cycles." In *Stabilization of the Domestic and*

International Economy, edited by K. Brunner and A. H. Meltzer, Carnegie-Rochester Conference Series on Public Policy, vol. 5, pp. 7–29. Amsterdam: North-Holland, 1977.

Lucas, R. E., Jr. "Rules, Discretion, and the Role of the Economic Advisor." Paper read at National Bureau of Economic Research Conference on Rational Expectations and Economic Policy, October 13–14, 1978, at Bald Peak, Melvin Village, New Hampshire.

Lucas, R. E., Jr., and Sargent, T. "After Keynesian Macroeconomics." *Federal Reserve Bank of Minneapolis Quarterly Review* (Spring 1979): 1–16.

McCallum, B. T. "Price Level Adjustments and the Rational Expectations Approach to Macroeconomic Stabilization Policy." *Journal of Money, Credit, and Banking* 10 (November 1978): 418–436.

McCallum, B.T., and Whitaker, J. K. "The Effectiveness of Fiscal Feedback Rules and Automatic Stabilizers under Rational Expectations." *Journal of Monetary Economics* 5 (April 1979): 171–186.

McCarthy, M.D. *The Wharton Quarterly Econometric Forecasting Model Mark III,* Studies in Quantitative Economics, no. 6. Philadelphia: University of Pennsylvania, 1972.

McNees, S. K. "An Empirical Assessment of 'New Theories' of Inflation and Unemployment." In *After the Phillips Curve: Persistence of High Inflation and High Unemployment,* pp. 29–46. Boston: Federal Reserve Bank of Boston, June 1978.

MacRae, E. C. "Optimal Estimation and Control: A Structural Approximation." Special Studies Paper, no. 27. Washington, D.C.: Board of Governors of the Federal Reserve System, July 1972.

Marschak, J. "Economic Measurements for Policy and Prediction." In *Studies in Econometric Method,* edited by William C. Hood and T. C. Koopmans, Cowles Foundation Monograph, no. 14. New Haven: Yale University Press, 1953.

Meiselman, D. I., and Roberts, P. C. "The Political Economy of the Congressional Budget Office." In *Three Aspects of Policy and Policymaking: Knowledge, Data and Institutions,* edited by K. Brunner and A. H. Meltzer, pp. 283–333. Amsterdam: North-Holland, 1979.

Muench, T.; Rolnick, A.; Wallace, N.; and Weiler, W. "Tests for Structural Change and Prediction Intervals for the Reduced Forms of Two Structural Models of the U.S.: The FRB–MIT and Michigan Quarterly Models." *Annals of Economic and Social Measurement* 3 (July 1974): 491–519.

Muench, T., and Wallace, N. "On Stabilization Policy: Goals and Models." *American Economic Review* 64 (May 1974): 330–337.

Phelps, E. S. "Inflation in the Theory of Public Finance." *Swedish Journal of Economics* 75 (March 1973): 67–82.

Poole, William. "Optimal Choice of Monetary Policy Instruments in a Simple Stochastic Macro Model." *Quarterly Journal of Economics* 84 (May 1970): 197–216.

Prescott, E.C. "The Multi-period Control Problem under Uncertainty." *Econometrica* 40 (November 1972): 1043–1058.

Sargent, T. "Rational Expectations, the Real Rate of Interest, and the Natural

Rate of Unemployment." In *Brookings Papers on Economic Activity,* edited by A.M. Okun and G.L. Perry, no. 2, pp. 429–472. Washington, D.C.: Brookings Institution, 1973.

———. "Comments on the Shiller and Kalchbrenner and Tinsley Papers." Paper delivered at the Conference on the Monetary Mechanism in Open Economies, August 4–9, 1975, Helsinki, Finland.

———. *Macroeconomic Theory.* New York: Academic Press, 1979.

Sargent, T., and Wallace, N. " 'Rational' Expectations, the Optimal Monetary Instrument, and the Optimal Money Supply Rule." *Journal of Political Economy* 83 (April 1975): 241–254.

Siegel, J. "Notes on Optimal Taxation and the Optimal Rate of Inflation." *Journal of Monetary Economics* 4 (April 1978): 297–305.

Taylor, J. B. "Aggregate Dynamics and Staggered Contracts." *Journal of Political Economy* 88 (February 1980): 1–23.

Theil, H. *Optimal Decision Rules for Government and Industry.* Amsterdam: North-Holland, 1964.

———. *Economic Forecasts and Policy.* Amsterdam: North-Holland, 1965.

Tobin, J. "Money Wage Rates and Employment." In *The New Economics: Keynes' Influence on Theory and Public Policy,* edited by S. Harris, pp. 572–587. New York: A. A. Knopf, 1947.

Townsend, R. "Market Anticipations, Rational Expectations, and Bayesian Analysis." *International Economic Review* 19 (June 1978):481–494.

Tse, E., and Bar-Shalom, Y. "An Actively Adaptive Control for Linear Systems with Random Parameters." *IEEE Transactions on Automatic Control,* AC–18 (April 1973): 109–117.

U.S., Congress, Congressional Budget Office. "A Simplified Wage-Price Model." Unpublished, 1975.

———. "A Methodology for Analyzing the Effects of Alternative Economic Policies." August 1977.

———. "Inflation and Growth: The Economic Policy Dilemma." July 1978.

———. "Aggregate Economic Effects of Changes in Social Security Taxes." August 1978.

Wallace, N. "Microeconomic Theories of Macroeconomic Phenomena and Their Implications for Monetary Policy." In *A Prescription for Monetary Policy: Proceedings from a Seminar Series,* pp. 87–98. Minneapolis: Federal Reserve Bank of Minneapolis, 1976.

———. "The Overlapping Generations Model of Fiat Money." In *Models of Monetary Economies,* edited by J. Kareken and N. Wallace, pp. 49–82. Minneapolis: Federal Reserve Bank of Minneapolis, 1980.

Zellner, A. *An Introduction to Bayesian Inference in Econometrics.* New York: J. Wiley and Sons, 1971.

Commentary

Robert Hartman

Allen Schick's paper highlights well many elements in the congressional budget process that have made it work over the period 1975 to 1979. One aspect of this success is an accommodation on the part of the budget committees to the other committees of Congress and to Congress in general. This is especially true in the House but applies to the Senate as well.

A second element in the success of the budget process, according to the paper, is an avoidance of direct confrontations over priorities. Whenever possible, there has been an avoidance of explicit considerations of tradeoffs between education, national defense, and so on.

Third, Allen Schick points out some interesting differences in how these compromises have developed in the two houses. Particularly illuminating is his discussion of how the budget consideration process in the House has become more or less a party issue. There, the question has been, How can the Democratic party get together on one set of numbers? Putting together a budget thus involves a balancing of the two tails of the Democratic party distribution. In the Senate, however, the approach has been much more a bipartisan and collegial one.

It is somewhat unclear—and I wish someone who is a political scientist would straighten me out—why these differences exist. Schick's paper does not evaluate alternative hypotheses for these differences. Is there a difference in the people involved in the two houses? Is it the nature of the election term in the two houses, or are there different rules of the two clubs? That part of the paper is a bit unsatisfying.

The paper put too little emphasis on the economic background that existed during these first years of the budget process. That had a lot to do with its success. Alice Rivlin is here. She was appointed the CBO director at the bottom of the recession, and, although she does not take credit for that coincidence, it is not unimportant that the budget process was started at an economic low point. Since accommodation—meeting the needs of the other committees—has, in general, meant adding money to what already existed and since adding on is not such a bad fiscal policy when moving up from the bottom of a recession (I am still enough of a believer in old-style macroeconomics to think that is true), there was a consistency between fiscal policy and the means of operation of the budget process. Accommodation meant a little bit more spending, a little bit of tax cutting, and that was okay fiscal policy. Fiscal policy was undertaken quite consciously during this period.

The future, unfortunately, may be different; as a matter of fact, as George Allen would say, the future is now. The difficulties of reaching agreement on the second budget resolution for fiscal year 1980 stem, in part, from a genuine desire on the part of Congress to restrain total spending. Congress cannot do that in the conventional manner because one cannot keep everybody happy by adding on if one has a tight overall target for expenditures. A lot of the budget resolution confusion comes from the attempt by each house to meet a goal unachievable by the usual rules of the game. The House has characteristically responded to this problem by inventing revenues to finance higher expenditures, and the Senate has responded by making what appear to be some hard-nosed cuts.

No matter what the outcome on the 1980 resolution, the problem of keeping restraint in the budget will continue for the next several years, for several reasons. First, the political signals are clear; the American public has become somewhat more conservative. People do want more budget restraint. The strength of the balanced budget and expenditure limitation movement has been felt in the Congress. While spending restraint is not necessarily a permanent condition of life, for the next few years it will be dominant unless we have a severe recession.

Second, even if there were no such thing as politics, there are other things happening that will also imply restraint in the budget. The defense budget seems to be going up in real terms, no matter what—I am not sure I can leave politics aside and say that, but that does seem to be the case—and under those circumstances there must be some pressure on domestic expenditures. This year's budget decisions have not given a long-term solution to how one restrains the domestic budget. A great deal of the restraint in the domestic budget this year comes from not adjusting a lot of grant-in-aid programs for inflation, which is a fine and dandy procedure if one does it one or two years. If one does it five years in a row, one makes substantial policy shifts. That will not go unnoticed. There is a big open question for the future of how domestic restraint will be exercised in the budget process.

The third reason that budget restraint will continue is the surprising amount of agreement—not many people have commented on this—among conservatives, liberals, and everybody that the next slug of stimulus in the economy ought to come in the private sector, in particular in domestic investment and in exports. There is a genuine consensus that the next big bang ought not to come from government spending, aside from defense, or from vast increases in transfer programs; there is general agreement that investment and exports are something that we have to strengthen.

The question then is, Can the budget process, as the author describes and analyzes it, survive the era of austerity that lies ahead? It seems—and here is my major quarrel with the paper—that it cannot survive an era of austerity if it simply accommodates committees that are organized as at present. Those committees, as the paper points out, will be pushing for more; that is, in a way, their role. If budgeting simply accommodates to that, there is no way to get restraint.

Budgeting cannot survive the future if it avoids confrontations between programs by simply adding everywhere and making everybody happy. There must be some more explicit consideration of priorities if these austerity goals are to be met. Congress cannot meet the challenge of the future if it abandons the budget process altogether. Some have suggested that the budget committees ought to set global aggregate goals and call it a day. That is fine, if one wants to kill the budget process. Such a procedure would be so lacking in teeth that expenditure restraint would be impossible.

While present budget procedures can use some improvement, recent innovations in the way the Senate deals with the budget have created a workable procedure for the future, even in an era of austerity when tough choices exist. First, the Senate has taken a longer-run view of the budget. This is important because, if one does not take this longer perspective, if one just looks to this next year's budget, it becomes nearly impossible to cut anything. Everything is predetermined; one bangs his head against the wall and goes home. The Senate attempts to look at future budget trend lines and adjusts current decisions to conform to a longer period plan.

Second, the Senate has confronted tradeoffs. The reconciliation recommendations from the Senate in its fiscal year 1980 budget deliberations represent direct confrontations with selected committees. They recognize the need to force unwilling committees to live up to the budget bargain. The Senate's procedures in 1979 included a feature that may be a bit phony but, on the other hand, set a worthwhile precedent. This is the explicit reference in the Senate resolution to the timing of tax cuts. The Senate did take into account the question of whether one wants to have a balanced budget and when one should have a tax cut if one wants a balanced budget. It was perhaps not an entirely satisfactory resolution of the issue, but at least it was there, which has not been the case in the past.

Finally, the Senate has been able to do this without creating a feeling in its own house that the Senate Budget Committee members are terrible usurpers, presuming to have the knowledge to dictate to expert committees and their staffs the fine points of detail. Although there is some such feeling in the Senate, on the whole, there has not been an outcry against the Budget Committee's usurping powers. Unfortunately, this situation does not exist in the House, where power positions play a major role.

Improving the Process

In the future, if both houses of Congress behave as the Senate has, it will be possible to hold down domestic expenditures in a satisfactory way. There are three things that should be considered to improve the process. First, it is nearly impossible to have a rational consideration of budget changes under present circumstances when everybody, every player in the game, uses a different budget base line. The Office of Management and Budget (OMB) uses something that it calls "current services," the concept of which is changed from time to time; the CBO has gone through "current policy," and "current law." There is an opportunity to set a common base line. OMB is moving a bit in the congressional direction. If everybody started at the same place, then we could say, "Here are the dollar implications of current programs." We could then look at what policy changes are in an intelligible fashion. Too much time is spent in reconciling different people's budgets. No constructive policy decisions are made when people exhaust themselves in fighting over whether to base changes on the CBO's estimate of the administration's budget or the budget as proposed by the administration.

Second, it is made unnecessarily difficult to set priorities when budget functions are called things like "veterans' benefits and services" or "health." That is too directly linked to special interest groups. There is a way of making the budget add up to the total that would not involve quite as much explicit association with interest groups. Some of the items might be broader, but relevant, categories like grants-in-aid. We could intelligently discuss grants-in-aid policy, set goals in the budget committees for grants-in-aid, and then distribute those goals among grants-in-aid committees without getting into the health versus education business. Another category might be research and development.

Third, we can improve the budget process by getting some of the detail that exists on the spending side into the tax side. We have an idiotic situation in the resolutions, where there are nineteen categories of spending times three years (fifty-seven little items dealing with expenditures); all it says is that total receipts this year should be *X*. There is tremendous imbalance between the treatment of taxes and expenditures. This is not to say that the budget committees should exhume the tax code every year and go through it line by line; setting broad goals in the tax area by having three or four or five major breakdowns under the heading of taxes would create some balance for giving overall guidance to tax policy.

Finally, if one accepts the premise that the future requires austerity, if one accepts the premise that the prospects for a super-strong president leading the way are not too high, if one accepts the current structure of Congress, we had better have a budget process or there is no way to make all this come together. The budget process has come through spring training fairly well, but it will be a long, hot summer before we reach the world series.

William Beeman

Despite the sweeping title of their paper, Miller and Rolnick have investigated only a small portion of the work of the CBO's fiscal analysis division, which itself includes only one-tenth of the CBO's staff. The restricted scope of this study is underscored in that they cite only three CBO publications. Moreover, even this limited analysis is seriously flawed: first, by a misunderstanding of the use of models by the CBO, and second, by their judgment that the CBO should abandon macroeconometric models altogether and adopt a rational expectations approach to policy analysis.

CBO's Methodology

The first part of the Miller-Rolnick paper relates to macroeconomic models and the CBO's use of them. The authors briefly examine the CBO's Multipliers Project, which was an attempt by the CBO to develop "consensus" multipliers by comparing the responses of several large econometric models to selected fiscal policy shocks.[1] Their examination of that model and its use at the CBO leads the authors to conclude that the CBO's fiscal policy analysis is biased, not because of any bias in the multipliers model itself but because of its misuse. Specifically, they assert that (1) the CBO analysis ignores uncertainty and (2) the CBO's analysis has too short a time horizon. These two shortcomings, according to the authors, bias the CBO's analysis toward activism.

We hope we all can agree that it is important for policy analysts to emphasize uncertainty and to report longer-run effects. Among the hundreds of macroeconomic estimates that we have made, there have been instances when we were not sufficiently attentive to this issue. The authors, however, leave the impression that such shortcomings are a

[1] U.S., Congress, Congressional Budget Office, *The Multipliers Project,* August 1977.

general practice or perhaps even a policy at the CBO. This impression is contrary to fact.

Indeed, readers of the CBO publications frequently complain that we overstress uncertainty—or less kindly, that we are too concerned with protecting our flanks. They object to the CBO's insistence on ranges, rather than point estimates, for our published gross national product (GNP) forecast. They object to our refusal to analyze proposals when we feel that available methodology is inadequate, even though others will do so.[2] They complain about the repeated qualifications and references to uncertainty and lengthy discussions on the sources of uncertainty in our economic reports.

Critics of the CBO's emphasis on uncertainty should not be dismissed out of hand. A case can be made that continued emphasis on uncertainty is not always consistent with the requirements of the budget process. After all, the budget committees and Congress are required to vote on specific budget aggregates. These budget figures must be derived from point estimates, rather than ranges, of projected economic activity and of the incremental effects of alternative policies. Confronted with the requirement for point estimates, we grit our teeth and do the best we can. Despite the obvious uncertainty inherent in these exercises, such estimates cannot be avoided if there is to be a vote on the budget. Unlike most other public institutions, we make our estimates and methodology public to insure objectivity and to encourage suggestions for improving our analysis.

The authors have the luxury of being able to ignore Congress's ability to absorb a massive amount of technical information. The CBO does not. The authors have not considered whether technical error analysis applied to economic and budget estimates would be regarded as meaningful by members of Congress, the primary customer for the CBO analysis, and would contribute to constructive debate. The budget process is already quite complex and members of Congress expect the CBO to come forward with the best point estimates and judgment we can muster.[3]

Miller and Rolnick might reply that their complaint pertains not to the judgment supplied by the CBO but to the forecast errors of macroeconometric models used by the CBO. The authors raise some in-

[2] The CBO, for example, has previously indicated that it was not able to estimate the impact on the economy of proposals for integrating the personal income tax and the corporate income tax.

[3] In response to a question about the macroeconomic effects of expanding federal credit programs, for example, my answer—true to my economic training—emphasized uncertainty, with ample reference to diverse views. With some annoyance, the congressman asked if the witness did not know that he had to make a decision, adding that he wanted the CBO's best guess.

teresting, though not new, criticisms of macroeconomic models in general. Specifically, they worry that the forecast errors of such models are so large that they can only mislead policy makers. They question the stability of the macroeconomic models and the frequent use of intercept adjustments.

If, however, that is the basis of their complaint, they do not understand policy analysis as it is done at the CBO, the Council of Economic Advisers, or, for that matter, their own employer, the Federal Reserve System. The CBO does not use large macroeconometric models mechanically. Nor do those other agencies. In practice, our policy analysts examine all evidence available to us, which includes the output of these models. In the end, our forecasts and estimates of policy impacts are heavily influenced by judgment, hopefully reasoned and well-informed judgment. There has always been a debate within the CBO as to the usefulness of large econometric models. Some at the CBO have argued that the major contribution of these models is consistency. Even their most avid defenders would not think of using pure model forecasts. Is there any serious policy analysis where reasoned judgment is not critical? Do not all analysts consider valuable information not incorporated in models?

Since Miller and Rolnick failed to talk to anyone on my staff prior to writing their paper, it certainly is possible that they misunderstand how we operate. The forecast errors of the large econometric models have only a tenuous relationship to our forecast, a fact that could easily have been ascertained by little investigation. The CBO's forecasts draw upon the judgment of a wide variety of opinion among prominent economists. Given the important role that CBO's analysis plays in the budget process, it would be irresponsible for us to do otherwise. Of course, the outcome of this is that our forecasts and analysis are heavily influenced by judgment and tend to be quite close to the so-called consensus forecasts.

Incorrect Assumptions

Consequently, we were surprised by the authors' assumption that the CBO uses the multipliers model for forecasting. It is not true. In fact, it cannot be used for that purpose. The authors should not be so surprised, then, that our projections do not emphasize the forecast errors of the multipliers model or of large econometric models. Their speculation about the size of the forecast errors using these models is pointless. The same should be said for their conclusion that these errors "would be considered large by most policy makers and would give them little confidence in CBO's ability to forecast the future course of the economy." Actual CBO forecast errors, however, are readily available but

FIGURE 1

THE MONETARY RESPONSE AND THE IMPACT OF A $10 BILLION INCREASE IN FEDERAL PURCHASES

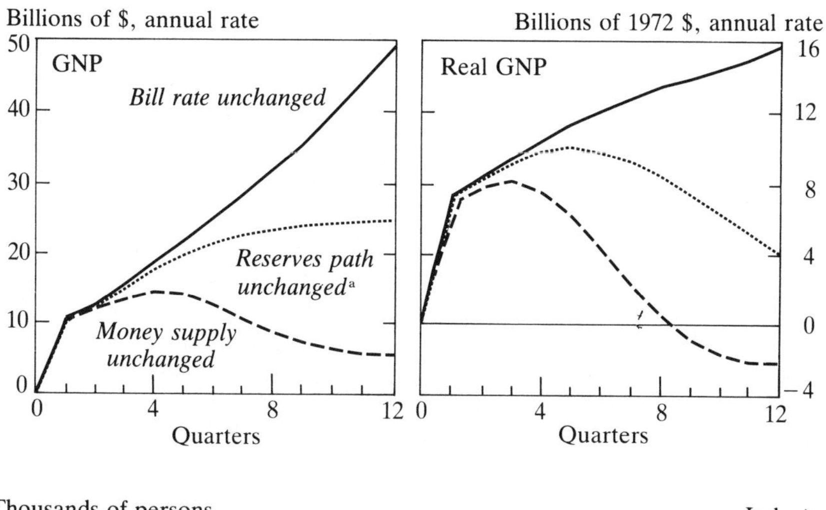

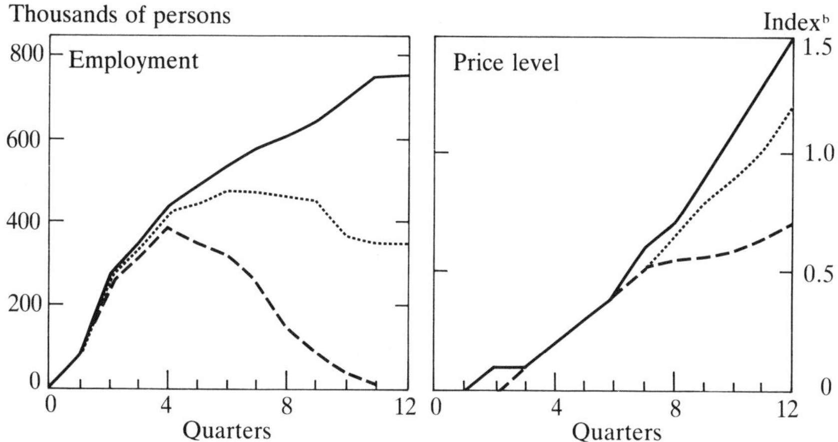

NOTE: Step changes begin in first quarter.
[a] Unborrowed reserves only.
[b] Records number of point changes in the index.

difficult to evaluate statistically because they are few in number and of necessity incorporate a "current policy" fiscal assumption.

The CBO does make greater use of large econometric models and the multipliers model in analyzing alternative policies, but judgment plays an important role here as well. The report on social security referred to by the authors is an example.[4] The authors reviewed the literature on the economic effects of social security taxes as well as the results of large econometric models and presented their best judgment as to the economic impact. The output of large macroeconometric models was not a critical aspect of the study.

The second criticism of the CBO's use of models involves the question of truncating forecasts. The CBO's GNP forecasts have been limited to six or eight quarters ahead, the minimum period necessary for calculating the budget costs for the budget resolution under consideration. This self-imposed limitation is an attempt to minimize uncertainty, which increases with the forecast horizon. The CBO is not alone in that practice. The authors may not know that the Federal Reserve forecast is generally limited to six quarters. For the years after the forecast, the CBO's five-year projections incorporate a noncyclical growth assumption that is influenced heavily by the specification of goals.[5] Estimates of the incremental effects of alternative policies usually cover the forecast period, with additional data or specific mention of the price effects in later years. Miller and Rolnick have identified an instance when such longer-run effects were not included; there are others.

A wider reading would have shown that longer-run effects are generally presented in our reports. Figure 1, from the CBO publication *Understanding Fiscal Policy,* is an interesting illustration of a longer-run model simulation with properties similar to those mentioned by the authors, which they assume we ignore.[6] CBO does not discourage consideration of longer-run effects. Unfortunately, we often find that there are not adequate tools available for analyzing long-run supply effects, which may be important indeed.

Among the deficiencies in the first part of the Miller-Rolnick paper is the suggestion that the CBO has recommended direct intervention in the wage-price determination process with some form of incomes policy. This is not true. The reference given by the authors does not describe incomes policy options in a favorable light, nor does the CBO background paper on the history of U.S. incomes policies, which the authors ignore.[7] It is also well known that the CBO report issued in January 1979 included an analysis of the administration's incomes program and predicted that it would have little or no effect on union wages or the

[4] U.S., Congress, the Congressional Budget Office, *Aggregate Economic Effects of Changes in Social Security Taxes,* August 1978.

[5] See, for example, U.S., Congress, the Congressional Budget Office, *Five-Year Budget Projections and Alternative Budgetary Strategies for Fiscal Years 1980–1984,* January 1979, chap. 1.

[6] U.S., Congress, the Congressional Budget Office, *Understanding Fiscal Policy,* April 1978.

[7] U.S., Congress, Congressional Budget Office, *Incomes Policies in the United States: Historical Review and Some Issues*, May 1977.

consumer price index.[8] We came under heavy fire for that analysis. Moreover, our view that inflationary pressures would remain strong was the major consideration in the CBO's forecast of a recession.

Rational Expectations

The second part of the paper argues for adoption of a rational expectations, general-equilibrium approach to policy analysis. Here, one encounters an interesting shift from profound worry about uncertainty to profound certainty.

Many economists have serious doubts about the conclusions of rational expectations theory. The advocates have not convinced the economics profession that their model adequately describes the actual behavior of the economy. The major deficiency seems to be the analysis of labor markets. Prolonged periods of high unemployment can be explained only by the assumption of an incredible amount of ignorance. Otherwise, it is a full-employment model. The model is clearly naive about institutional arrangements in labor markets. On the one hand, wage decisions are sophisticated, incorporating inflation expectations that in turn fully reflect the effect of expected policy adjustments. Experts know of no instance where future monetary and fiscal policies entered in wage negotiations. On the other hand, the model has no room for catch-up wage adjustments that *are* widely observed in wage negotiations. Incorporating catch-up in the wage decision alters the outcome of the rational expectations model in such a way that announced policy changes to restrain inflation also cause large losses in output.

The basic argument of rational expectations against the use of macroeconometric models to analyze monetary and fiscal policy is that it does not take into account changes in behavioral relationships that may be brought about by changes in government policy. The problem is that the rational expectations model has not shown that these reactions to policy changes are sufficiently large and quick that macroeconometric analysis should be rejected on this account. The empirical basis of rational expectations theory is, as yet, thin. The authors have skipped an important step in the sequence from a novel theory to policy application. In today's world, they must demonstrate—not just assert—their case.[9]

[8] U.S., Congress, Congressional Budget Office, *The Fiscal Policy Response to Inflation*, January, 1979, appendix A.

[9] It appears that critics of rational expectations do not have to argue that the rational expectations model does not describe the real world adequately. Some scholars have argued that macroeconomic policies can stabilize output even in a rational expectations world. See Edmund S. Phelps and John B. Taylor, "Stabilizing Powers of Monetary Policy Under Rational Expectations," *Journal of Political Economy*, vol. 85, no. 1 (February 1977); John B. Taylor, "Estimation and Control of a Macro Economic Model with Rational Expectations," *Econometrica* (September 1979); and Ray C. Fair, "A Critique of One Class of Macroeconometric Models with Rational Expectations," *Journal of Money, Credit, and Banking*, vol. 10, no. 4 (November 1978).

Given the state of the art and the CBO's responsibility for providing Congress with analysis that is defensible and widely accepted, it would be irresponsible for the CBO to toss out macroeconometric analysis and adopt the rational expectations approach. Rational expectations has a long way to go to explain reality and, despite important theoretical achievements, the theory remains well outside the mainstream of economics today.

Despite the authors' interpretation, it is not correct to say that the CBO favors activism. I share the authors' concern for more stable monetary and fiscal policies, a view that does not depend on rational expectations. I am also sympathetic with the view that greater emphasis should be placed on efficiency and income distribution considerations, issues not neglected at the CBO. I also agree that the questions that the CBO addresses are not always the best questions. Of course, most of the time we are not the framers of the questions that we try to answer. The CBO staff did not initiate the question that the authors claim was asked by the CBO—whether high interest rates cause inflation. At this moment, I have on my desk a letter from a member of Congress asking the CBO to study the question of whether the currently tight monetary policy and high interest rates are major causes of inflation. It is not clear, however, that Miller and Rolnick have provided good advice for responding to this request. Can one imagine the reaction if the CBO replied: "Dear Senator, we think a more relevant question is: 'What is the optimal mix of fiat money and fiat bonds in an economy with a risky bank sector?'" I would rather see that response come from the Federal Reserve Bank of Minneapolis than from the CBO.

Contrary to Miller and Rolnick's conclusion, rational expectations literature does not appear to be sufficiently well developed to provide answers to difficult questions encountered by the CBO. The authors do cite a few issues that have been studied, but even here the analysis has not yet been tested and given rigorous review by the economics profession. Let me cite a portion of the conclusion of one such study produced by Neil Wallace and John Bryant for the Federal Reserve Bank of Minneapolis:

> We hope, by now, to have convinced you that the conventional wisdom about the effects of different ways of financing a deficit is seriously in error. Perhaps, the best way to emphasize how much in error is to summarize what our model says about the inflationary consequences of deficits and how they are financed.
>
> Our analysis suggests that it is the deficit that is crucial for inflation. To the extent that financing matters, money-financing is, in general, less inflationary than bond-financing. The shocking way to state this last conclusion is to consider what it implies about Federal Reserve open-market operations.

> Most of us have been "taught" that open-market purchases are inflationary and open-market sales deflationary. Our model says the opposite. Indeed, it suggests that as regards open-market operations, the least inflationary action the Federal Reserve could take would be to buy up all outstanding government securities and to henceforth buy all new issues.[10]

I would like to congratulate the authors for having the courage to publish their views under the auspices of the Federal Reserve. There is no better example to show that the conclusions of the rational expectations approach are far from consensus economics of the 1970s.

John T. McEvoy

My basic philosophy toward the budget process, which only reinforces my basic philosophy about government, is that it is only as good (1) as the people in it, (2) as the public demands it to be, (3) as the people themselves, the government and the citizens, want to make it. There is a tendency, especially in Washington, to think of the government the way that the public does elsewhere, as an abstraction from the public in the sense that somehow the people are in one place and the government is in another. In my experience, especially in the budget process, the government can be no better than the people expect it to be, because it is a part of the people. People and the government are so intertwined in this democracy that there is no way to deal with one without the other.

One of the commentators this morning spoke of being uncomfortable with ad hominem analysis in dealing with the budget process. Political science, though, offers little understanding of politics in general, and certainly not of the budget process. That kind of abstract analysis applied to our process tends to yield the wrong answers.

One cannot deal with the budget process except in ad hominem terms. Look at the difference between two presidents. President Ford seemed not to understand that the process existed. Indeed, there was a hostility between the Office of Management and Budget (OMB) and the budget process, partly because the process in those years was used by congressional Democrats to justify what they wanted against the more conservative policy of President Ford. Congress was reflecting what it thought the public was demanding of it; in 1976, the president found that Congress had been on the right side of that argument, as far as electoral politics are concerned.

President Carter is very different from President Ford in terms of the congressional budget process. It began when he called Senator Mu-

[10] Federal Reserve Bank of Minneapolis, *The Inefficiency of a Nominal National Debt*, staff report no. 28, October 1977, p. 23.

skie to Plains, Georgia, to interview him in connection with the vice-presidential choice in 1976. Senator Muskie began, at that time, to inculcate him in the budget process. Mr. Carter then sent Jack Watson to spend a day with us on the Senate Budget Committee staff explaining the process, in August 1976, when they were just formulating the campaign. He assigned a staff man, full-time, to work with us during the campaign, to help prepare issue papers for the president once he took office.

Partly on account of that initiation, and partly on account of his reputed engineering bent, the president sees this as an orderly process. He also has found, as a conservative president working against a more liberal, Democratic Congress, a use for the budget process in advancing his own programs; he has paid a great deal of deference to it, to the chairman, and to the staffs, clearing things with us that we never would have heard of from President Ford; assigning people, full-time, to work with us on various projects. It has made a world of difference in the stature of the budget process in the Congress and its effectiveness. There are two personalities, both using the institution of the presidency but producing radically different results, based on their approach to government and their basic understanding of the process.

One could take another case where personality has been the determining factor. The contest for the appointment of the first CBO director was between the House candidate, who was in favor of a kind of a passive information service, and the Senate choice, Alice Rivlin, who seemed able to make the CBO what the Senate thought that institution was supposed to be—an analytic as well as information-supplying arm of Congress. The House, for six months, held out for a caretaker regime; the Senate held out for an activist regime and the Senate happened to win. What the CBO is today, as opposed to what it could have been had the other candidate been selected, is entirely a function of personality, view, and energy, all of which were factors in the choice between the two candidates.

A look at the ranking members on the congressional budget committees is also illuminating. Delbert Latta (Republican, Ohio), the ranking member of the House committee, is a man well known—and this is not a criticism of him—as a political gut-fighter in the House. There is no reason to believe that it was an accidental choice when he was put on the House Budget Committee.

Senator Roman Hruska (Republican, Nebraska)—not Senator Bellmon, but Senator Hruska—was going to be the first ranking member of the Senate Budget Committee. Senator Hruska was different from Senator Bellmon. Had he remained the ranking member after 1974, when he served for a brief period, the committee would have been substantially different.

If Senators Muskie and Bellmon had not had a common experience as governors of their states, we would also have had a different experience. In Muskie and Bellmon, we have two former governors of the minority party in their own states, who dealt with legislatures overwhelmingly of the other party. They both had to learn how to come to agreement with people whose views they did not accept, or they would have had no program.

We have had an accommodation in the Senate toward more conservative budget numbers than on the House side. In the House, there is a Republican abstention from the process; it means that the House has to pass its resolutions by Democratic majorities.

The 1979 resolution was deadlocked because not one Republican in the House would vote for it. Therefore, the left wing of the Democratic Party in the House of Representatives had to be appeased in the final version of this budget resolution in order to achieve its passage in the House. The amounts of money, even though on the margin they are not overwhelming, required for that appeasement are much greater than the Senate is willing to agree.

Again, it comes down to a policy choice between the houses and between the parties. In the Senate, the parties work together. In the House, they do not. The difference is not the result of the different characteristics of the two legislative bodies or of the different characteristics of the two parties. It is the result of the different personalities.

Even in the Senate today, there are others on both sides of the aisle who would not have the same stake in making the process work that Senators Muskie and Bellmon feel. It is possible to destroy this process. I would like to think, as Allen Schick does, that we are going to be around ten years from now. I am pleased that we have been around for five. It does depend on people being devoted to make that process work.

This brings me to my second great reservation about political science analyses that I have seen of the process: they tend to analyze the congressional budget process in classic congressional turf terms—the Senate committee does this or does that in order to advance the committee.

I do not want to eschew or criticize all the political science analyses of our process; many of them may be accurate to an extent I do not recognize because of my involvement in it. But, there is an overriding objective on the Senate side and on the House side—whose members have an even more thankless task than the Senate members because they do not even have an independent committee—to build an independent institution. There is an overriding concern, which I have seen year in and year out for five years, to make the process work, to try to achieve a system of discipline.

Senator Muskie has frequently described the budget process as a cloak which Congress cannot put down; it is a cloak which Congress put on and with which Congress must learn to live. In this present budget conference, when some members have advocated waiting to see what the finance committee would do or an appropriations subcommittee would do and then raise the budget totals or lower them to accommodate that, Muskie has made a point that all the committees are part of the process, and the process will only survive if all the committees accept it. The purpose of the budget committees is only to offer guidelines for the other committees and members to criticize and amend if they want, but, once amended and enacted, guidelines with which they must live if the process is to survive.

If there is a power theory, it is the power of making the process work that is applicable. Public attitudes, vastly more than parochial or institutional interests, determine what our committee does, not its relationship with other committees.

Let me offer one note with regard to the future of the process and then make one brief comment on the constitutional issue that has been discussed here. There is an institutional weakness in the House committee that everybody recognizes. It was not created to be as strong a committee as the Senate committee. It was not made permanent. More than that, certain of the powers delegated to the Senate committee are reserved, reasonably enough in historical perspective, to the House Rules Committee with regard to legislation that offends the Budget Act and otherwise would be out of order.

The House committee is not a permanent institution, in the sense of its membership being permanent; no member of the House committee can serve more than six years of any ten. The tendency to be a committee of committees keeps that House committee relatively less vigorous, so far, in pursuing the objectives of making the process effective, in disciplining the Congress once budget resolutions are adopted than has been true in the Senate.

A second weakness is what one might call the problem of reinventing the wheel. More than half of Congress sitting in 1979 was not in office in 1974 and does not remember the chaos, the governmental demoralization, and the political deterioration in those years when the congressional spending process was essentially out of control.

To many members elected after the 1974 Budget Act, that act, the budget process, and the budget committees seem about as ancient as the appropriations process itself. There is a tendency on the part of those people, on the one hand, to say, "Gee, what a terrific process, and we'll adhere to it." All of the members are like that part of the time. There are other members who view the budget process as something to avoid, something to be evaded, and something to be suspended when it is appropriate politically to do so. That is a long-term political problem.

There is also a situation that the budget drafters never contemplated. That is that it would be a one-party process in the House, where one party would be stuck with passing budget resolutions. As long as that is true, the chance of the budget process collapsing from the inability to pass a budget resolution will exist. It took the House two tries on the first conference report, it took two tries to get to conference in the case on which we are now working.

Finally, let me just say this with regard to constitutional amendment. I think that a Congress so profligate as to require a constitutional amendment to limit its spending propensities will certainly be ingenious enough to figure ways to avoid it. Before we get into a constitutional amendment, we ought to be sure that it is not going to make a bad situation worse because of the collapse of public confidence altogether.

The analogy frequently advanced that the states have constitutional amendments and live within them is particularly pernicious and inaccurate, given the fact that those state limits have led the states to shift the burden upstream, so that now the federal government supplies $84 billion, or about 30 percent, of all state spending, in one form or another.

In the end, rather than a constitutional amendment or even the Budget Act, the one controlling law that we confront, and are sometimes confounded by, but also the only one that can save us is the law of human nature. Human beings can be progressive—and they were in enacting the Budget Act—or they can be retrograde. There is no question—although people do not recognize this fact—that practically every federal dollar in the budget, except the small amount that goes to foreign economic assistance and to our military bases overseas, reaches some American hand. The money is spent in our own country. For every dollar that goes out of the Treasury, there is almost always an American hand at the other end. One hears plenty from those folks, whichever recipient of that $550 billion a year it happens to be, when one pulls back a little on that dollar. The tension is expressed in loud political terms.

When I think of constitutional amendments I am reminded of what President Kennedy said about Vietnam shortly before he died. "If they cannot save themselves, surely nothing we can do can save them." If we are at a state in our political life and our attitude toward the role of government and the role of tax dollars and deficit spending that we need some kind of a law to try to get us to do what we ourselves have been unwilling to do, then surely we have given up self-discipline and no law can save us.

Summary of Discussion

In response to Mr. Hartman, Mr. Schick noted that when he referred to the budget process as being accommodating, he did not mean that it made everyone happy. He would, in fact, expect the terms of accommodation to change greatly depending on whether the budget situation was tight or loose.

With respect to the differences between the behavior of the House and the Senate, Mr. Schick noted that he was not satisfied with explanations that depended on an analysis of the personalities involved—Muskie, Bellmon, Giaimo, and Latta. Instead, he guessed that the current situation was not stable. Over time he would expect the Senate to become somewhat more partisan and the House less partisan.

In response to Mr. Beeman, Mr. Rolnick said that the main point of the Miller-Rolnick paper was that current macroeconomic models were simply not good enough for policy analysis. While Mr. Beeman indicated that CBO forecasts relied less on macro models than did their policy analysis, Mr. Rolnick felt strongly that current macro models are better at making a forecast for a given set of policies than they are at analyzing the impact of policy changes.

Stephen Entin suggested that macro models were primarily deficient in not adequately portraying micro incentives to save, to invest, and to work. He also noted that heavy reliance on Keynesian models created confusion for congressmen. Those models, which are inherently short-run, imply that savings is bad, whereas we know that it is good in the long run.

Mr. Beeman agreed with Mr. Entin's basic criticism, but noted that CBO does not have the resources to do basic research and has to rely on the economics profession for information on micro responses. So far, the profession has not reached a useful consensus on how such issues should be built into macro models.

Frank de Leeuw suggested that much of the criticism of CBO was, "We don't like your model. Use ours instead." Such criticism comes from groups such as fiscal supply-siders, monetarists, and labor unions, and seldom leaves any room for compromise or consensus building. He wished that the criticism took the form, "Here are some thoughts on modifying your approach and here is the way that we think it would improve your policy analysis and forecasting."

Robert Hartman suggested that the use of Keynesian models might bias government spending upward, because simple, short-run analysis always shows that changes in spending have higher multipliers than changes in taxes. Obviously, such analysis tells us little about the longer-run implications of tax and outlay changes, and it is essential that the process focus more on the long run.

Bruce Bartlett asked Allen Schick whether CBO analysis did, in fact, bias spending upward. Mr. Schick said that he felt that the budget process provided a new forum for stating claims on the budget, but this was very different from saying that spending responded to those claims.

Alice Rivlin said that the only thing worse than having an upward bias in the budget process was to have no process at all. Before the budget process, a congressman could vote for a spending increase without ever having to vote explicitly for a deficit increase. That situation resulted in a very strong upward bias. Now Congress has to "face the music" and ask how all of its individual actions fit together in a comprehensive aggregate strategy. This does not force the Congress to do anything it doesn't want to do, but it provides a systematic way of deciding what it really wants to do.

Jan Olsen suggested that the arguments for the budget process were analogous to the arguments for economic planning. Many thought planning was the way to guide the "disorderly" market system to superior results, but it never worked in practice. Similarly, the "disorderly" procedure prevailing before the new budget process may have given us more restrained and sensible budgets.

Part Two

Constitutional Expenditure Limitation and Congressional Budget Reform

Aaron Wildavsky

Had the Congressional Budget Act explicitly been designed to lower and even limit expenditure, it could not have achieved the widespread agreement essential to get reform going, even in the crucibles of Vietnam and Watergate. Its purpose was to show that Congress was in control of the budget by facilitating explicit consideration of total expenditures as well as individual items. These totals might go up or down but they would be approved and adhered to at some stage. To serve this end, Congress was to create new machinery to monitor expenditures, improve data, and analyze policies.

The budget reform has been a success. Whether it has been a huge success in obtaining modest objectives like improving data, or a modest success in encouraging consideration of larger issues of public finance, the reform has prospered. If it has not altered totals much so far as anyone can tell or if it has influenced major items only occasionally, as seems to be so, it was not supposed to be (nor could it have started or survived as) a super government.

The budget reform was not supposed to hold spending down as a virtue in and of itself, to balance the budget, if Congress felt otherwise, or to limit the growth of federal expenditure to a predetermined level. Precisely because it is an incremental rather than radical change, the budget reform is quite compatible with constitutional expenditure limitation. I shall argue that the budget reform could operate within an expenditure limitation to the benefit of both. To explain why, I shall discuss the logic of limitation: Why do some people, of whom I am one, think it is necessary to limit expenditures to the existing level plus the increase in gross national product? Why do they want to fix the size of the public as compared to the private sector by constitutional rather than legislative means? Once expenditure limitation is recognized as radical, it should become obvious that the budget reform cannot (and, some would say, should not) prevent the public sector from continuing to expand into the private. Nor would the reform enforce competition within the bureaucracy. One's views of whether this or another position is more nearly correct depend on why one thinks federal expenditure has increased so much in our time. Whatever the cure, it must be related to the cause.

Where is the Breakdown?

Public spending is like a game of reverse musical chairs, when the singing stops, there are extra chairs to fill.[1] The golden rule is that each spending sector may do unto the other as the other does unto it, as long as there is more for both. What must never happen to shatter the chain is one sector taking resources from another. "Beggar thy neighbor" is verboten.

Federal spending programs evolve up but rarely down; they change only by growing larger. Extraordinary programs, with special appeal, may grow as long as others do not decrease. Thus, defense will not decrease but may be kept constant while welfare grows. How are these happy accommodations possible? The public sector has been able to solve its internal problems both by absorbing the growth and decreasing the share of the private sector.

To sum up the system of incentives in central government spending, addition is easier than subtraction. Whenever there is a crunch, administrative agencies will add on the costs of their programmatic proposals; they will not, unless compelled, subtract one from the other. (They do not, to be sure, ask for all they would like, only for more than they already have. Their proposals are cuts; only their spending is not.) Subtraction suggests competition in which there have to be losers; addition is about cooperation in which (within government) there are only winners. When the economy produces sufficient surplus, spending grows painlessly. When there is not quite enough to go around, spending grows noiselessly, as inflation increases effective taxation or tax expenditures, and loan guarantees substitute for amounts that would otherwise appear in the budget. The budget grows. A downward dip now and again does not slow its inexorable progress. Why does this imperfection in political processes occur?

Why has the invasion of the private by the public sector—from under 10 percent in 1900 to well over 30 percent now—been allowed to begin and able to succeed? Perhaps the answer is simpler than anyone suggests: Working their will through democratic procedures, people are doing and getting what they want. Otherwise, as Brian Barry states so well, it is

[1] This material is taken from my Fels Lectures at the University of Pennsylvania, April 1979, on constitutional expenditure limitation, and is now published as *How To Limit Government Spending* (Berkeley/Los Angeles/New York: University of California Press, 1980).

> important to know if the forces of electoral competition can be expected to operate in some systematic way to give people what they don't want, or more specifically to give them something that would be defeated by some alternative in a straight vote. For this would suggest that there is some kind of internal flaw to democracy. . . . [2]

Barry is inclined to believe there is no such flaw or, if there is, not one of the kind that would lead to undesired high expenditures. Those who hold opposing views are also troubled by the thought that the political process is right and they are wrong. Their perplexity is worth pursuing; according to James Buchanan and Richard Wagner:

> The question we must ask, and answer, is: Why do citizens support politicians whose decisions yield the results we have described? If citizens are fully informed about the ultimate consequences of alternative policy choices, and if they are rational, they should reject political office seekers or officeholders who are fiscally irresponsible. They should not lend indirect approval to inflation-inducing monetary and fiscal policy; they should not sanction cumulatively increasing budget deficits and the public-sector bias which results. Yet we seem to observe precisely such outcomes.[3]
>
> There is a paradox of sorts here. A regime of continuous and mounting deficits, with subsequent inflation, along with a bloated public sector, can scarcely be judged beneficial to anyone. Yet why does the working or ordinary democratic process seemingly produce such a regime? Where is the institutional breakdown?[4]

I emphatically do not subscribe to theories of bureaucratic conspiracy or manipulation by politicians to explain the growth of public expenditure. "What," Barry says, "could anyone hope for from a system characterized by a collection of rogues competing for the favors of a larger collection of dupes?"[5] I wish to puncture the preposterous Parkinsonian proposition that bureaucrats expand their programs indefinitely by hoodwinking the population. Were these programs not deeply desired by strong social elements, they would not prosper. As Frank Levy said, it is not the conspiracy theory but the Pogo theory that is applicable: *We have seen the enemy and they is us.*

[2] Brian Barry, *Does Democracy Cause Inflation?* Brookings Institution Project on the Politics and Sociology of Global Inflation, Washington, D.C. (September 1978), p. 53.

[3] James M. Buchanan and Richard E. Wagner, *Democracy in Deficit: The Political Legacy of Lord Keynes* (Academic Press: New York, 1977), p. 125.

[4] Ibid., p. 94.

[5] Barry, *Does Democracy*, pp. 34–35.

A Critique of Conspiracy Theories. The elegant theory of bureaucracy propounded by William Niskanen is far more intuitively appealing and aesthetically pleasing. By what criteria, he asks, are bureaucrats judged and rewarded? The difference between the results that they achieve and the resources that their agencies consume are not among them. Bureaucrats cannot appropriate savings; neither can their agencies carry over funds. Rather, their opportunities for promotion, for salary, and for influence increase with size regardless of success. They will want more—much more—for their agencies and programs than citizens would prefer under similar circumstances.[6] So far, so good. Why would citizens as voters elect governmental officials who would agree with this? If citizens think taxes are too high or expenditures too large, what stops them from using the ballot box to enforce these views?

I reject the conspiratorial views of the left, known as "false consciousness," or of the right, called "fiscal illusion," not because they are wholly wrong but because a partial truth is often worse than none at all. Baldly stated, the doctrine of false consciousness alleges that the masses of people in a capitalist country are indoctrinated to prefer policies contrary to their real interests by a biased transmission of culture, from schools and churches and the media of communication. No doubt all of us mistake our interests; no one can jump out of his skin and pretend that he was born anew, untouched by human hands or immune from the presuppositions of his society. None of this, however, signifies that others have a "true consciousness," enabling them to claim authoritatively that they know what is better for us than we do. In any event, in the current context, false consciousness would signify that expenditures are too low rather than too high, led by corporate propaganda to prefer private to public spending. This is not, as social workers say, the presenting problem.

Stripped of its surface of complex calculation, everyone can understand fiscal illusion because no one understands ramifications of innumerable taxes and expenditures.[7] Citizens may systematically underestimate what they pay and what the government spends. That they pay a lot in sales, real estate, state and federal income taxes, and all the rest, however, is obvious to most people. Witness Proposition Thirteen. At the federal level, the United States uses far fewer indirect taxes, which might escape notice, than do most Western industrial nations. Undoubtedly, in view of the unfathomable billions involved, citizens also underestimate the costs of various programs. Since it would take

[6] William A. Niskanen, *Bureaucracy and Representative Government* (Aldine-Atherton: Chicago, 1971).

[7] On fiscal illusion, see Richard E. Wagner, "Revenue Structure, Fiscal Illusion and Budgetary Choice," *Public Choice*, vol. 24 (Spring 1976), pp. 45–61.

only a few minutes for them to discover the costs, however, this does not matter much. Illusions exist, but it is doubtful whether they result in the euphoric feeling of escape from taxation. Both false consciousness and fiscal illusion serve the function of explaining to followers why a left- or right-wing movement fails. They are the doctrines of inveterate losers.

Other observers find the public sector underfinanced. In explaining "Why the Government Budget Is Too Small in a Democracy," Anthony Downs argues that a fully informed majority would want larger expenditure. Voters (whom politicians try to please in party competition) are consistently misinformed; they perceive the tax burden that they bear far more severely than the advantages of programs, many of which do not benefit them personally. This poor perception leads to the erroneous conclusion that government costs more than its programs are worth.[8] The difficulty with Downs is that the opposite assumption—benefits are palpable and appear to be free, because they are not paid for in cash, whereas taxes have to be paid anyway or are hidden in the price of commodities—appears equally plausible. Were Downs correct, it would be hard to explain why taxing and spending, spending and taxing, go up and up instead of down and down. Since total taxes and spending are widely perceived to be too high, not too low, an expenditure limit tied to economic growth would appear well aimed to restore the relationship between individual items and total expenditures, whatever the reasons they have drifted apart.

Arguing that society was affluent but public facilities were starved, John K. Galbraith insists that individuals were indoctrinated by advertising into artifical wants—consumption for its own sake. Government, by contrast, he claims, is unable to advertise. Citizens would be better served, he asserts, if they gave more income to government for public purposes.[9] Aside from the fact that advertising is not always successful and that people in countries without advertising appear to have remarkably similar preferences, the great question is, Why is what Galbraith wants or what government does superior to private preferences? Governmental advertising, in the form of public relations, actually is ubiquitous; Galbraith's complaint must be that it is ineffective. Is he arguing that politics is superior to economics? He is not quite doing that. Is he saying that some wants are superior to others? No doubt he is. What then distinguishes his or my preferences from yours and theirs?

Another view, with which I also disagree—though, as with the others, only in part—is Gordon Tulloch's theory that "the growth of the

[8] Anthony Downs, "Why the Government Budget Is Too Small in a Democracy," *World Politics*, vol. 12 (July 1960), pp. 541–563.

[9] John K. Galbraith, *The Affluent Society* (Houghton Mifflin: Boston, 1958).

bureaucracy to a large extent is self-generating."[10] The trouble with bureaucrats is that they vote; the more of them there are, the more votes they have, the larger they grow. In support of this hypothesis, (un)certain evidence may be adduced. Civil servants on average are about twice as likely to vote than other people. Governments at the state and local levels, where most civil servants are employed, are much more labor intensive than private industry, not only where they perform services, as William J. Baumol's theory of increasing cost of service suggests,[11] but across the board. The larger the size of government, the higher its proportion of administrative costs.[12] All this is tantalizing but far from conclusive. Bureaucrats are by no means a majority. If in their role as citizens they do not like big government much more than the rest of us, they would not vote for expansion in general. They defend only their part of the public purse. Indeed, according to poll data, 48 percent of state employees in California said they would vote for Proposition Thirteen. The grand queries remain, Why don't the rest of us stop them or, even better, why don't their private stop their public selves?

Doing It to Ourselves

The Pogo theory, by contrast, is that we-the-people (including citizens, politicians, and civil servants) are doing this to ourselves. This is a cooperative game. We do not like it—who said that people necessarily like what they do to themselves—but we do it.

Not only the big bad bureaucrats and their political protectors but also, as the song says, "you and me babe" are at the root of our own problems. All of us are pure as the driven snow, it is just that we keep pushing expenditures up. Citizens like some of those programs, not all, of course, but enough to want to see them go up. Unfortunately, the only way to do that is to push everything up, partly because that is the price of support from other citizens (you provide the scratch for my program and I will provide the scratch for yours), partly because that

[10] Gordon Tulloch, "What Is To Be Done?" in Thomas E. Borcherding, ed., *Budgets and Bureaucrats: The Sources of Government Growth* (Duke University Press: Durham, North Carolina, 1977), p. 285.

[11] William J. Baumol, "Macroeconomics of Unbalanced Growth: The Anatomy of the Urban Crisis," *American Economic Review*, vol. 57 (1967), pp. 415–426.

[12] Work by Elinor Ostrom and her colleagues on police suggests that size leads to overspecialization, which results in a top-heavy administration without equivalent increases in productivity. Thus, small police forces keep as many men on patrol per unit of population as the larger ones. See, for example, Elinor Ostrom and Roger B. Parks, "Suburban Police Departments: Too Many or Too Small?" in Louis H. Masotti and Jeffrey K. Hadden, ed., *Urban Affairs Annual Review*, vol. 7 (1970), pp. 367–402.

is the necessary exchange with politicians who support our programs but others as well, and partly because there is usually no way to express a position on total spending aside from the items that make it up. Citizens want some spending more than others. They want their priorities to prevail; among these priorities is a preference for lower expenditure. Only the existence of the referendum route in California permitted voters to say that real estate taxes were too high without simultaneously repudiating their political parties or their representatives in the state legislature whom they may still have preferred on other grounds. Public policy requires not only an aim but an avenue of redress.

Bureaucrats are not better. Because they actively want more or passively cannot resist, does not mean that they want the government to grow, at least not so fast. Everybody is doing the same thing, however, or they cannot get theirs without going along with those other programs. Like the citizenry (they are the citizenry, at least a good part of it), bureaucrats bid up the cost of government, hardly knowing that they are doing it. As the hero would say in those old-fashioned seduction scenes, when he was inexperienced and she was eager, "It's bigger than the both of us." How did we (not they but we), the people of the United States of America, get to be expenditure junkies? How, more to the point, do we kick the habit?

Alphonse and Gaston on Public Expenditure. Who would take the lead in reducing expenditures? Each sector of policy is concerned with its own internal development. More money makes it easier to settle internal quarrels. Those who believe more is better for their agency or their clientele come to this position naturally. Those who favor radical restructuring of programs soon discover that this is exceedingly difficult to do without sweetening the pie. All internal incentives work to raise expenditures. The price of policy change is program expansion.

Nonetheless, in viewing welfare from the perspective of popular preferences, the people have approved the criteria according to which policies are created vastly increasing expenditures. Without bothering with a formal announcement, Americans apparently agreed on three things: (1) No category of people, once covered, may be denied future benefits; (2) no level of benefits, once raised, may be reduced; and (3) given a choice between bringing benefits to all who qualify, even if some unqualified get in, or leaving out all the unqualified, even if some qualified do not make it, the former, accentuating the positive, is preferable. Thus, there are headlines when people are underpaid but none when they are overpaid. Following these rules guarantees that every new program, if it is not just to do more of the same, must be larger than its predecessors. Otherwise, the most conceivably comprehensive coverage for the largest number of potential beneficiaries could not be guaranteed.[13] Yet, excessive welfare costs are a common contemporary complaint.

Congressmen complain, too, but they do nothing about it. Periodically in its history, Congress has been tightly organized under central leadership or committee chairmen chosen under a seniority system that gave weight to longevity, with appropriations positions occupied by people from safe districts who could afford to say *no*. The ability of individual legislators to express themselves has increased as their internal cohesion has decreased. As a consequence, appropriations have steadily risen and, where they would not, tunnels have been dug around them in the form of entitlements and tax expenditures, annual authorizations to put pressure on appropriations committees, varieties of back-door "spending," subsidized credit, and all the rest. Congress has become fragmented; its members and their substantial staffs are as much a part of the sectors of policy as anyone else.

Of all those writing on these subjects, William Riker's explanation of legislative expansion of the public sector comes closest to the correct spirit:

> I think it is probably the case that, if everyone (or if all rulers in a society) agreed to do so, they could obtain the benefits of reducing the size of the public sector. But no such agreement occurs and our question is to explain why it does not. The explanation I offer is that rulers are trapped in a system of exchange of benefits that leads to disadvantageous . . . results.
>
> The system works in this way:
>
> Step 1: Some legislator (or the leaders of some identifiable group with access to legislators) sees an opportunity for gain for some of the legislator's constituents by the transfer of some activity from the private sector to the public sector. Usually such gain involves the transfer of a private cost to the public treasury. . . . Typically, of course, the beneficiaries of the transfer are relatively small groups of citizens and only a minority of legislators have constituents in the benefiting groups. Typically also there exist other groups and other minorities of legislators who see opportunities for private gain in other transfers from private to public sectors. The combination of several minorities of legislators acting to benefit constituents are enough to make a legislative majority and so together they can produce significant expansions of the public sector.
>
> Step 2: Such a coalition would be socially harmless (though perhaps unfair) . . . . But, of course, this successful coalition is only one of many. Entirely different coalitions, some over-

[13] See Aaron Wildavsky, *Speaking Truth to Power* (Boston: Little, Brown & Co., 1979).

> lapping, some not, obtain other kinds of transfers to the public sector: coalitions around public works, around military bases and contracting, around regulatory bodies and the favors they pass out to various small economic interests, etc. Beyond economic interests there are ideological interests around which legislators can ally themselves to win support by satisfying deeply felt values of some constituents: racial, ethnic, linguistic, religious, moral, patriotic, etc.—all of which can be promoted by expansions of public sector activities.
>
> The consequence is that nearly every conceivable interest, economic and political, has some legislators promoting their own fortunes in future elections by promoting governmental service to that interest.
>
> Step 3: Since each citizen with one or several interests served by these (usually minority) coalitions of legislators benefit as the coalitions succeed and since each legislator benefits in some degree from the gratitude thus generated in marginally important voters, nearly everyone benefits from successful actions to expand the public sector. Consequently, every legislator has a driving motive to form more or less ad hoc majority alliances of these minority coalitions in order to obtain some public benefits for every interest represented in the alliance. Were a legislator to refrain either from promoting some minority interests or from joining in larger alliances to obtain benefits, he (and his constituents) would merely suffer the costs of paying for the benefits for others while obtaining no benefits for themselves.
>
> Yet in the end the society has a greatly expanded public sector with very high costs and considerable inefficiencies. It seems very likely to me that these disadvantages are so great that nearly everybody is worse off than if the public sector expansion had never taken place. It might be supposed, therefore, that everybody would have a motive to agree to forego public sector benefits—and indeed they do. But an agreement for a grand coalition for abstinence seems well-nigh unenforceable. Everyone has a motive to desert the grand coalition in the hope of getting some public sector benefit before others do so.[14]

The only difference between us is one of emphasis: Riker sees the governors doing in the governed and I see all of us in it together.

Among the political puzzles of recent years has been the support shown for congressmen by their constituents amid a general decline in esteem in Congress. Aside from the advantages of incumbency, citizens

[14] William H. Riker, *The Cause of Public Growth* (Rochester, N.Y.: University of Rochester, 1978), pp. 24–28.

seem to have high regard for their representatives, whom they return to office with increasing regularity. The explanation offered by Richard Fenno—congressmen support themselves by campaigning against Congress—cries out for extension. Why do both congressmen and their constituencies like what they do in the small but not in the large? Perhaps the puzzle may be pieced together by the observation that constituents are in fact getting what they want from their representatives but what they want and get on each matter does not turn out to be what they want in total. Their representatives feel the same way. By thinking that in this respect all of us may be in the same boat, it becomes easier to accept the argument that choices on individual programs are not serving collective purposes.

Is Item-by-Item Intelligent? I have not yet specifically stated the most obvious and direct alternative to a constitutional expenditure limitation—acting intelligently on major items of expenditure. If we believe that expenditures are too high, the argument goes, we should say specifically which ones should be cut and by how much. From this standpoint, a general injunction to keep within expenditure limits, without dealing with individual programs, is the height of irresponsibility. As Jude Wanniski wrote in the *Wall Street Journal*,

> The trouble with a constitutional amendment requiring a balanced budget [the stricture holds against expenditure limitation as well] is that it doesn't tell us how to do it, nor do its proponents confront the issue in these terms. Surely most of those aboard the bandwagon, if asked, would tell us they would slash federal spending. But then the public-opinion polls tell us that more than 95% of the American people want federal spending reduced.
>
> This bit of information, though, is also of no value. Each individual citizen wants spending cut according to a list of priorities. Some would cut defense spending, some social spending. Urban citizens would cut rural spending, and vice versa. It's the South against the North, the West against the East, sunbelt versus snowbelt, and so forth. But these priorities are already reflected in the voting patterns of the Congress, and still the budget is out of balance and has been for decades.[15]

Somehow, he seems to feel that if what we are doing does not work, we should do nothing else. The questions Wanniski raises are crucial. Why have a constitutional amendment if it escapes, instead of grasps, responsibility? Why have an amendment if ordinary action is more efficacious?

[15] *Wall Street Journal*, March 5, 1979.

If one wants to cut expenditures, one must cut programs. Simply stated, these words have much to commend them. Talk about improving efficiency, reducing overlap or duplication, perfecting procedures, which may be valuable as far as it goes, ordinarily does not involve substantial sums that quickly cumulate into large savings. One only fools oneself if he thinks nibbling at the edges is a substitute for the main meal. This is true enough as far as it goes, truer than the alternative mentioned, true under the conditions considered, but not necessarily a timeless and circumstanceless truth. I do not regret having agreed with it on micro matters, but investigating individual items is misleading as a general guide to expenditure decision making.

For one thing, that is what we have always done; "item-by-item" got us where we are today. For another, the lack of a limit, especially since the decline of the balanced budget ideology, means that items need not compete with one another. Comparison of increments at the margins might indeed be intelligent if it ever happened. We know better. What really happens is that each item is not compared but added to the others; what we want is to substitute some subtraction for all the addition.

The Rationale. This is the rationale for a constitutional amendment: Not only a particular public policy at a point in time is being negotiated but a social contract into which no one will enter without some assurance that it will last. The relative shares of the public and private sectors are fixed so that the private is protected from diminution and the public guaranteed the availability of its part of the national product. If the alleged advantages are to be obtained, sacrifices must be symmetrical. I will sacrifice today because I know that your turn will come tomorrow. (Put less pejoratively, there is no point in your sacrifice if I do not make mine, because the end result depends on both of us.) We must know that we are in this together to make it worthwhile to do at all. Since "everybody is for it [cutting the federal budget] in general" as Vice President Walter Mondale observed, "as long as it doesn't affect them specifically,"[16] everybody must know, to paraphrase Franklin, that they are going to hang separately before they will be willing to hang together.

Without expectation, the rules will remain the same; few will play the expenditure game. A grand rule is also necessary in order to reflect public opinion accurately. Were substantial spending desired by strong and lasting majorities, the rules of the political game permit this opinion to be registered in budgetary decision. Should there be an opposite opinion, reflecting a desire to slow down spending, it would not have

[16] *New York Times*, March 2, 1979, p. A 11.

an equal opportunity to manifest itself in the budget. Without an amendment, there would be no way for slow spenders to get together to enforce equal sacrifice so that the general rule became part and parcel of the calculations involved in individual spending decisions. To increase spending, no coordination is necessary; to decrease it, an enormous amount is. If my gain is not to be your loss, a ground rule establishing limits is essential.

There is a difference between ordinary decisions and constitutional rules for regulating those daily choices in the light of how we expect them to turn out in total. The sum of our actions over time is not necessarily subject to the same considerations as a single one at a single time. We can (and do) want this or that expenditure now and still object to the total amount of spending to which our actions have contributed. Because we wanted it, does not mean that we like it. Unlike other creatures, like lemmings plopping into the sea, mankind is doomed to observe its own disasters; we know that we are doing it to us. For self-protection, like the dieting man who walks home without passing the bakery, we can safeguard ourselves against the temptation of eating so many desserts that we spoil the meal.

The outcome that we would choose for total spending is smaller than the sum of individual items that we choose to compose it. Deciding with a total in mind is different from deciding without one. Unless we all work within the same total, at the same time, however, some of us stand to get more for our favorite programs. Unless we all slow spending simultaneously, therefore, your forebearance will be my reward. In order to be free to pursue what we know is best, we must bind ourselves against our worst inclinations. To do this, we need a structural change—constitutional expenditure limitation.

Congressional Budget Reform

What has happened with congressional budget reform? It is superior to what it replaced but it is a modest, meliorative move rather than a radical reform. It does for Congress what the Budget Act of 1921 did for the executive, namely, help get its act together. Its purpose is to increase the sense of self-mastery in Congress, with appropriations made within a sense of total expenditures. Congress passes a first concurrent resolution, containing an approximation of this relationship, which is then modified to take account of decisions on individual items and is codified in a second resolution whose total cannot be raised without special procedures. The budget process is somewhat more orderly, with running totals taken of decisions along the way. The Congressional

Budget Office has improved the accuracy of budget numbers by providing a competitive source of expertise, and it has made competent analysis more widely available to those who want it.

The Budget Act is not designed as a one-way street to reduce expenditure. Congress is encouraged to consider totals, but it has no greater incentive than before to reduce these totals. Indeed, it is quite possible for legislators to vote to increase individual items and simultaneously to vote to lower the target totals. Old entitlements are entirely outside its jurisdiction; Congress must only be notified of new ones. When Congress is so disposed, the Budget Act enables it to relate desired totals to individual appropriations. This is desirable. It is not meant to be (and it is not) inevitable. As a close student of the reform recently summed up the evidence, "Congress expanded upon the fiscal policy of the President somewhat more with its budget process than without it."[17]

Conceived as an accompaniment to constitutional expenditure limitation, however, the budget reform gains in strength. As soon as every spending agency and interest knows that for every big increase there must be a corresponding decrease, not only this year but in years to come, they will become partisans of policy analyses. Their activities are desirable and others, that would take from theirs, are not. Thus, the analytic activities of the CBO would become much more important. Data on rates of current and estimates of future spending would also be more highly valued. The penalties attached to bad data and poor estimates would be far more severe than in the past; an agency and program would have to do without because all spending must fit within a genuine constraint.

Activities of economic management, which most sharply distinguish the budget committees from their predecessors, would also be enhanced. Since totals would be fixed by formula, the most difficult and disagreeable tasks would be taken away. What remains would be determining the size of the deficit by varying the tax take and the composition of spending to aid the economy. Because limits would be set by constitutional rules, congressional committees could not set totals (unless, of course, they were to be lowered, which is unlikely).Yet, it is hard to say that the budget reform as it exists now does much more than add up the totals. The task of budget control is to make total expenditures low enough to bite and not large enough to be inconsequential. If they are set too low politically, the budget committees will be overridden;

[17] Joel Havemann, *Congress and the Budget* (Bloomington and London: Indiana University Press, 1979).

if too high, they will be rendered superfluous. A limit on the low side, which will be produced by expenditure limitation, puts the budget committees in the best possible position—limits without losing—without having to exhaust themselves to achieve this result.

It is understandable that every administration feels it can accomplish what others could not, believing that other administrations have lacked political will. The Reagan administration is proposing massive budget reductions on an item-by-item basis. Maybe it will succeed; if so, it will see no need for Constitutional spending limits. But if, as I expect, it gets worn down with endless negotiations, the Reagan administration may discover that while the spirit is willing, the flesh may also be weak. Then it may welcome a mechanism for deflecting all this pressure. If every program is a potential threat to every other, presidents and budget committees will no longer be the only ones worried about spending.

Constitutional Limits and the Federal Budget

Donald G. Ogilvie

For the first time in our history, the American people are giving serious thoughts to applying constitutional limits to the federal government's ability to tax and spend public funds. Opinion polls show overwhelming support for such limits; thirty states (of thirty-four needed) have passed resolutions calling for a convention to draft a constitutional amendment requiring a balanced budget. Dozens of bills have been introduced in Congress that would amend the Constitution in some way to limit taxes or spending.

This paper examines the major issues raised by constitutional limits to the federal budget. The first section reviews the current state of government spending and taxes, how we got where we are today, and the forces that led to the current demand for constitutional limits. The second section reviews the options available, including constitutional amendments, to balance the budget or in some way limit federal spending or taxes and recommends a cause of action.

Let us start with the problem, because the remedy (especially if it is a constitutional one) should relate to the nature of the problem. Unfortunately, there is widespread disagreement about exactly what that problem is and, therefore, what the proposed constitutional amendments should accomplish. Some believe that they should eliminate the imbalance between receipts and outlays. Others are convinced that constitutional limits are needed to control the shift of resources from the private to the public sectors. Some believe that amendments are necessary to limit excessive growth of federal taxes, which have reduced private investment and productivity.

Many of these objectives are interrelated. Cause-and-effect relationships, however, are difficult to define, and much of the empirical research is controversial, ideological, or both. Nevertheless, two widespread concerns about our economic and political system constitute the problem that we are trying to resolve with the suggested constitutional amendments.

First, there is a growing conviction that the shift of resources and responsibility from private individuals to public institutions has gone too far or at least far enough. At issue is the fundamental relationship between the individual and the state. Government absorbs a large and growing share of our national wealth; there is a general uneasiness that government solutions to complex social, political, and economic problems are no longer the best answers, if they ever were. For over thirty years, we have grown accustomed to putting our faith in government solutions; our traditional reliance on private individuals and institutions has declined. The problem is to redefine the appropriate role for public and private America and to establish effective mechanisms to achieve and maintain it.

Second, there is, for the first time since the 1930s, widespread concern about our economic future. Fifteen years of rising inflation, increasing unemployment, and sluggish growth have shaken our faith in government's ability to manage economic policy and sustain the levels of real growth to which we have grown accustomed. Inflation has changed the ways that we think about our salaries, savings accounts, pension plans, and consumer credit of all kinds. We are uneasy with these changes and their implications for our economic futures. Many of us suspect that the days of 3–4 percent annual increases in our real standard of living are gone forever. We are concerned about government's apparent inability to stop inflation and restore real economic growth.

Government is bigger today than it was in the 1920s because we, through our votes and our elected representatives, asked it to assume a greater role in managing economic growth through monetary and fiscal policy, in redistributing income, and in attacking the complex problems associated with a modern technological society. At the same time, there is growing reason to believe that stagflation has been caused by increased government activity at all levels. Although the precise cause-and-effect relationships between these forces are controversial, there is little question that the relationship between government and the economy and the balance of power between the citizen and the state lie at the heart of what concerns Americans today.

The Current State of Government Spending, Taxes, and Deficits

The federal government spent over $530 billion in 1979. That is, by any measure, a great deal of money, and the way it is spent directly affects all of us. Federal spending today accounts for over 23 percent of the gross national product; state and local government spending absorbs an additional 14 percent. Altogether, government either spends or decides how to spend over one-third of the national income each year.[1]

[1] The federal government will provide $80 billion in grants to state and local governments in fiscal year 1980. These grants are designed to implement federal programs through local government mechanisms. Because of the nature of state, local, and federal accounting systems, some or all of these grants may be double counted.

Federal Spending Trends. The historic record of federal spending reflects our wars, our changing social beliefs, and a changing attitude about which social and economic functions are best left in private hands and which are best performed by federal, state, or local government. In the long run, government in America represents what the majority of us feel is necessary and appropriate. It mirrors our goals, our fears, our frustrations, and our personal desires.

Few of us understand how this change in the pattern of government spending happened. Major changes have occurred during the last fifty years that for many of us represent the full span of our personal involvement with the federal government. It is useful for us to look at the pattern of change because, as Robert Bork has said,

> One of the uses of history is to free us from a falsely imagined past. The less we know of how ideas actually took root and grew, the more apt we are to accept them unquestioningly as inevitable of the world in which we move.[2]

Life in modern American society has changed significantly in 200 years, and the scope of government activity at all levels has changed to keep pace with these developments. Our population has increased (from less than 4 million in 1790 to 216 million in 1979), the land area in the United States has grown (from less than 1 million square miles in 1800 to 3.5 million), and the population density per square mile has risen (from 4.5 to 57.5 persons per mile). Major metropolitan areas have developed and increased the need for public services and protection. The decline of the extended family, the rise in geographic mobility, and the increase in life expectancy have combined to produce new requirements for federal programs—income assistance and health and social services to a large population of older Americans. Industry, commerce, and transportation have increased in scope and complexity; science and technology have heightened the need to educate all Americans. These changes have complicated and expanded the role of the public sector in social, economic, and political affairs. A close look at the record of federal spending, however, shows that the rapid growth in government spending is a relatively recent phenomenon. In fact, most of the growth has occurred since 1935; table 1 shows the growth of federal spending in constant and current dollars as well as in real dollars per capita since 1800. These figures illustrate some of the major shifts that have occurred in the role of the central government in American society.

The original role of the federal government was limited both by the precise language in the Constitution and by the prevailing social consensus that powerful central governments should be avoided. As a result, federal activities were restricted to those traditional "public good" func-

[2] Robert H. Bork, *The Antitrust Paradox* (New York: Basic Books, 1978), p. 15.

TABLE 1
U.S. FEDERAL GOVERNMENT EXPENDITURES
(in millions of dollars)

	Current Dollars		*Constant 1972 Dollars*	
Year	Amount	% GNP	Amount	Per capita
1800	11	—	36	7
1850	39	—	200	9
1900	50	2.8	2,800	36
1920	6,357	6.9	12,300	116
1930	3,100	3.7	9,900	80
1940	9,456	9.1	40,100	304
1950	42,597	13.9	101,400	666
1960	92,223	18.6	150,800	895
1970	196,588	19.9	220,800	1,078
1980[a]	531,600	21.2	286,200	1,288

[a] Estimated.

SOURCES: Current dollar and GNP figures 1960–1980 from *Budget of the U.S. Government, FY 1980,* p. 578; for 1800–1950 from U.S. Department of Commerce, *Historical Statistics of the United States, Colonial Times to 1970*; and M. Slade Kendrick, *A Century and A Half of Federal Expenditures.* Constant dollar figures for 1940–1980 from U.S., Office of Management and Budget, *Federal Government Finances*; for 1800–1940 from author's estimates using price index from *Historical Statistics of the United States, Colonial Times to 1970,* and OMB methodology. Population figures from U.S. Bureau of the Census, *1977 Statistical Abstract,* and, *Historical Statistics of the United States, Colonial Times to 1970.*

tions such as the maintenance of national security forces, management of the monetary system, and the operation of the executive, congressional, and judicial branches of government. It was widely agreed that most decisions about how to spend our national income were best left to private individuals and institutions and to local governments.

Because of its restricted role, the federal government consumed only a small (and fairly constant) share of the national wealth until the Civil War. In 1865, federal spending exceeded a billion dollars per year for the first time; almost all of the funds spent that year supported the war effort. At the close of the Civil War, federal expenditures dropped sharply as the nation demobilized, and they remained relatively level for the next fifty years. The federal budget did not again exceed a billion dollars until 1917, when expenditures for the First World War pushed annual federal spending to almost $20 billion at the height of the war. Then, as with the post–Civil War period, government spending declined sharply as military expenses were cut back. Federal spending remained relatively level at about $2–3 billion per year for the next decade.

As recently as 1900, the federal government spent only 2.8 percent of the gross national product. The federal budget that year was only \$500 million; adjusted for inflation, that represents \$2.8 billion in 1972 prices or approximately \$36 per year for each American citizen. Decisions about how to spend the rest of their incomes were left to individuals and organizations outside Washington.

The Turning Point. The Great Depression of the 1930s represented a significant turning point in the role of the federal government in American society. The nation turned to massive federal programs to pull the economy from the worst economic recession it had experienced. President Roosevelt and Congress initiated one program after another to provide jobs to the unemployed and income assistance to those most in need. Spending for domestic assistance programs jumped from less than \$1 billion in 1930 to almost \$7 billion in 1939.

Prior to the 1930s, three-quarters of the federal peacetime expenditures were directly related to expenses for military, veterans, or interest on war-related debt, as shown in table 2. This changed radically during the 1930s, when civil expenditures accounted for 60 percent of the total. Domestic programs continued to account for the bulk of federal programs until 1941, when the buildup in military expenditures began for World War II.

The Second World War pushed federal spending to new heights. Increasingly complex military technology, a massive buildup in the number of American servicemen (over 56 percent of the eligible male population), and inflation combined to increase federal expenditures to \$95 billion per year at the peak of the Second World War (almost ten times the prewar level). Military expenditures of \$85 billion far exceeded the \$14-billion peak during the First World War and the \$1.3-billion Civil War peak.

TABLE 2

U.S. GOVERNMENT EXPENDITURES, 1923–1937
(in billions of dollars)

	War-Related Expenditures		*Civil Expenditures*		
Period	Amount	% Total	Amount	% Total	*Total Expenditures*
1923–1930	17.4	75	5.9	25	23.3
1931–1937	16.9	40	25.5	60	42.4

SOURCE: M. Slade Kendrick, *A Century and a Half of Federal Expenditures,* National Bureau of Economic Research 1955, occasional paper 48, table B-1.

Military spending declined sharply at the end of the Second World War, although it remained considerably above prewar levels. Increased U.S. military responsibilities in Western Europe and Asia required a higher level of American mobilization and spending for national security forces. During the decade just prior to the Second World War, only 1.5 percent of the eligible male population was in the armed forces and 13 percent of the federal budget was devoted to military purposes. During the peace years between the Second World War and the Korean War, approximately 7 percent of the eligible male population and 30 percent of the federal budget were allocated to support the nation's security forces.

Federal expenditures rose sharply again with the onset of the Korean War, as mobilization began in 1951. The budget doubled in five years from about $36 billion in 1948 to $77 billion in 1953. Military expenses, of course, accounted for most of the increase, although civil programs remained at their relatively high postwar levels.

The major growth in the federal budget, however, has occurred since the end of the Korean War. In 1954, government outlays were approximately $70 billion. Twenty-six years later, they exceed $530 billion. The Vietnam war accounted for some of that spectacular growth, but the bulk of the spending reflects new domestic roles and functions that have been assumed or created by the federal government. These fundamental changes and their causes will be reviewed in detail later.

Although federal spending has increased significantly, the increases have been neither regular nor routine (see table 3). As pointed out, until the 1930s, major increases occurred only during war years. Federal expenditures rose predictably as the nation mobilized its military forces and fell (although not to previous levels) as demobilization occurred. During the intervening years of peace, the federal budget either declined or increased at modest (less than 5 percent) rates each year. During the first 102 of the 185 years for which we have reliable data on federal expenditures, spending either declined or increased only slightly. In the last twenty years, spending has decreased only three times, and not at all since 1969. It took 186 years for the federal budget to exceed $100 billion; it took only 9 more years to reach $200 billion; 4 more to exceed $300 billion; 2 more to reach $400 billion; and an additional 2 years to go to $500 billion. Federal spending is increasing at an average rate of almost $500 billion a year.

Another way to measure federal spending is in terms of constant dollars, which eliminate the effect of inflation. Even after adjusting for inflation and population growth, the increases in federal spending have been dramatic, particularly since the turning point in the 1930s. Annual

TABLE 3

CHANGES IN FEDERAL EXPENDITURES, 1794–1979

Periods	*Decline* Years	*Decline* %	*Increase < 5%* Years	*Increase < 5%* %	*Increase > 5%* Years	*Increase > 5%* %
1794–1818	12	48	2	8	11	44
1819–1843	15	60	3	12	7	28
1844–1868	9	36	2	8	14	56
1869–1893	13	52	5	20	7	28
1894–1918	10	40	7	28	8	32
1919–1943	10	40	4	16	11	44
1944–1968	5	20	5	20	15	60
1969–1979	0	0	0	0	10	100
Total	74		28		83	
Average		40		15		45

SOURCE: *Historical Statistics of the United States, Colonial Times to 1970,* U.S. Department of Commerce, and calculations by the author.

real federal spending per capita (in 1972 dollars) has grown from $80 in 1930 to almost $1,300 in 1979.

The final way to measure federal outlays is in relation to the total amount of income that the nation produces each year, the so-called gross national product (GNP). The individual citizen can allocate his income in three ways—he can save or invest it, he can consume it himself, or he can give it to the government, in one form of taxes or another, to spend for him. It is a true zero-sum game; money spent by government is (or could be) the same money that we would have spent instead.

The relationship between the gross national product and government spending, therefore, is one indicator of the relative distribution of spending *decisions* between the public and the private sectors of the economy. I emphasize the word *decisions* to distinguish it from the benefits of government spending. Government often decides how to spend money, but the benefits of those decisions go, directly or indirectly, to private individuals and organizations. Washington, for example, sets policies and program levels for food stamps, Medicare, and social security, but the benefits of these programs accrue directly to individuals. These income transfer programs redistribute income from one group of Americans to another. Washington decides how to spend the money and who should receive it, but the benefits are returned to private individuals.

TABLE 4

FEDERAL OUTLAYS AS PERCENTAGE OF GNP, 1900–1978

Year	*Federal Outlays As % of GNP*
1900	2.8
1910	2.0
1920	6.9
1930	3.7
1940	9.1
1950	13.9
1960	18.5
1965	18.0
1970	20.5
1972	20.9
1974	20.0
1976	23.6
1978	23.1

SOURCE: *Historical Statistics of the United States, Colonial Times to 1970,* U.S. Department of Commerce, and the *Budget of the U.S. Government, 1980.* All figures include off-budget federal entities.

Until 1930, with the exception of the major war years, the federal government spent, or decided how to spend, a relatively small and constant share of the national income. Federal outlays varied between 2 percent and 4 percent of the GNP for almost 160 years, except those war periods when government spending increased sharply to finance a national mobilization. Table 4 shows federal spending as a percentage of the GNP since 1900.

Since the 1930s, however, the federal government's share of national income has increased rapidly. The most rapid growth came during the 1935–1960 period, although there has been a substantial (25 percent) increase in the federal share since 1960. Some of the recent growth resulted from increases in real spending for national security following World War II, but most of the increase represents new functions and new programs developed by the federal government since the depression.

Three Major Developments

Whichever way one chooses to view federal spending, the figures show that something truly significant happened to federal spending during the 1930s. Three major developments combined at that time to alter the role of the federal government and to affect the allocation of national income. For the first time, during those depression years, the federal government assumed direct responsibility for the nation's economic growth and stability. Congress initiated direct and broadbased programs designed to stimulate economic recovery. This represented a fundamental change in the role of government in America—away from the traditional belief that the economy was basically self-regulating and toward a new Keynesian doctrine that direct government intervention was needed to ensure stable economic growth and prosperity.

Keynesian economics provided a theoretical justification not only for direct government intervention in the economy but also for deficit spending. Prior to the 1930s, deficit spending was effectively precluded by a "fiscal constitution" that called for a balanced budget except in times of war.[3] The abandonment of the balanced budget requirement in the late 1930s stimulated spending by allowing the federal government to avoid the pain of directly imposing the cost of new programs on the people through higher taxes; the true cost of these programs was disguised through deficit spending and inflation. In addition, government lost its only yardstick by which to determine how many worthy federal programs the country could afford.

The second major development was that the federal government began a wholesale redistribution of income from one group of Americans to another, from one region of the country to another, and from one set of institutions to another. Over the next forty years, this income redistribution function dramatically changed the structure of the federal budget and increased its share of national wealth. For the first time, federal officials and elected legislators began to influence the distribution of wealth significantly, initially through the tax system and then increasingly through direct spending programs of the federal government.

All of this might have never occurred without the leadership of Franklin Roosevelt.

> He came at a time when the society was ready for vast political and economic change, all of it enhancing the power of the President and the Federal government, and he accelerated that change. The old order had collapsed, old institutions and old myths had failed; he would create the new order. In the new order, government would enter the everyday existence of almost all its citizens, regulating and adjusting their lives. Under him, Washington became the focal point, it determined how people worked, how much they made, what they ate, where

[3] James M. Buchanan and Richard E. Wagner, *Democracy in Deficit* (New York: Academic Press, 1977).

> they lived. Before his arrival, the Federal government was small and timid; by the time he died it reached everywhere . . . .[4]

After the Roosevelt era, a pattern of government spending subtly evolved until, in the 1960s, it entered a new phase, the federal stage. Since the Great Depression, we have seen the gradual development of government programs that benefit all Americans more or less equally. Their distinguishing characteristic is that they exist not to redistribute income from wealthy to poor Americans but to provide to all of us certain goods and services that traditionally we had provided for ourselves. These federal subsidies exist in great numbers, affect most of us in significant ways, and are largely unnoticed by most Americans. They include subsidies for the food that we eat, the cars that we drive, the homes that we live in, the health care that we receive as senior citizens, and a host of income security programs.

Unlike income redistribution, which generated heated debate not only about the appropriate level of spending, but also about the legitimacy of redistribution as a function of the federal government, the federal stage arrived almost unannounced. Like income redistribution, the federal stage significantly increased the government share of national income because it added significant new functions to the federal role in society. Unlike income redistribution, which cast the federal government only in the role of taxing one group and paying out to another, the federal stage shifted functions that were traditionally left to individuals and local governments to the federal government. In essence, almost without knowing it, we decided to tax ourselves at the federal level and to commission the federal government to provide goods and services that we had historically provided for ourselves. The profund implications of this trend for the nature of our social, political, and economic institutions, and the difficulties of reversing it, should not be underestimated.

In addition to carrying out its activities, the federal government has developed a series of budget and legislative procedures that make it extremely difficult to affect the course of government spending significantly. The budgetary process has become so complicated and bureaucratic that only a small number of technicians—many of whom devote their entire careers to the budget—are capable of influencing the budget process that ultimately spends (or decides how to spend) about one-fifth of our national income each year.

Most importantly, however, Congress has begun to define spending levels for government programs in substantive law and effectively remove them from the annual budget review. These entitlement programs

[4] David Halberstam, *The Powers That Be* (New York: Alfred A. Knopf, Inc., 1979), pp. 8–9.

(such as social security), which are defined as "relatively uncontrollable" without a change in substantive law, account for three-quarters of all federal spending. Ironically, these efforts to ensure that federal spending does not get out of control have produced a budget that is, on one hand, almost completely controlled by law and, on the other hand, increasingly removed from the annual budget review process. We have developed a budget that is, for all practical purposes, on automatic pilot. We do have the option to turn off the autopilot, but, at least in recent years, Congress and the president have not chosen to take control again.

Demise of the Fiscal Constitution. It is worth reviewing how we moved from a fiscal constitution to this federal stage in order to understand the changes we may be able to make. James M. Buchanan and Richard E. Wagner have argued that federal spending in the pre-Keynesian era was guided by a fiscal constitution that was based on

> the central principle that public finance and private finance are analogous, and that the norms for prudent contact are similar. Barring extraordinary circumstances, public expenditures were supposed to be financed by taxation, just as private spending was supposed to be financed from income. The pre-Keynesian or classical fiscal constitution was not written in any formal set of rules. It was, nonetheless, almost universally accepted. And its importance lay in its influence in constraining the profligacy of all persons, members of the public along with the politicians who acted for them. Because expenditures were expected to be financed from taxation, there was less temptation for dominant political coalitions to use the political process to implement direct income transfers among groups. Once the expenditure-taxation nexus was broken, however, the opportunities for such income transfers were increased. Harry G. Johnson, for instance, has advanced the thesis that the modern tendency toward ever-increasing budget deficits results from such redistributional games. Governments increasingly enact public expenditure programs that confer benefits on special segments of the population, with the cost borne by taxpayers generally. Many such programs might not be financed in the face of strenuous taxpayer resistance, but might well secure acceptance under debt finance. The hostility to the expenditure programs is reduced in this way, and budgets rise; intergroup income transfers multiply.[5]

Income Redistribution and the Federal Stage. In response to the widespread unemployment and hardships caused by the depression, the fed-

[5] Buchanan and Wagner, *Democracy in Deficit.*

FIGURE 1

BUDGET OUTLAYS
(constant 1980 dollars)

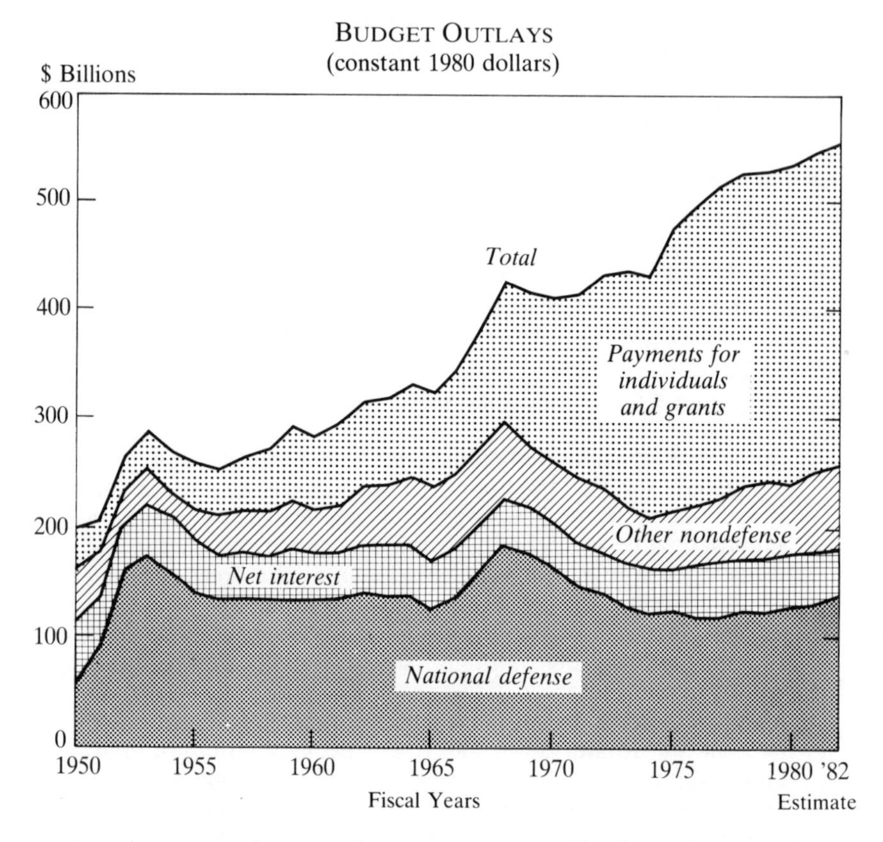

eral government developed programs to redistribute income from wealthy to needy Americans. These countercyclical programs were intended to be temporary and to be phased out as the economy recovered. Many did disappear after a few years, but their existence established two important principles that affect federal programs to this day. First, they built a broad social consensus for programs that redistribute income to needy citizens. These programs were the forerunners of the so-called income transfer programs (such as public assistance, social services, Medicaid, and food stamps), which today account for a sizable share of the federal budget. Second, they established the demand for federal programs that provide economic security for all Americans (not just the poor) during temporary periods of hardship (such as social security, Medicare, and unemployment compensation).

The impact of these programs on federal spending was great (see figure 1). From relatively modest beginnings in the 1940s and 1950s,

TABLE 5

FEDERAL OUTLAYS, 1955–1980
(percent)

Program	1955	1965	1975	1980
National Defense	58.1	40.1	26.2	23.7
Human Resources				
Income security	13.3	21.7	33.3	33.7
Health	0.4	1.5	8.5	10.0
Education, training, etc.	0.6	1.8	4.9	5.7
Veterans	6.9	4.8	5.1	3.9
Subtotal	21.3	29.9	51.8	53.2
All Other	20.6	30.0	22.0	23.1
Total	100.0	100.0	100.0	100.0

SOURCE: *Budget of the United States Government, Fiscal Year 1980,* pages 84–85. Figures may not add to totals because of rounding.

these payments to individuals grew rapidly in the 1960s and accelerated during the 1970s. As a percentage of total federal spending, payments for individuals and grants increased from 22 percent in 1951 to 54 percent in 1979.

Table 5 shows the programs mainly responsible for the rapid reversal of national priorities in the federal budget, away from defense and toward spending for human resource programs. As a percentage of total federal outlays, defense spending has declined steadily from 58 percent during the Korean War to 24 percent in 1980. During the same period, spending for human resource programs increased from 21 percent in 1955 to 53 percent in 1980. The major human resource programs are for income security (which almost tripled during the period), health care (which now accounts for 10 percent of the total), and education, training, unemployment, and social services.

All of these federal programs benefit the poor. Most, however, also increasingly benefit middle- and upper-income Americans as well. Social security, for example, undoubtedly is the only source of income that keeps many senior citizens from poverty; it also provides supplementary income for millions of retired citizens who have "adequate" incomes provided through their individual savings and pension plans. Medicare benefits all Americans over age sixty-five, not just the poor. Numerous unemployment, training, and education programs provide hundreds of millions of dollars worth of benefits to middle-income citizens. Literally hundreds of direct federal programs and tax expenditures subsidize goods or services that we traditionally provided for ourselves or received from state or local governments. A few examples are:

TABLE 6

GOVERNMENT BENEFICIARIES, 1960–1977
(millions of people)

	1977		*1960*	
Kind of Beneficiary	Number	% of population	Number	% of population
Government employees and dependents	29.9	12.9	24.1	13.3
Private employees dependent on government spending	19.3	8.3	16.9	9.3
Federal income transfer and pension recipients	71.4	30.6	30.8	17.0
Other beneficiaries of government programs	4.5	1.9	1.2	0.7
Total	125.1	53.7	73.0	40.3

SOURCE: A. Gary Shilling & Company, Inc., New York, New York.

• Washington today is the primary source of loans or grants for higher education, regardless of income.

• The homes that we own are subsidized heavily by the federal government.

• The planes, trains, buses, and subways that we ride are funded substantially from Washington.

• A great many city governments depend on CETA funds from Washington to pay for up to 45 percent of their employees in order to provide essential safety and sanitation services.

• State and local governments receive approximately 25 percent of their annual income from Washington, up from only 10 percent in 1955.

As a result, a surprising and rapidly growing number of Americans are dependent on the government (federal, state, and local) for a significant share of their annual expendable funds. Table 6 shows the number of citizens who are direct beneficiaries of government programs. Many of these individuals (39 million in 1977) are federal, state, or local government employees and their dependents. Another 19 million (8 percent of the total) are employees of private enterprises that are dependent on government purchases for annual earnings. However, 71 million Americans (31 percent of the population) receive direct federal income transfer or pension benefits. An additional 5 million (2 percent) receive federal assistance for food stamps, educational assistance, or subsidized housing. Altogether, 125 million Americans (54 percent of the population) receive a significant income supplement of one form or another from government today. That is a dramatic increase from the estimated 40 percent in 1960.

The political significance of this development should not be underestimated. We have, in effect, created a special-interest group that includes a majority of the population. Federal efforts to reduce benefit levels in any of these programs will directly affect millions of voters (30 million citizens, almost all of voting age, receive social security, for example). It should come as no surprise that President Carter's recent proposals to make modest changes (cuts) in social security benefits were not considered seriously by Congress. Because we all benefit from these programs, it will take a brave (or foolhardy) set of representatives and senators to cut them. This is a significant consideration in the debate over constitutional limits and the federal budget to which we turn shortly. We may need something to save us from ourselves.

The Size of Uncontrollable Spending

The popular view that federal spending is out of control is correct, despite the fact that there have never before been so many restrictions and preconditions on federal spending. The number of program planners, budget analysts, auditors, and accountants on the federal payroll has increased significantly in recent years. Spending is out of control because the myriad of legislative restrictions and preconditions (which were imposed, ironically, to ensure congressional control) have effectively removed most of the federal budget from the annual review process. The Budget Reform Act in 1974 imposed further controls on the spending process. All these were intended to control expenditures.

Yet, from the perspective of the president, who many of us (incorrectly) believe determines federal spending, most of the budget appears to be uncontrollable. Federal expenditures are defined as relatively uncontrollable, either because they are mandated under present law or because they represent fixed obligations of the government. Three-quarters of the budget is defined as relatively uncontrollable by the Office of Management and Budget (OMB), as shown in table 7. This share has grown almost 20 percent in the last decade alone.

Direct payments to individuals account for $251 billion of relatively uncontrollable outlays in 1980, almost half of the federal budget. These legislatively defined payments include social security, unemployment assistance, Medicare and Medicaid assistance, housing subsidies, federal pensions, and veterans' benefits. Eligibility and benefit level criteria are written into the law for these programs. The president's budget proposals each year are not really budgets at all; they are merely estimates (guesses

TABLE 7

CONTROLLABILITY OF FEDERAL OUTLAYS, 1969–1979
(percent)

	1969	*1971*	*1973*	*1975*	*1977*	*1979*
Relatively uncontrollable	63.1	66.4	70.0	72.9	73.0	74.9
Relatively controllable	38.0	34.8	31.1	28.4	28.1	26.1

Note: Totals do not add to 100 percent because of the undistributed employer share of employees retirement (about −1.2 percent per year) not shown.
SOURCE: The *Budget of the U.S. Government, 1979,* table 14, p. 470.

is probably more appropriate) about what will happen to inflation, unemployment, and demographic changes, all of which combine to determine the level of federal spending for these programs each year. Most of the growth of federal spending occurs automatically, untouched by the budgeters or congressional "control" processes. Presidential and congressional "budgets" in no way control federal spending in these uncontrollable areas; inflation, unemployment, and demographic changes do.

We will return to this subject shortly when we consider constitutional limits to the federal budget. For now, it is sufficient to note that three-quarters of the federal budget is already uncontrollable under present laws and that significant legislative and political changes must occur to bring these programs once again into the annual budget review and appropriation process.

The Current State of Government Taxes

The rapid rise in government spending programs has not been free. In one way or another, either now or in the future, we pay for all that we receive from Washington or city hall, through a complex system of federal, state, and local government taxes.

Since 1900, there have been significant shifts in the level, nature, and structure of government taxes that bear heavily on our review of constitutional limits and the federal budget. First, it almost goes without saying that, in both current and constant dollars, government tax revenues have increased dramatically to keep up with the pace of government spending. Total federal receipts, for example, grew from $4 billion in 1931 to $502 billion in 1980.

Second, total tax revenues as a share of the gross national product increased from 6 percent in 1902 to approximately 35 percent in 1979. In effect, there has been a massive shift of national wealth from private individuals and institutions to government. Hidden within these totals,

TABLE 8

TAX REVENUE AS PERCENTAGE OF GNP, 1902–1972

Level	*1902*	*1922*	*1940*	*1960*	*1972*
Federal	2.3	4.6	5.7	18.2	17.7
State	0.7	1.4	4.4	4.5	6.2
Local	3.2	4.2	4.5	3.8	4.3
Total	6.2	10.2	14.6	26.5	28.2

SOURCE: Musgrave and Musgrave, *Public Finance In Theory and Practice;* McGraw-Hill, 1973, table 9-1.

however, there lies an even more significant shift; while local governments maintained a relatively constant share of the GNP (3–4 percent), federal tax revenues grew from 2 percent in 1902 to almost 20 percent in 1979. Not only was there a dramatic shift of resources from the private to the public sector, there was also a significant centralization of these resources at the federal level. (Table 8 shows federal, state, and local tax revenues as a percentage of the GNP since 1902.) At the same time, federal tax receipts grew from 37 percent of total tax revenues in 1902 to 62 percent in 1972, while local taxes fell from 51 percent to 15 percent during the same period and state taxes increased from 11 percent to 21 percent (see table 9).

A third significant change in government taxes is the shifting nature of the taxes themselves. The tax structure has evolved from heavy reliance on direct (visible) taxes on property and wealth to indirect taxes on income and earnings. In 1902, for example, almost 70 percent of all government tax receipts were raised through property taxes (51 percent) and customs duties (18 percent). By 1972, however, two-thirds of all taxes were generated by individual income taxes (34 percent), corporate income taxes (11 percent), and payroll taxes (20 percent).

TABLE 9

TAX LEVELS AS A PERCENTAGE OF TOTAL TAX BURDEN, 1902–1972

Level	*1902*	*1922*	*1940*	*1960*	*1972*
Federal	37.4	45.2	38.8	68.5	62.7
State	11.4	13.9	30.0	17.1	21.9
Local	51.3	40.9	31.2	14.5	15.4
Total	100.0	100.0	100.0	100.0	100.0

SOURCE: Musgrave and Musgrave, *Public Finance In Theory and Practice;* McGraw-Hill, 1973, table 9-1.

As a result of these changes in the tax structure, the gap between the spending and the taxing decision has widened. The theory of public choice establishes the ideal of associating all spending decisions with a comparable taxing decision. In theory, individuals and public officials can only make fully rational decisions about government programs when they can simultaneously associate the costs with the benefits. The centralization of tax receipts at the federal level (far removed from most of us), the increased reliance on income taxes, and the introduction of withholding taxes have made it increasingly difficult for the average citizen to assess rationally the costs and benefits of government programs, even in the aggregate.

Federal Surpluses and Deficits. The primary public concern with the federal budget appears to be over the imbalance between receipts and expenditures. The impetus behind most efforts to amend the Constitution is the desire to force Congress and the president to balance the budget. The historical record supports this concern. (Table 10 shows the number of years in which the federal budget has been in surplus or deficit since 1792, the first year for which governmentwide data are available.) During the first fifty years of our history, Washington ran a deficit only fourteen times or 28 percent of the years, and then almost entirely to finance major wars. Deficit years dropped slightly during the second fifty years to 24 percent. The third fifty-year period saw a rapid rise of deficit spending years to 60 percent as a result of defense spending for the Spanish-American War and World Wars I and II. The pattern of deficit spending continued to increase during the 1945–1946 period when deficits occurred two of every three years. Since 1965, the federal budget has been in deficit in all but one year; the outlook for balance in the foreseeable future is dim.

TABLE 10

U.S. GOVERNMENT FINANCES, 1792–1980

	Budget Surplus		*Budget Deficit*	
Period	Number of years	Percent	Number of years	Percent
1792–1842	36	72	14	28
1843–1893	38	76	12	24
1894–1944	20	40	30	60
1945–1965	7	35	13	65
1965–1980	1	6	14	94

SOURCE: *Historical Statistics of the United States, Colonial Time to 1970,* U.S. Department of Commerce, p. 1104, and *Budget of the U.S. Government 1980,* p. 579.

The pattern of change from little government spending and rare deficit budgeting to extensive spending and consistent deficit budgeting is clear. The crux of the current debate about constitutional amendments to require balanced budgets is whether the recent growth in deficit spending represents a significant national problem that can and should be resolved by a constitutional requirement to equalize taxes and spending.

Constitutional Amendments

Constitutional amendments are serious remedies that should be applied to the federal budget only if:

- Significant national problems exist that, without corrective action, will impose unacceptable social, political, or economic costs.
- Other remedies, short of constitutional limits, have been tried and have failed.
- The proposed constitutional amendments can be reasonably expected to eliminate the problems without unacceptable costs.

Numerous constitutional amendments have been proposed to limit the federal budget. Although there are many variations, the amendments usually fall into one of three categories: (1) those requiring a balanced budget; (2) those limiting spending; and (3) those limiting taxes. The proposed constitutional amendments are designed to apply different types of limits and, therefore, have significantly different implications for federal spending and taxes and the role of government in society. People trying to solve different problems naturally propose different remedies. Most of the anxieties that produced these remedies, however, fall into one of the two areas of concern discussed at the beginning of this paper: first, the growing imbalance between the public and the private sectors, and second, the inability or unwillingness of the federal government to use monetary and fiscal policy to produce consistent real economic growth.

The Public-Private Imbalance. Many Americans believe that the massive shift of resources and power from private to public hands, and from local to federal governments, has gone too far: "Ever-increasing expenditures by government may lead to an ever-contracting private sector, with all the implications that has not only for the economy but for our political democracy."[6] A significant and continuously growing share of the population depends on the federal government for all or part of

[6] Ralph K. Winter (Remarks made at a conference on the constitution and the budget, American Enterprise Institute, Washington, D.C., May 24, 1979).

its annual income. Many of our finest private institutions could not exist as we now know them without federal money.

Our traditional political, economic, and social strengths are derived in large measure from the creativity, innovativeness, and humanity of private individuals and institutions. At some point, the shift of authority and resources from private into public hands will significantly weaken these traditional roles of the private sector. Proponents of constitutional limits on federal spending and taxes believe that this shift has already gone too far, that government taxes and regulation are too much of a burden, and that serious damage has been imposed on the private sector.

John Gardner states the dangers this way:

> with Federal money comes the Federal rule book. . . . Preserving a role for the private citizen encourages creativity and keeps alive in individual citizens the sense of personal caring and concern so essential if a mass society is to retain the element of humaneness. . . . We must stop thinking in terms of solutions concocted in Washington and imposed on every locality. At a time in history when we are ever in need of new solutions to new problems, the private sector is remarkably free to innovate, create, and engage in controversial experiments.[7]

The Fiscal-Monetary Debate. The second major concern is over government's inability to ensure stable economic growth. It is widely believed that deficit spending in Washington lies at the heart of these economic difficulties. Some or all of the following arguments apply:

- Deficits cause inflation and/or crowding out, both of which are undesirable.
- Inflation increases the government share of national wealth through "tax bracket creep,"[8] fuels the boom-bust economic cycle and stagflation, and causes significant economic dislocation and hardship.
- The ever-increasing real tax burden caused by inflation, and the crowding out caused by deficit spending combine to weaken private investment and individual initiative. The ultimate result is declining productivity and lower real economic growth.

All of these propositions are controversial, to say the least. Volumes have been written on both sides of each issue; I will attempt little more than a summary at this point.

Despite Keynesian economics, most Americans still believe that

[7] John W. Gardner, "The Private Pursuit of Public Purpose," *The Chronicle of Higher Education*, January 8, 1979.

[8] To my knowledge, this phrase first appeared in a *New York Times* article by William Safire, June 1, 1978.

governments, like everybody else, should live within their means.[9] Individuals and organizations that consistently spend more than they earn eventually become bankrupt. The popular view is that this phenomenon applies to governments as well, at least in the long run. Except in emergencies, budgets should be balanced. The old-time fiscal religion was set back significantly by Keynes's theoretical justification for deficit spending and debt accumulation. Proponents of the balanced budget amendment, fearing that they will be unable to reinstate the "fiscal constitution" through the normal legislative process, want to achieve the same goals by amending the Constitution to require balanced budgets except during national emergencies.

The Problem with Deficits. Budget balancers argue that deficits cause inflation (which is bad) or crowding out (which is equally undesirable). There is, unfortunately, a great deal more emotional argument than empirical research on these cause and effect relationships.

In his recent article on "Balancing the Budget," Herbert Stein has perceptively summarized the arguments about deficits and inflation:

> 1. An increase in the deficit will increase government borrowing, which will raise interest rates. That, in turn, will reduce the quantity of money people want to hold; that is, at higher interest rates they will prefer to hold more of other assets, such as government bonds, and less money, which yields no interest. This will permit aggregate demand to rise even if there is no increase in the money supply.
>
> 2. Even if a deficit is not accompanied by an increase in the money supply, it does lead to an increase in the supply of quite secure and liquid assets—namely, the government debt—and that is likely to cause an increase in private spending.
>
> 3. Although a deficit may not raise aggregate demand unless it is accompanied by an increase in the money supply, a deficit will cause an increase in the money supply.
>
> While all of this is controversial, it is probably true that cases 1 and 2 are not likely to explain a steep and prolonged inflation without an increase of the money supply. They may, however, explain spurts of inflation. The interesting case is the third one, in which the deficit is alleged to cause the increase of the money supply.
>
> A good deal of effort has been devoted to trying to determine whether deficits cause an increase in the money supply. The linkage is thought to be that deficits cause interest rates to rise, that monetary authorities wish to moderate increases of interest rates, and that they try to do this by making the money supply

[9] The Gallup Poll taken in early 1979 showed that 78 percent of the population supported a constitutional amendment to require a balanced budget.

> grow more rapidly. Studies of this relationship have been inconclusive. The factors determining the behavior of the monetary authority are numerous and variable, and some of them are hard to quantify. Therefore, the effect of one factor, the size of the federal deficit, cannot be isolated with any confidence.
>
> Still, the proposition that deficits cause an increase in the money supply is clearly too simple.[10]

William Niskanen has attempted to test the thesis in Stein's case 3 situation, namely, that deficits cause an increase in the money supply which in turn causes inflation. Niskanen's analysis indicates that, over the period 1948–1976:

> • About 15–20 percent of the Federal deficit appears to have been monetarized. This effect, however, nearly disappears when one controls for the substantial shift in monetary policy in the last decade. In any given year, the Federal deficit does not appear to have any significant effect on the rate of change of the money supply.
>
> • In a given year, the rate of inflation appears to be most strongly dependent on the rate of money growth two years ago and the rate of inflation in the prior year. In the long run, the rate of inflation appears to have a negative trend of around 2.2 percent a year and increases more than proportionately with an increase in the money supply. These results are generally consistent with those of other studies.
>
> • Federal deficits do not have any significant effects on the inflation rate operating either through or independent of the rate of money growth."[11]

The controversy over the cause-and-effect relationships between deficits and inflation will not be resolved easily or soon. To be perfectly fair, there are compelling arguments on both sides of the issue. This conclusion, however, has important implications for our review of constitutional limits and the federal budget. Two of the criteria that I proposed for assessing constitutional amendments are, first, that there be a significant national problem and, second, that the proposed remedy be likely to eliminate it. There is widespread agreement that today's inflation meets the first criterion and that the costs of continued inaction are unacceptably high. There is serious disagreement, however, about whether balanced budget amendments or spending/tax limitations by themselves would have any impact on inflation. If inflation is the national

[10] Herbert Stein, "Balancing the Budget" in *Contemporary Economic Problems 1979*, ed. William Fellner (Washington, D.C.: American Enterprise Institute, 1979), pp. 213–214.

[11] William A. Niskanen, "Deficits, Government Spending, and Inflation," *Journal of Monetary Economics*, 1978, p. 601.

problem, the proposed amendments (however appealing for other reasons) are probably not the solution.

The Crowding-Out Thesis. Deficit spending can be financed either by increasing the money supply or by borrowing from the private sector. Traditional economic theory held that borrowing to finance the deficit absorbs savings that would otherwise be invested in the private sector; private capital formation is crowded out by government borrowing, and productivity and economic growth decline.

This thesis has been challenged empirically and emotionally on many grounds, and the issue is far from resolved. For our purposes, however, it is not clear that we need to reach a final resolution of the issue in order to consider the proposed constitutional amendments. If deficits do not necessarily crowd out private investment, then a balanced budget amendment is not necessary (at least for this reason). If, on the other hand, deficits crowd out private investment and cause significant economic harm, the most effective remedy must surely be to attack the problem of private saving and investment directly (through increased earnings on savings accounts, more rapid capital depreciation schedules, investment tax credits, or lower capital gains and corporate income tax rates). Given the controversy and uncertainty over this issue, conventional remedies are probably more appropriate than constitutional amendments.

Conventional Remedies Have Failed. Clearly, the best solution is to solve some or all of these problems through normal legislative and political processes. Congress can pass laws designed to accomplish the same results as a constitutional amendment. In fact, the comprehensive flexible nature of the legislative vehicle should produce better results than an amendment, which is difficult to modify as conditions change. If we as voters do not like the results or the pace of legislative reform, we always have the option of voting into office a new set of elected officials who will do better.

There are two compelling counterarguments to this line of reasoning. First, we have already tried conventional remedies and they have failed. Second, we have had ample opportunity to vote the big spenders out of office during the last twenty years, but most remain in office.

Conventional efforts to deal with increased government spending and deficits have been tried for many years. In the executive branch, every president since John Kennedy has launched his own management efficiency campaign against waste. Presidents Kennedy and Johnson instituted program, planning and budgeting (PPBS); President Nixon had management by objectives (MBO); President Ford tried presidential management initiative (PMI); and President Carter committed his administration to zero-based budgeting (ZBB). None of these made much of an impact in the sense that they did not significantly restrain the growth of federal spending and deficits. Management of the federal government is arguably more efficient because of these systems, but they will never resolve the problems of growing government spending or inflation, which concern the proponents of constitutional limits to the federal budget.

On the legislative side, Congress itself recognized the need to reform its budget process and passed the Budget Reform Act in 1974. There are undoubtedly ways to improve on the provisions of the act, but most observers agree that the mechanisms are in place to limit spending and deficits if Congress chooses to use them. The fatal flaw is that the act merely specifies a process to achieve an unspecified objective. Even that process has not been carried out, as Congress has repeatedly failed to comply with the provisions of the act. On the question of substance, the new procedures have had little or no impact on limiting federal spending or reducing the size of the deficit. Some critics of the new system (I am not among them) argue that the 1974 act may have increased spending by getting the budget committees' stamp of approval for programs that otherwise might not have been passed.

All of these conventional remedies have been useful in attempting to limit federal spending; with a few exceptions, they have probably contributed more than they cost. None of them, however, have effectively addressed the real problems; as I argue in the next section, similar conventional remedies that have been proposed as alternatives to constitutional limits probably have no greater chance of success.

The Constitutional Flaw Thesis. There is a growing conviction that we need constitutional rather than conventional remedies because there is an inherent flaw in our current political structures and procedures that, short of constitutional restraints, will generate increased government spending and deficits indefinitely. This line of argument takes many forms and has been effectively articulated by numerous political scientists and economists.[12]

The political and social philosophy that dominated the thinking of the Founding Fathers and that strongly influenced our Constitution held that "so long as politicians and political parties were required to submit their record to the voters at periodic intervals, the overall results really couldn't get far out of bounds. . . . This mythology embodied a blind

[12] See, for example, Buchanan and Wagner, *Democracy in Deficit*. Henry C. Wallich argued along these lines as early as 1962 in "Public vs. Private: Could Galbraith Be Wrong?" in *Private Wants and Public Needs* (New York: W. W. Norton, 1962).

faith that somehow the competitive pressures of electoral politics made explicit consideration of further constitutional constraints unnecessary."[13] Herein lies the flaw.

Political scientists long ago demonstrated the perverse effects of logrolling, block voting, and the political process on government spending. Elected officials gain political support by increasing taxes to pay for those benefits. It is easier to vote for spending programs, which provide visible benefits today, than it is to vote for the tax programs, which will raise the revenues to pay for them tomorrow. As a result, there is a strong inclination to finance today's benefits through deficit spending and to disguise the real costs imposed later in the form of inflation and/or lower economic growth.

The constitutional flaw argument can also be explained in terms of the interaction of two theories—the *tragedy of the commons* and a variation of the *prisoner's dilemma*. The tragedy of the commons describes what will happen to public goods offered for public consumption at no cost. The English public commons were overgrazed and destroyed until access to them was controlled through some form of price mechanism or rationing. The same phenomenon applies to all of us when it comes to accepting "free" benefits. In effect, once we have paid our taxes (almost all of which are established years in advance of the benefits), we have strong incentives to get as many benefits as possible. Henry Wallich compares it to a group of people who sit down at a restaurant table, knowing that they will split the check evenly. In this situation everyone orders generously; it adds little to one's own share of the bill, and for the extravagance of his friends he will have to pay anyhow. What happens at the restaurant table explains—though it does not excuse—what happens at the public trough.[14] The recent increases in health care utilization as a result of third-party insurance is a modern variant of the tragedy of commons.

This thesis at least partially explains the process that leads to overuse of a public resource in the first place and demonstrates how totally rational individual behavior can produce an irrational and undesirable community result. The prisoner's dilemma helps to explain why it is so difficult to eliminate overuse or overspending once it begins. The dilemma describes the choices facing a group of prisoners who have been charged with a common crime. Each prisoner, kept in isolation from the others, is offered a deal by the authorities: a lower sentence if he confesses and testifies against the others or the maximum penalty if he does not cooperate and is subsequently found quilty. If they all refuse

[13] James Buchanan (Remarks made at a conference on the constitution and the budget, American Enterprise Institute, Washington, D.C., May 24, 1979).

[14] Wallich, "Public vs. Private: Could Galbraith Be Wrong?" p. 53.

to confess, they have a reasonable chance of being acquitted. Not fully trusting each other and unable to communicate together, they face a significant dilemma about whether to plead innocent or confess.

Taxpayers face a similar dilemma. With their taxes already paid, it is in their rational self-interest to get as many benefits as possible in return. The net effect of large numbers of individuals and interest groups pushing for ever-higher benefit levels may be to produce an aggregate level of government spending that is higher than desired by any individual or group. All of us, acting in our own best interests through our existing political system, may produce too much of a good thing. Like the diners in the restaurant, we are likely to overindulge in the process of getting our fair share. If this is true, we face a difficult type of prisoner's dilemma.

The ideal solution would be for everyone to cooperate and agree to moderate individual demands for the good of the society. Because these acts of self-denial cannot all occur simultaneously and because (like the prisoners) we can never be sure that everyone else will cooperate, there is little chance of such voluntary restraint. The inability to communicate effectively with each other and a long history of experience with self-interest politics make it unlikely that many Americans will agree to certain personal losses today in exchange for potentially greater (but uncertain) community benefits tomorrow. Thus, government spending, facilitated by deficit spending and "inflation taxes" generated through tax-bracket creep, continues to increase.

Almost all proponents of constitutional limits for the federal budget argue, in one form or another, that some type of social restraint is needed to save us from ourselves. The classic solution to the tragedy of the commons is to create private property rights and provide individuals with the proper incentives to manage their lands efficiently. That solution is impossible to apply to the federal budget. The classic response to the prisoner's dilemma is to form a pact to cooperate (and all plead innocent). That requires considerable individual risk taking, trust, communication, and a high probability of future benefits, all of which are unlikely in today's environment.

It should be clear, then, why conventional remedies have failed and will continue to do so. The restraints imposed by the traditional "fiscal constitution" cannot be effectively restored. Only some type of constitutional amendment, which removes the issue from the conventional political arena, will effectively limit federal spending and define the appropriate role of government in society.

Three major questions remain:

- What type of amendment is most likely to solve the problem?

- Can any amendment be implemented effectively?
- Are the costs acceptable?

Which Way Should We Go?

Ideally, we should adopt the constitutional amendment that will most directly solve the problem. That, of course, is easier to say than to do, if for no other reason than, as pointed out, most proponents of constitutional limits do not agree on a common definition of the problem. It is important, therefore, to distinguish between good intentions and desirable outcomes. Proponents of constitutional limits on federal activity may—with the best of intentions—propose amendments that will produce unpredictable and undesirable results. With that possibility in mind, let us review what each type of amendment can be expected to accomplish.

Balanced budget amendments are obviously intended to eliminate deficit spending. Their basic goal is to substitute a real constitutional limit for the "fiscal constitution" that prevailed prior to the 1930s and ensured balanced budgets except during war. If deficit spending is the real problem to be resolved, balanced budget amendments of one form or another are surely the most direct and probably the most effective remedy.

On the other hand, if the level of government spending is the problem, the balanced budget approach will only by coincidence, if at all, get us where we want to go. The fatal flaw of balanced budget amendments is that they specify only that balance must be achieved; they give no guidance about how the budget should be balanced or what level of federal spending is appropriate. The requirements for balance could be achieved, for example, by raising both taxes and spending to 50 percent of the gross national product. That is, of course, not at all what the proponents of the balanced budget approach have in mind, but it could happen (at least, the constitutional amendment would not prevent it). Finally, if the goal is to reduce taxes, the balanced budget amendment will not solve the problem for the same reasons that it will not limit spending. Balance can be achieved in too many ways to give any assurance that the amendment will keep taxes at their current or lower levels.

The best argument for the balanced budget amendment is that, in addition to balance, it may *indirectly* limit spending and taxes by taking advantage of the political and economic phenomena that originally got us into trouble. Proponents of this approach argue that the political resistance to higher taxes will effectively prevent balancing the budget by increasing receipts. They also believe that the requirement for balance changes the rules of the spending game significantly. In effect, it creates a zero-sum game in which whatever I get, you lose, and vice versa. There is no longer any way we both can be better off by increasing the total budget through deficit spending. This will serve to hold down total spending, intensify the review of national priorities, and focus the debate on how much we can afford to spend.

These indirect effects of the balanced budget amendment will not happen. We will discuss these arguments in detail in the next section. With so many ways to escape even the *primary* limits of any constitutional amendment, it is completely unrealistic to hope that the indirect limits will be effective.

Tax limitation amendments are typically designed to limit or reduce federal tax receipts. Americans are feeling decidedly overtaxed, and proponents of the tax limitation approach are searching for a way to curb future increases and/or to roll back certain tax rates (such as social security).

If the problem to be solved is narrowly defined in terms of effective limits on federal taxes, the tax limitation amendment is the most direct remedy. If, on the other hand, the problem is to restrict the shift of resources from private to public institutions, the tax limitation amendment will not help. The popular justification for California's Proposition Thirteen (a tax limit amendment) was that one cannot spend what one does not have. This may have been true in California, but it is clearly not true for the federal government. Congress routinely spends more than it has and simply borrows the difference. One way or another, through taxes, inflation, or lower growth, we all pay for what we get from Washington. The tax limitation amendment may effectively limit direct taxes, but it will not in any way reduce the total cost of government spending, the aggregate level of federal outlays, or the ability to engage in deficit spending.

Preliminary evidence from California appears to support this conclusion. To date there have been few, if any, cutbacks in government spending. Business as usual has been maintained by drawing upon state surpluses (instead of refunding them to the taxpayers) and by imposing new taxes in the form of user charges to cover the shortfalls. Unless direct spending limits are imposed in conjunction with tax limits, it is unreasonable to expect spending restraint. There are simply too many ways to invent new taxes to pay for old programs.

Spending limitation amendments are designed to reduce either the rate of growth or the absolute level of federal spending. Their primary goal is to halt effectively the shift of resources and power to the public sector. Spending limits are the only constitutional amendments that directly address the public/private balance issue.

The amendment's proponents hope that, by directly limiting what government can spend, the amendment will also indirectly limit taxes because no administration would propose large federal surpluses for long. While such an indirect benefit is unlikely, the amendment would establish a bias in favor of a balanced budget, although it would by no means require or guarantee it. Finally, spending limits are the only ways to change directly the "uncontrollable" nature of the federal budget. Spending limits would force Congress to examine the entitlement programs in detail and modify them where necessary to bring them more effectively under the influence of the annual budget review cycle. Changing social, economic, and political situations justify different spending levels for these programs, and we should move quickly to take them off automatic pilot and return them to the mainstream of the annual economic and political processes that we use to establish national priorities.

Will Any of the Amendments Work? One major argument against any constitutional limits on the federal budget is that—regardless of how desirable their theoretical goals may be—they simply will not work in practice. There are many variations on this theme, some of which are discussed here, but they all basically argue that the amendments cannot be implemented effectively. The crux of these arguments is that the pressures behind increased government spending and deficit financing are so strong that they will successfully evade the intent of any constitutional amendment, regardless of how cleverly written and implemented. If these arguments are valid, the real danger is not that we will pass an ineffective amendment but that we will force the spending pressures from their conventional forms into alternative channels that will be more difficult to detect and control.

Arguments about the effectiveness of constitutional amendments fall into four categories:

1. Creative accounting. Literally hundreds of accounting details, definitions, and procedures would have to be developed to implement a constitutional amendment. There is always a possibility that creative accounting at any point in this process would seriously weaken the impact of the amendment. How would outlays and receipts be defined, for example? Would forecasts or actual results be used to control spending? If forecasts are used, who would develop the estimates? How would off-budget spending, direct loans, and loan guarantees be handled? Would quasi-government operations (like the post office) be covered by the amendment? What type of changes to government accounting conventions (such as a separate capital budget) would be permitted? Whose data would be used to determine compliance and when would corrective action be required?[15]

2. *Nonbudget spending.* The federal government could devise numerous ways to spend money without increasing the budget. Approximately $12 billion of annual expenditures are already off-budget. Loans and loan guarantees can be designed to have the same effect as direct spending, but their budget effects are significantly different. The Department of Defense, for example, could build and fully pay for a new oil tanker or it could arrange a twenty-year lease with a private shipbuilder, thereby spreading the full cost over twenty years rather than one. The possibilities are infinite.

3. *Nonspending spending.* Government can achieve its desired effects in some areas without spending a dollar. Health, safety, and environmental regulation are good examples. If Washington wants to clean up a particular river, it can develop and pay for water pollution control devices directly (which would show up as a budget outlay) or it can pass a law requiring the affected individuals and institutions to buy the devices themselves (in which case, the federal budget is not affected). The water is cleaned in both cases and approximately the same resources are shifted from the private sector to this public service, but the federal budgetary implications are significantly different. Effective limits on spending, taxes, or deficits may generate pressure for ever-increasing amounts of direct regulation.

4. *Enforceability* Finally, opponents of constitutional limits argue that, even if they are desirable, they cannot be effectively implemented because there is no way to enforce them. This argument is unconvincing. If the amendment has been approved by the necessary three-quarters of the states and if Congress and the courts are given appropriate authority they will find or develop ways to enforce the Constitution. Many of the proposed constitutional amendments already contain language that would establish enforcement mechanisms.

The effectiveness argument is really a debate about *how well* constitutional amendments will work. Nobody believes they will work perfectly; on the other hand, even the most vocal opponents concede that they will have some effect (it may be undesirable, but there will be an impact). There are four possible conclusions:

[15] Along the line of these concerns, Herb Stein has defined the balanced budget amendment as "an amendment to the Constitution proposed by politicians who have never balanced the budget, requiring their successors to achieve and maintain equality between two undefined conditions for undefined periods subject to undefined penalties, unless they decide to do otherwise. "Verbal Windfall on Language," *New York Times Magazine*, September 9, 1979, p. 14.

• *They will not work well enough to offset the costs imposed by the constitutional amendment.* There are simply too many technical and definitional loopholes available for the amendments to achieve even their primary goals. In fact, the situation could be worse with an amendment than without one because the national budget debate will shift from a consideration of federal programs to technical arguments over definitions and accounting procedures.

• *They will work reasonably well.* That is all we should expect.

• *They will work reasonably well (in the sense that they will effectively achieve their major goals)*, but the final results will be undesirable. Their effectiveness will force the development of less visible forms of government intervention (such as tax expenditures and direct regulation). This line of reasoning assumes that government will continue to grow (no matter how hard we try to constrain it) and that the best course is to keep it as visible and conventional as possible.

• *They will work reasonably well and produce the undesirable side effects discussed above, but they are still worthwhile.* Effective amendments will undoubtedly generate pressures for new types of government growth and intervention, but these new forms take considerable time to develop and implement. If three-fourths of the states have passed a constitutional amendment and there is continuing public support, the conventional political, economic, and judicial procedures should be sufficient to respond appropriately to these new developments.

What Price Will We Pay? Constitutional limits on the federal budget will not be free. The two principal arguments against the proposed amendments to limit federal spending, taxes, or deficits have already been discussed—first, that they are not necessary or desirable and, second, that they cannot be implemented effectively. In addition to these reservations, however, critics of constitutional limits have questioned whether they are worth the price we will pay in at least three other ways.

First, constitutional amendments impose unacceptable limits on our ability to respond to changing economic needs. Opponents of constitutional limits argue that they will put government in a straitjacket and preclude legitimate government activity to promote stable economic growth. "Economics is so inexact a science and the future is so unpredictable that it is an act of arrogant folly to try to specify constitutional formulas applicable for the indefinite future."[16]

The most common argument (and certainly the easiest with which to deal) is that constitutional amendments would prevent an effective

[16] Paul A. Samuelson, statement presented as testimony before the Subcommittee on Monopolies and Commercial Law of the Committee on the Judiciary of the U.S. House of Representatives, in *The AEI Economist*, April 1979, p. 6.

government response to a national crisis such as a world war or depression. Almost every draft constitutional amendment has an escape clause to deal with the problem of national emergencies. Although they vary considerably, most escape clauses would suspend the constitutional limit for one year at a time when a national emergency is declared by the president and approved by two-thirds or three-quarters of both houses of Congress.

The more difficult argument to resolve is that serious economic difficulties (which are threatening to become but are not yet a national crisis) will not be dealt with in a timely and effective manner because of the constitutional limits. Spending limits would curtail spending at precisely the time that increases are needed to stimulate economic recovery. Balanced budget amendments will prevent deficit spending when aggregate-demand stimulation is most appropriate. Tax limitations will preclude tax cuts when they would be most effective in promoting economic recovery.

Proponents of constitutional amendments cannot have it both ways. Either the amendments will effectively limit spending, taxes, or the size of the deficit (in which case, we have to pay that price in terms of a loss of policy flexibility in noncrisis situations), or they will not be effective (in which case, we do not need the amendment at all). Each type of constitutional amendment will exact a different type of price:

• The balanced budget approach is the most restrictive limit on economic policy because it restricts government action to stimulate the economy through direct spending *and* tax cuts.

• Tax limits are probably the least restrictive in the sense that they do not preclude either deficit spending or increased government countercyclical programs during an economic downturn. They would, however, prohibit the use of tax increases to moderate an overheated economy.

• Spending limits would preclude increases in direct government spending during a (less-than-crisis) slowdown of the economy. They would not, however, prevent deficit spending or tax cuts to stimulate economic growth. Proponents of spending limits argue that tax cuts are not only the most effective fiscal policy but that they logically separate the desirability of government programs from the need for economic stimulation. We have approved some highly questionable programs and increased the base of government spending unnecessarily in the past under the guise of economic stimulation.

Second, constitutional amendments unfairly burden and restrict future generations of Americans. This intergenerational argument is to some extent true for all constitutional amendments because they require considerable time and effort to pass and to rescind. Once established, future generations would have to mobilize a significant effort to remove any constitutional limits on the federal budget; in that sense, these limits do bind our descendents. On the other hand, the ways in which the proposed amendments would limit future generations would be only in terms of the amount of debt and the size and role of the government that they inherit from us. It is far easier to increase spending and debt than to decrease it; if we have to err in one way or another, our democratic tradition dictates that we should leave our descendents less public debt and a strong private sector.

Third, constitutional amendments will needlessly inject the judicial system into economic and public policy issues that are best resolved by the executive and legislative branches of government. The Constitution lies at the heart of the judicial system; an amendment will undoubtedly require greater legal activity in budget and policy issues than in the past. That is clearly part of the price that we will pay for setting a limit on the federal budget. Appropriate drafting of the constitutional amendment and the necessary implementing legislation, however, should limit the judicial intervention.

A Reluctant Conclusion

In the final analysis, I have reluctantly concluded that we should amend the Constitution to limit the growth of federal spending. I am reluctant because I recognize fully the seriousness of such a step. I am reluctant because a constitutional amendment is not a panacea that will solve all of our problems, and it carries with it clear political, social, and economic costs. I am reluctant, frankly, because the issue has valued arguments on both sides and requires complex and uncertain personal judgements about our economic and political systems.

The current conditions, however, justify constitutional remedies. The criteria necessary for constitutional actions have been met. Significant economic problems have developed during the last fifty years that will remain indefinitely unless direct remedies are imposed. Although there is widespread agreement that these problems would be best solved through conventional remedies, that approach has already been tried and failed. Most importantly, similar conventional approaches are unlikely to succeed in the future because of the inherent nature of our political and economic incentive systems, structures, and procedures.

The costs of inaction are high. The reallocation of resources and power between the public and the private sectors has already gone too far and threatens the traditional role of private citizens and institutions. The inability of government to manage fiscal and monetary policy prudently and effectively in order to stabilize economic growth and productivity has imposed a heavy burden on all Americans through high inflation and unemployment and slow growth. The fundamental relationships between government and the economy and the allocation of power between citizens and the state are in jeopardy.

On balance, some form of constitutional amendment that directly limits federal spending is preferable to the balanced budget or tax limitation approaches.

> The idea of restricting Federal outlays to a given percentage of the Gross National Product is a powerful and compelling one. Its power resides in the wonderful simplicity with which it states its case. It proposes, simply, to limit spending to a specific percentage of the Gross National Product. And that is all. It does not say that any particular Federal program is too expensive or that it is or is not a wise employment of our finite resources at any given point in time. It does not speak to the issue of how or with what instruments we shall raise the revenues to pay for this level of expenditure. It does not, as has happened so often previously, confuse the logically distinct goals of spending limitations and a balanced budget. It does not fail to take into account the growth of our population and our economy and, thus, the necessity of an absolute growth in the level of Federal spending. The power of this kind of limitation lies in its overarching simplicity. It simply states that however desirable programs may appear in isolation, the cumulative effect of too many desirable programs will be harmful. There can indeed be coherent parts which make up an incoherent whole; there can indeed be too much of a good thing.[17]

Such an amendment will be neither easy to live with nor free. It will not solve all of our problems, and it will not fully resolve even those problems it is designed to mitigate directly. The potential benefits and the costs of continued inaction, however, more than justify an amendment to limit federal spending. We owe it to ourselves to take the steps necessary to preserve a vital and a creative role for private individuals and institutions, to define the limits and the rules of government intervention in the economy, and to establish these as constitutional principles of the United States.

[17] Jeffrey T. Bergner, "Federal Spending Limitations: An Idea Whose Time Has Come," *Policy Review*, 1979.

Commentary

Kenneth W. Dam

Donald Ogilvie has given us a masterful review of federal fiscal history. Nevertheless, that history cannot be properly interpreted without greater attention to the role of state and local governments. Specifically, I should have preferred greater recognition of the role of intergovernmental transfers in the federal budget. Moreover, I should have avoided what I regard as an overemphasis in his paper on federal spending and employment and given greater attention to the more spectacular growth in recent decades of state government spending and employment.

Ogilvie, who is well aware of these trends, no doubt chose to concentrate on the federal government for what appeared to him to be good and sufficient reasons. But such an emphasis, so natural in Washington, D.C., obscures some of the crucial forces at work in the country and here in Washington as well.

Let us look at the facts. First, state and local spending has been growing much faster than federal spending. Federal spending (after deducting transfers to state and local governments) has gone up about 22 percent in constant dollars in the last decade. In contrast, state spending is up almost 50 percent and local spending is up nearly 30 percent.

Second, state and local employment has risen by well over 3 million employees in the last decade while federal civilian employment has been virtually unchanged. Today fewer than one in five of all public sector employees work for the federal government.

Third, federal grants to state and local governments have gone from $24 billion in 1970 to about $82 billion in 1979. Until this year such grants-in-aid have been growing at an average of about 15 percent a year since 1955.

Taking a very long view, as Ogilvie does, it is possible to regard these comparisons of relative growth over the past decade or two as static tending to drown out some more important message. But ten years is a long time in politics. Although there are some developments that augur well for controlling state and local spending—especially demographic changes suggesting that there will be relatively small needs for, say, school construction—we nevertheless cannot prudently ignore trends of a decade and more.

A large part of our present problem lies in the explosive growth of grants-in-aid. The resulting mismatch between taxing and spending generates a lack of accountability and creates perverse incentives. Federal grants to state and local governments create two and sometimes three levels of government that can claim the credit for particular spending programs. But only the federal government has to raise the taxes. This situation generates an unfortunate coalition in favor of spending, especially since both houses of Congress are elected on a geographic basis.

Consequently, a reasonable hypothesis is that the persistent federal deficit can be explained to a substantial degree by the built-in pressure to increase federal grants-in-aid. If that hypothesis is correct, then any remedy has to involve limits on the grants-in-aid process.

In the light of this analysis, the tax limitations movement in the states may actually exacerbate the federal budget problem. If the states cannot increase taxes, then the pressure on the federal government to take up the slack will grow. On the other hand, a balanced budget or spending limitation rule at the federal level might help because it would tend to force state and local governments either to raise their own taxes or to reduce their own expenditures.

Despite this possible advantage of a federal rule, I oppose a constitutional amendment. Many of the principal arguments, pro and con, have been well summarized by Ogilvie. In the limited time available to me, I should like to discuss only one of the considerations weighing against a constitutional amendment. That one is that such an amendment would, if it were to be of any budgetary value at all, surely thrust the Imperial Judiciary into the budget process. The standard answer to this objection is that the number of potential plaintiffs could, by artful drafting, be so greatly reduced that only responsible plaintiffs would present only the weightiest budget issues to the courts.

The problem is not, however, the number of plaintiffs. It is rather the number of issues—serious ones to boot—that would be immediately raised. What is an outlay? What is revenue? Anyone who has worked professionally on the budget knows about negative outlays and revolving funds and all the thousand and one other little anomalies that would be likely to generate litigation. Even more serious, what is the crucial moment in time when the budget must be balanced? With changing economic conditions, a budget that is balanced when the president submits it, or when the budget resolution passes, or even when the final appropriations bill passes may become seriously unbalanced as economic conditions change.

My objection is not simply that, as a lawyer, I believe that the judiciary is poorly equipped for these kinds of issues and that, in the end, it would be bad for the courts to become even more deeply involved in the political process. My objection is also that the budget process is so complicated that it cannot be expected to accommodate still another level of complexity and continue to deliver rational decisions. Even today the budget process is so complex that budget decisions can hardly be said to be taken. Rather, they simply happen, results of an obscure, often purposely obscured process. Perhaps we should have Tolstoy to describe it for I am certain that Napoleon knew more about what was actually happening at the line of battle than, say, a president knows about what is happening in his executive branch budget process.

The reasons for the growing complexity and intractability of the budget process have often been detailed. Perhaps the most important factors are the decline of the appropriations committees, the growth of backdoor spending, and the consequent increase in the percentage of uncontrollable items in the budget. The result is that federal budgeting is not what the public thinks it is. When I teach constitutional law, my favorite aphorism is: "To govern is to choose." But when I talk about the budget process I have to amend that phrase to: "To govern is to estimate." Any real decision tends to have been made years or decades ago and all that is left to the budget official, or the Budget Committee for that matter, is to estimate the consequences. The 1974 Budget Act did little to arrest these trends away from accountable decision making and nothing to reverse them. Indeed, it exacerbated a key underlying problem, the long time-lag between presidential and congressional deliberation and the actual expenditure, by lengthening the budget cycle by a full three months.

What is necessary, I conclude, is to reverse these institutional trends and establish a system in which decisions can be more clearly and cleanly made and in which accountability for those decisions is more directly imposed. I would be the first to say that there are no easy formulas to achieve these objectives. But if these are the proper objectives, then one can say that the 1974 act was at best a small step in the right direction and that a Constitutional amendment would likely be a step back.

Summary of Discussion

Mr. Ogilvie accepted Mr. Dam's point that his paper said little about state and local budgets, which are growing much more rapidly than federal budgets, but, though Mr. Ogilvie expressed concern about state and local growth, he noted that it was his task to concentrate on constitutional limits as they might apply to the federal sector. With respect to the point that a constitutional budget limit may be no more effective than the prohibition amendment, Mr. Ogilvie expressed the belief that the latter had been imposed on the majority by a minority of voters whereas a clear majority seems to favor limiting budget growth.

David Sitrin did not see how a constitutional limit would avert the "tragedy of the commons" since everyone would still want to cut the other fellow's favorite program. Mr. Ogilvie replied that placing an artificial limit on spending was exactly analogous to placing a limit on the number of animals grazing the commons and would require a rationing mechanism. Mr. Sitrin said that he wished the paper had been more explicit about the nature of the rational mechanism that would be necessary to complement a constitutional budget limit.

Bruce Bartlett suggested that Mr. Ogilvie's goal would be better achieved by requiring a balanced budget and limiting the tax burden constitutionally. Mr. Ogilvie agreed that such an approach might achieve the same goal as a spending limit, but it would require a much more complicated amendment and he wanted to keep things as simple as possible.

Alice Rivlin worried that a limit on spending would simply induce politicians to shift to regulation for reallocating resources and noted that the costs of regulation are harder to document than the costs of budget programs. Mr. Ogilvie admitted that this is a real problem and that we would have to develop new mechanisms for controlling regulation.

Part Three

A Congressman's Perspective on the Budget Process

Timothy E. Wirth

It is fair to make one generalization from the history of the budget process: it is fortunate, and perhaps lucky, that the budget process has survived at all. The budget process in the House has gone through some close calls. The first budget resolution under Brock Adams's chairmanship, in spring 1975, passed by the landslide margin of, I believe, 200 to 197. The margins in the House since then, in terms of overall votes, have not been much greater, and we have lost a couple of budget resolutions, some for tactical reasons and some for political reasons.

But the budget process has survived and has created a terribly important potential for the Congress to resolve the greatest political problem that we have now. That political problem is the ambivalence of the American public toward its government.

As one dominant theme, there is an overriding concern in the country to balance the budget immediately, and there is a predominant sense that the primary cause of inflation is the federal deficit. Argue as one might about oil prices or food prices or whatever, there is a conventional wisdom that we would not have serious inflation were the budget in balance.

The other dominant theme is one of increasingly well-organized special interest groups that are doing a better and better job of organizing, funding, and then presenting their case to Congress to increase spending. I can remember any number of meetings with various groups in the district that I represent—whether those are highway contractors, defense contractors, space contractors—that are saying, "Why don't you spend more on my budget function?" While the opening discussion will ask to balance the budget tomorrow, the specifics of that discussion will be, "Our program is so deserving that we ought to have funds added to it." To paraphrase Huey Long, who once said, "Don't tax me, don't tax thee," it is appropriate to say about the budget, "Don't cut me, don't cut thee, cut the man under yonder tree."

How we are going to go about reconciling these two dominant themes in the country? With the collapse of the party system in the country and the increasing vulnerability of individual candidates, we need some mechanism for resolving those two strong but conflicting forces.

The budget process is the single most promising one in allowing us to react to all of that pressure on individual members, within a rational context. This is the context of the overall budget ceiling. No other mechanism allows us to reconcile in some way the demands of interest groups for more and the demands of the country as a whole to balance the budget. Certainly, the various appropriation committees and authorizing committees, while they have been cooperative with the budget process in the House, are not ones that can take on that overall view, nor should they. The budget process has survived, surprisingly enough, in the face of all of the jurisdictional issues and the threats that it brings to existing power structures, because the budget process is the most promising vehicle that we have.

Let us look down the line at some of the problems that we face. There is some feeling in the House that the Budget Committee is acting not so much in a policy making manner as in an adding machine capacity—that all the budget process does is add up what the authorizing or the appropriating committees will do and then come up with some sort of a total that becomes the budget ceiling.

That is increasingly untrue. I cannot speak to what happened in the first four years of the budget, but in 1979 there has been a great deal of hard negotiation, conciliation, and discussion with the various groups—the veterans' lobby or the defense groups, the veterans' committees or the defense committees or the other appropriation committees, the highway lobby, and so on—to try to get them to understand that they have to bring their demands down. We have increasingly begun to play that kind of a policy function to allow other committees to put less pressure on themselves, in other words, to use us as the whipping boy for many of the decisions that they make. In the future, we are going to see more and more of this approach to policy making.

The second problem that we have had is clearly the burgeoning of the federal budget under provisions of the entitlement programs already enacted. Seventy-five percent of the budget is called "uncontrollable." That demands a different kind of thinking in the Congress about all those programs. If one projects the size of the budget, leaving the uncontrollables alone, one finds that there will be nothing left for new initiatives. There will be nothing left for addressing many unresolved problems, like productivity.

How will we get on top of the uncontrollable situation? It will be tough and will demand the best of the kind of work that we can do with AEI, the Brookings Institution, the Urban Institute, and other research groups to put together the political agenda for attempting to break into some of those uncontrolled programs.

One of the ways in which we can do that is an approach advocated by Congressman Bolling to change the cycle of appropriations and authorizations in Congress from a one-year cycle to a two-year cycle. One problem that we have is the "squirrel cage" nature of the process. One no sooner finishes in one year—running to complete that by the deadline—than the next year immediately begins with the same set of decisions. There is little time for Congress to sit back and take a look at what it has already done and will do in the longer term.

What Mr. Bolling and a number of us have discussed, is switching to a two-year cycle with some longer-term five-year planning in the process. That would allow, for example, an authorizing committee to work for a year on oversight of a particular program, to come to understand what is in that program and what it is doing, and then to return the next year to rewrite the legislation, if necessary.

That, for the first time, is beginning to have a good deal of appeal in the country as many people are annoyed by the regulatory process. There is an increasing crescendo of complaints about the bureaucracy: Why doesn't Congress do something about it? Why doesn't it exercise more oversight over existing programs?

The reason has been twofold; first, Congress does not have time and second, there has not been any political reward for that kind of oversight. Those two things must be changed. We can help develop the time through a two-year cycle. We also need to recognize that there are political rewards now, for the first time, for sitting on top of an agency, getting it to change its behavior, policing it better, and exercising the oversight for which we have responsibility. That will be an important precedent that will give us the opportunity to review closely many of these entitlements and quasi-entitlement programs.

A final item is a problem on the House side that is unfortunate and does not characterize the Senate Budget Committee. In the House, the budget resolution effectively must be passed with a majority of Democrats only, with almost no help from the Republican party. I cannot speak to the history of how all of that evolved except to say that it is unfortunate. By having to pass a budget resolution with 200 plus votes on the Democratic side, we miss a reflection of a national consensus. That is beginning to show signs of changing, but 1980 is an election year and partisan politics seem to have more appeal at the moment.

There are possibilities of developing a broader coalition on the Budget Committee and on the floor of the House. We have an obligation to try that in the next budget cycle, to work with the minority members of the Budget Committee, who are more likely to develop a coalition with the Democrats on the committee. That has the possibility for bringing the budget more in tune with the national consensus.

We have survived so far. The budget process is the best means for reconciling the two deep pressures on us to balance the budget and to protect increasingly well-organized special interests. We have an obligation and the opportunity to get more into policy, particularly on the "uncontrollable" programs. That, combined with a change in the cycle, will give us more tools to do that.

Summary of Discussion

Alice Rivlin stated that she was encouraged by Representative Wirth's favorable remarks on introducing longer-term planning not only into the budget process, but into authorizing legislation as well.

Representative Wirth replied that it will be difficult to change to a longer planning cycle, but the Congress has already made some progress in areas such as public broadcasting and advanced funding for education.

Stephen Entin asked Representative Wirth whether the typical member of Congress who is not on the House Budget Committee has a clear understanding of the rapid growth of uncontrollables and the difficulty these will pose for funding other initiatives.

Representative Wirth replied that the typical congressman is flooded with information and is expected to be an expert on absolutely everything. As a practical matter, he cannot be an expert on everything and tends to specialize. So far there is not a broad enough understanding of the problems posed by uncontrollables, but because the members must vote on a budget ceiling, they will learn about them fast. They will be forced to say no to more and more pressure groups like highway lobbyists, veteran's groups, and defense groups.

Attiat Ott asked Representative Wirth's view of Robert Hartman's suggestion that we redefine spending categories to get away from "good" labels such as "veteran's" and "health" toward more neutral labels such as "grants" and "transfers."

Representative Wirth said that would not help much. The competing factions might change somewhat, debating between rural and urban or New England and Texas rather than between veterans and health, but the battles would be just as bloody.

Representative Wirth believed it would be more useful to move to longer-term budgeting and to focus attention on trade-offs, as the Senate has attempted through the reconciliation process and the House through clearly identifying legislative savings. More and better information is necessary. Representative Wirth hoped that in the future it will be possible to work more closely with research institutes such as Brookings, the Urban Institute, and AEI in an effort to inform congressmen about the economic effects of programs.

Louis Fisher commented that the trend toward putting more and more legislation into appropriations bills tends to delay the appropriations process and foul up the schedule of the budget process. Some oppose this trend, but others feel that if the authorization committees will not place constraints on spending growth by controlling entitlements, the appropriations committees must do so. He asked Representative Wirth to comment on this conflict.

Representative Wirth replied that the best example of the trend described by Mr. Fisher is the abortion language in various appropriations bills. But Representative Wirth noted that the authorization committees are concerned about the trend, and he predicted that they will soon reassert their authority over legislation.

William Lilley asked Representative Wirth's opinion of the House rules that rotate the membership on the Budget Committee. Representative Wirth replied that he did not believe it was a major issue. The term of membership is now six to eight years, and there is no shortage of talented congressmen seeking membership.

Jan Olsen expressed some concern about a two-year budget cycle. There is no guarantee that the extra time would be used productively. Instead of using the time for more intensive oversight, Congress might think up new programs. Moreover, a two-year cycle would halve the number of programs available for cutting each year.

Representative Wirth agreed that these are valid concerns. But he believed that since he entered Congress oversight activities have become politically popular and congressmen are now anxious to engage in them.

Alice Rivlin asked Representative Wirth's view of constitutional amendments requiring a balanced budget. Representative Wirth thought such efforts absurd; he had not seen any language for such an amendment that made any sense whatsoever. He felt constitutional amendments allowed congressmen to avoid the tough decision to say no to interest groups.

Part Four

Effect of the Budget Act of 1974 on Agency Operations

Louis Fisher

The Congressional Budget Act of 1975 assumes that a change in legislative operations will produce legislative control. By creating budget committees, establishing floor procedures for budget resolutions, and adding the expertise of the Congressional Budget Office, Congress responded to the trenchant criticism of President Nixon, whose 1972 reelection campaign featured an attack on the "hoary and traditional" budget procedure of Congress.[1]

Changes in congressional organization and procedure cannot fully protect the fiscal prerogatives of Congress. Legislators had to do more than rearrange the congressional furniture. They had to give greater attention to agency operations. As illustrated so vividly by the Nixon impoundments, whatever Congress did during the appropriations phase to fix budget priorities, was easily undone by officials during the budget execution phase. By 1974, it was necessary for Congress to plunge far more deeply into administrative matters.

The major statutory response to budget execution is Title X of the 1974 act, covering impoundment control. There are, however, other important congressional efforts to monitor the spending of funds: (1) committees and subcommittees are far more active in reviewing reprogramming actions by agencies; (2) personnel ceilings imposed by the Office of Management and Budget (OMB) are subjected to increasing scrutiny and control by Congress; and (3) OMB's absorption policy for pay increases has come under searching review by Congress. These four areas—impoundment, reprogramming, personnel ceilings, and absorption—all are part of the congressional effort to assure that agencies respect and faithfully carry out legislative priorities. Administrators may complain about the intimate involvement of Congress in executive details, but it was administrative behavior in the first place that required Congress to intervene.

NOTE: The views in this paper are those solely of the author.

[1] U.S., *Public Papers of the Presidents*, 1972, p. 742.

Impoundment Control Act

Congressional efforts to decide budgetary priorities were undermined by the Nixon administration in two ways. Executive officials seized on discretionary language in statutes to suspend or cancel programs. Through strained legal analyses, administrative officials contended that permissive language in authorization and appropriation bills allowed the president to terminate programs. Also, the Nixon administration treated the president's budget as a ceiling on Congress. Any funds that Congress added to the president's budget could be set aside and left unobligated.[2]

Although this two-pronged attack gravely threatened congressional fiscal prerogatives, legislators were reluctant to pass legislation curbing impoundment. They feared that constituents would interpret the move as pro-spending. Also, separate legislation on impoundment faced an almost certain veto by the president. Statutory controls on impoundment were politically acceptable only as part of more general legislation that promised to revamp congressional procedures and organization on the budget. Through such calculations, Title X was appended to the Congressional Budget Act of 1974.

Title X establishes two types of impoundment: rescissions and deferrals. The president may seek to rescind (cancel) budget authority (1) whenever he determines that all or part of such budget authority will not be required to carry out the full objectives of a program, (2) whenever a program is to be terminated, or (3) whenever he determines that all or part of one-year money should not be obligated. He must transmit to Congress a special message requesting the rescission. Unless both houses approve the request within forty-five days of continuous session, the president must make the budget authority available to the agencies for obligation.

The president must also submit to Congress a special message whenever he proposes to defer (delay) budget authority. Deferrals include any delay in obligating budget authority or "any other type of Executive action or inaction which effectively precludes the obligation or expenditure of budget authority."[3] The budget authority must be made available for obligation if either house passes an "impoundment resolution" that disapproves the deferral.

The General Accounting Office (GAO) received major new responsibilities in monitoring Title X. The comptroller general must review

[2] See Louis Fisher, *Presidential Spending Power* (Princeton, N.J.: Princeton University Press, 1975), pp. 175–197; James P. Pfiffner, *The President, the Budget, and Congress: Impoundment and the 1974 Budget Act* (1979).

[3] 31 U.S.C. 1401(1)(B).

each presidential message on rescissions or deferrals and report his evaluation to Congress. Essentially, this consists of a review of the factual accuracy of the messages. The comptroller general must report any action by the president or any other executive officer who impounds funds without a notification to Congress. The comptroller general's report on these omissions is treated as though it originated with the president, triggering the procedures for rescission and deferral. The comptroller general must also inform Congress whenever he believes that the president has incorrectly classified a rescission or a deferral. The comptroller general's reclassification of an impoundment action is final and conclusive. He is empowered to sue in federal court to enforce the provisions of Title X.

The Ford Administration. Over a period of two and a half years, President Ford proposed 480 impoundment actions: 330 deferrals and 150 rescissions. He also submitted 146 supplementary messages to revise actions already reported. These awesome statistics do not reflect the occasions when the Ford administration used a single deferral request to cover deferrals in more than one program. In 1976, for example, Ford proposed in one action the deferral of $596 million that affected ten separate appropriation accounts for the Defense Department.[4] Neither do these figures include actions by the comptroller general to reclassify presidential impoundment requests or to report omissions.

To analyze these actions, it is essential to distinguish between "routine" and "policy" impoundments. Routine impoundments normally serve the specific purposes of the antideficiency act—to promote savings or to set aside funds for contingencies. Routine impoundments do not restrict programs and activities. They do not interfere with the budget priorities established by Congress. Policy impoundments, on the other hand, reflect a determination by the president to substitute executive spending priorities for those enacted by Congress. Here the administration acts "with prejudice" toward congressional preferences.

Distinctions between routine and policy are sometimes awkward and arbitrary but not impossible. Prior to 1972, the Office of Management and Budget prepared impoundment reports that distinguished routine actions ("budgetary reserves") from nonroutine actions ("impoundments").[5] In carrying out the Impoundment Control Act, Ford indicated in his messages to Congress when a proposed impoundment was made pursuant to the antideficiency act, suggesting that the executive branch is capable of separating routine actions from policy impoundments.

[4] D76–86 as reported in 41 Fed. Reg. 1707 (1976).

[5] U.S., Congress, Senate, *Congressional Record*, 92nd Congress, 2nd session, p. 8032.

Of the 330 deferrals by the Ford administration, 209 were routine. In contrast, most of the rescission proposals were for policy reasons; only 17 were routine. Of the 146 supplementary impoundment messages, 99 were to revise routine impoundments. The large number of routine proposals generated a tremendous amount of paperwork for Congress and the agencies. Agencies had to supply information to OMB, which OMB then organized into special messages for the president. Congress referred the messages to congressional committees for evaluation, while GAO and the committees reported their recommendations to each house for floor action.

Congress could reduce this burden by eliminating presidential reports on routine impoundments. Routine impoundments could be defined as impoundments authorized by the antideficiency act or any other law (except the Impoundment Control Act). As an alternative, Congress could require the president to submit abbreviated reports on routine impoundments to the comptroller general, who would decide whether the proposed impoundment had policy implications that required congressional review and action. This type of mechanism to screen impoundments was proposed in 1973 by the Senate Government Operations Committee[6] but was not included in the 1974 act, despite the concern that a large number of routine impoundments would overload the process.[7] Preliminary GAO review, in addition to eliminating unnecessary paperwork for Congress and the executive branch, would rivet congressional attention on policy impoundments. Both GAO and OMB have recommended that the requirement to report routine impoundments be repealed.[8]

The large number of policy rescission proposals shows that Ford attempted to continue the presidential custom of reshaping budget priorities enacted by Congress. The federal courts had overturned dozens of Nixon impoundments precisely on that ground. The courts decided that it was not the president's prerogative to disregard the budget decisions made by Congress. The Nixon administration was not permitted to impound funds appropriated for the Office of Economic Opportunity simply because the president had not requested funds in his budget. The president's budget was a mere starting point, "nothing more than a proposal to the Congress for Congress to act upon as it may please."[9] In a decision involving mental health funds, a federal judge noted that

[6] S. Rept. No. 121, 93rd Cong., 1st sess. 14 (1973).

[7] U.S., Congress, Senate, *Congressional Record*, 93rd Congess, 2nd session, Statements of Senators Humphrey and Ervin. June 21, 1974, pp. 11238–11239.

[8] U.S., Congress, House, Committee on the Budget, *Oversight Hearing on the Impoundment Control Act of 1974*, 95th Congress, 2nd session, 1978, pp. 24–25.

[9] Local 2677 v. Phillips, 358 F. Supp. 60, 73 (D.D.C. 1973).

Nixon did not have "complete discretion to pick and choose between programs when some are made mandatory by conscious, deliberate congressional action."[10]

Nevertheless, even after passage of the Impoundment Control Act, Ford used the rescission-deferral mechanism to frustrate congressional adjustments to his budget. Ford sent up many more policy impoundments than Congress had anticipated. During floor action on the Impoundment Control Act, Senator Ervin (Democrat, North Carolina), as floor manager, said that he expected that there would be no more than "a few dozen policy impoundment actions a year."[11] Yet, the Ford administration, in less than three years, proposed more than 120 policy deferrals and 133 policy rescissions.

Although Congress rejected most of those proposals, Ford was successful nonetheless. Funds could not be obligated until the congressional review procedure was exhausted. Members of Congress complained that Ford misused Title X. House Appropriations Committee Chairman George H. Mahon (Democrat, Texas) said it was not appropriate

> for the Executive to transmit a rescission proposal that only contains funds which have been enacted into law as a result of the initiative of the Congress. I do not subscribe to the theory that everything the Executive does is correct and right and defensible, and that everything the Congress does by way of providing additional sums or modifying sums is all wrong.[12]

Senator Ted Stevens (Republican, Alaska) drew a parallel between the Nixon impoundments and the rescission proposals by Ford: "We have gone through it before. Everything that was added on by the Congress was impounded. Now almost everything that is added by the Congress is rescinded. You just have a new mechanism for delay."[13] In addition, Ford used Title X to penalize domestic programs, primarily agriculture, housing, environment, and health, education, and welfare. Precious few of the policy impoundments were directed against military programs.[14]

The Carter Administration. Policy deferrals declined sharply after Jimmy Carter took office. Congress took exception to far fewer actions.

[10] National Council v. Weinberger, 361 F. Supp. 897, 902 (D.D.C. 1973).

[11] U.S., Congress, Senate, *Congressional Record*, 93rd Congress, 2nd session, June 21, 1974, p. 11238.

[12] U.S., Congress, House, *Congressional Record*, 94th Congress, 1st session, February 25, 1975, p. 1054.

[13] U.S., Congress, Senate, Committeee on Appropriations, *Budget Rescissions and Deferrals: Hearings, Part 1*, 94th Congress, 1st session, 1975, p. 283.

[14] Louis Fisher, "Congressional Budget Reform: The First Two Years," *Harvard Journal on Legislation*, vol. 14, no. 3 (1977), pp. 413, 452–454.

Under Ford, Congress passed sixteen resolutions of disapproval in fiscal 1975, twenty-six in fiscal 1976, and three in fiscal 1977.[15] Thus far, under Carter, Congress has passed only six resolutions of disapproval in fiscal 1978 and two in fiscal 1979. The deferral mechanism is used primarily for routine impoundments.

Rescission proposals continue to be a vehicle for policy impoundments, but under Carter they strike at domestic and defense programs alike. Carter's actions against the B-1 bomber and the Minuteman III missile programs produced a groundswell of opposition within Congress. In each case, he took steps to terminate production contracts before sending rescission proposals to Congress. Stop-work orders were issued on the B-1 bomber on June 30, 1977, although Congress was not notified until July 19. Contract stop-work and termination orders were sent to the major Minuteman III contractors on July 11, 1977; the proposed rescission reached Congress on July 26.

Members of Congress complained that they were caught over a barrel. If they decided to withhold support from the rescissions, the administration would have to renegotiate contracts at substantial new costs to the government. Congress asked GAO to recommend procedures that would permit legislative review of proposed curtailments or terminations prior to their being put into effect. GAO suggested a review procedure under which Congress could disapprove (by concurrent resolution) proposed curtailments within fourteen days after they have been submitted.[16]

OMB wholeheartedly opposes this plan. It does not believe that Congress should be under pressure to decide major questions in such a short time. As evidence for its position, it pointed out that Congress took 148 days to review the proposed B-1 bomber termination.[17] OMB also disagrees with some members of Congress that no impoundment should take place while a rescission is being reviewed by Congress: "It seems irrational and undesirable to propose rescission of a specific sum and then to continue to obligate some portion of that sum proposed for cancellation."[18]

On other fronts, however, GAO and OMB agree that the Impoundment Control Act needs to be changed. GAO recommends that OMB identify all impoundments of congressional add-ons to executive

[15] Statistics on deferrals obtained from the House Committee on Appropriations. Two of the twenty-six actions in fiscal 1976 are duplications by the House and Senate.

[16] U.S., Congress, House, Committee on the Budget, *Oversight Hearing on the Impoundment Control Act of 1974,* 95th Congress, 2nd session, 1978, pp. 8, 12.

[17] Ibid., p. 25.

[18] Ibid.

branch budget requests; OMB agrees when the add-on influences the decision to impound.[19] GAO wants OMB to specify whether there have been previous impoundments proposed for each program presented to Congress for rescission or deferral; OMB agrees.[20] Both agencies see the value of excluding reports on routine impoundments.[21]

Members of Congress have objected to the length of the rescission procedure. The forty-five days of continuous session can stretch to four or five months because of congressional recesses and adjournment. The average length has been about eighty days.[22] To shorten this time, GAO suggests a definite time period of sixty calendar days. Instead of waiting for the sixty days to expire, GAO recommends that either house of Congress be allowed to disapprove the proposed rescission at any time, at which point the funds would be made available for obligation.[23] OMB agrees that the rescission period should be limited to a fixed period of days and recognizes the need for shortening that time even further if Congress has expressed its disapproval. Instead of a one-house legislative veto, OMB insists on action by a concurrent resolution.[24]

Reprogramming of Funds

In addition to actions reported under the Impoundment Control Act, there are any number of other opportunities for administrative delays and slowdowns. Agencies may take all of the funds from one program and "reprogram" them to another (within the same appropriation account), without submitting an impoundment message to Congress. If all of the funds are obligated, GAO contends that there is no impoundment. Writing in 1977, the GAO held that a

> lump-sum appropriation for programs A, B, and C used to carry out only program C would not necessarily indicate the existence of impoundments regarding programs A and B. So

[19] Ibid., pp. 7, 11.

[20] Ibid.

[21] Ibid., pp. 7, 24–25.

[22] Ibid., p. 7.

[23] Ibid., p. 8.

[24] Ibid., pp. 25–26. Congressman Max Baucus (Democrat, Montana) introduced legislation in 1975 to permit a two-house disapproval of rescission proposals; U.S., Congress, House, *Congressional Record,* 94th Congress, 1st session, March 11, 1975, p. 1548. Congressman Ottinger introduced legislation the following year to permit a one-house legislative veto of rescission proposals; U.S., Congress, House, *Congressional Record,* 94th Congress, 2nd session, March 23, 1976, pp. 2291–2292. Also on the early use of Title X, see Joel Havemann, *Congress and the Budget* (Bloomington: Indiana University Press, 1978), pp. 174–188.

long as all budgetary resources were used for program C, no impoundment would occur even though activities A and B remained unfunded.[25]

Legislative Constraints. Reprogramming has been a constant source of tension between the executive and legislative branches for a number of decades. Congress expects agencies to "keep faith" by following the itemized material found in their original budget justifications, as amended by committee reports and floor action. Yet Congress also recognizes that there are many legitimate reasons for agencies to depart from these nonstatutory controls. Over the course of a fiscal year, reprogramming may be necessary because of unforeseen developments, changing requirements, incorrect price estimates, wage-rate adjustments, and legislation enacted after appropriations.

The latitude for reprogramming increased markedly after 1949, when Congress began to consolidate a number of appropriation accounts. Congress, for example, cut the number of appropriation accounts for the Defense Department in half.[26] With this shift toward lump-sum appropriations, executive spending discretion increased substantially. To retain control, congressional committees insisted on various types of procedures to require agencies to notify committees of significant reprogrammings and, in some cases, to seek their prior approval.[27]

The heavy volume of defense reprogramming during the Vietnam war began to exasperate members of the House and Senate. Chairman Mahon of the House Appropriations Committee told a Pentagon witness in 1971 that "we cannot have double hearings on all programs every year. We are a little irritated—at least I am—that we are confronted with this sort of thing."[28] That same year John Stennis (Democrat, Mississippi), chairman of the Senate Armed Services Committee, warned Defense Secretary Melvin Laird that reprogramming had gone too far.[29]

Even with elaborate procedures to govern reprogramming, Con-

[25] U.S., Congress, Senate, *Congressional Record,* 95th Congress, 1st session, June 24, 1977, p. 10597.

[26] Louis Fisher, "Reprogramming of Funds by the Defense Department," *Journal of Politics*, vol. 36 (1974), pp. 77, 80.

[27] Fisher, *Presidential Spending Power,* pp. 78–86.

[28] U.S., Congress, House, Committee on Appropriations, *Department of Defense Appropriations for 1972: Hearings, Part 2,* 92nd Congress, 1st session, 1971, pp. 336–337.

[29] U.S., Congress, Senate, Committee on Armed Services, *Fiscal Year 1972 Authorization for Military Procurement, Research and Development, Construction and Real Estate Acquisition for the Safeguard ABM and Reserve Strengths: Hearings, Part 1,* 92nd Congress, 1st session, 1971, pp. 232–233.

gress discovered that agencies could use this tool to bypass congressional control.[30] Particularly repulsive was the Pentagon's practice of requesting funds for a program and, after Congress denied the request, using other appropriated funds to finance the rejected program. Legislation in 1974 specifically prohibited the Pentagon from asking committees for permission to reprogram funds to an item that had been previously submitted to Congress and denied.[31] This restriction is repeated every year in the defense appropriation bill.

As another way to limit reprogramming, the House gave its Appropriations Committee authority in 1974 to recommend rescission of unobligated budget authority. Congress felt that the existence of large carry-over balances constituted a standing invitation to agency officials to reprogram the available funds to other uses. The House Select Committee on Committees hoped that the recovery of unused funds "will discourage reprogramming of those funds."[32]

Legislative Invitations. By the time of the Carter administration, Proposition 13, and balanced-budget proposals, the political climate on reprogramming had changed. It became an attractive mechanism to avoid requests for supplemental funds. In 1977, OMB asked agencies to make "every effort to absorb costs from existing funds" instead of seeking supplemental appropriations from Congress. Even new programs or initiatives approved by the president should be "accommodated by reprogramming existing funds whenever possible."[33]

Congressional committees also urged agencies to rely on reprogramming rather than supplementals. Regarding Indian health services, the Interior Subcommittee of House Appropriations noted in 1978 that it would consider a reprogramming request to augment the program.[34] For the Smithsonian Institution, the committee said additional funds "may be obtained through the agreed upon reprogramming procedures of the Committee."[35] Some committees are more evenhanded, agreeing to give careful consideration either to a reprogramming action or a supplemental request.[36]

[30] Fisher, *Presidential Spending Power,* pp. 88–93.

[31] 87 Stat. 1046, sec. 745 (1974).

[32] House Report No. 916 (Part 2), 93rd Congress, 2nd session, 1974, p. 29. The rescission authority was adopted by the House on October 8, 1974, when it passed House Resolution 988.

[33] U.S., Office of Management and Budget, memorandum, "Requests for Supplemental Appropriations and Budget Amendments," October 18, 1977, p. 2.

[34] House Report No. 95–1251, 95th Congress, 2nd session, 1978, p. 89.

[35] Ibid., p. 100.

[36] House Report No. 95–1672, 95th Congress, 2nd session, 1978, p. 13.

Compared to a few years ago, committee interest in reprogramming is much more sharply attuned. Congress has monitored defense reprogramming with care for several decades. Domestic reprogramming is coming under the same kind of scrutiny. Guidelines are regularly published in committee reports. For the Interior appropriation bill, any project or activity that is initially deferred because of reprogramming (and therefore flagged by the agency as low priority) shall not later be accomplished by means of further reprogramming. Agencies are supposed to seek funds for the deferred project or activity through the regular appropriation process.[37] Reprogramming should be made only for "an unforeseen situation" and then "only if postponement of the project or the activity until the next appropriation year would result in actual loss or damage. Mere convenience or desire should not be factors for consideration."[38] Moreover, reprogramming should not be used to disrupt legislative priorities by changing allocations specifically denied, limited, or increased by Congress in a public law or a committee report.[39] Dollar thresholds have been established to indicate which reprogrammings must be submitted to review committees before implementation.[40]

Until the last few years, reprogrammings were controlled primarily by nonstatutory sources: committee reports, committee hearings, correspondence between agencies and committees, and various types of "gentlemen's agreements." Only in the case of the Defense Department did Congress resort to statutory restrictions.

Three new public laws, all passed in 1978, regulate reprogramming. All of the provisions come from committees that act on annual authorizations for the Department of Energy and the Department of Justice. The committees did not want to spend their time reviewing departmental budgets in great detail and pass authorization bills each year for the various activities, only to find their work frustrated by subsequent reprogramming agreements worked out by the agencies and the appropriations committees.

The annual authorization for the Department of Justice in 1978 contains a section that details a notification procedure for reprogramming. Basically the department is required to notify (in writing) the judiciary committees a minimum of fifteen days prior to reprogramming in excess of specified dollar figures or when any reprogramming action less than the amounts specified would have the effect of "significant

[37] House Report No. 95–1251, 95th Congress, 2nd session, 1978, p. 121.

[38] Ibid.

[39] Ibid.

[40] Ibid. For other guidelines on reprogramming, see Senate Report No. 95–1063, pp. 6–7; Senate Report No. 95–1076, p. 8; House Report No. 95–1253, p. 6; House Report No. 95–1246, p. 15; Senate Report No. 95–1060, pp. 4–5; Senate Report No. 95–1019, pp. 10–11; and Senate Report No. 95–1043, pp. 8–9.

program changes and committing substantive program funding requirements in future years." Notification is also required when increasing personnel or funds for any project or program restricted by Congress, creating new programs or significantly augmenting existing programs, reorganizing offices or programs, or "significant relocation of offices or employees."[41] To the Senate Judiciary Committee, this kind of information will permit the review committees to carry out their oversight mandate.[42]

Notification procedures for reprogramming also appear in two statutes for energy programs: one for national security programs in the Department of Energy and the other for the Nuclear Regulatory Commission.[43] Both statutes require the agency head to notify designated committees of certain types of reprogramming and to give those committees thirty days to review the contemplated shift of funds.

Personnel Ceilings

Personnel ceilings imposed by OMB can slow down a program in much the same manner as impoundment. While funds are not actually withheld from agencies, personnel restrictions prevent agencies from using all the funds. They have the money but lack the manpower to spend it. This type of quasi impoundment was recognized during the Nixon years. In 1973, during testimony before the Senate Appropriations Committee, an agency official described the effects of OMB policy:

> We had a ceiling placed on us. The authorized [by Congress] position level was 341. We never got up to that. We had a ceiling of 315. We were told by OMB that we should not exceed 315. The highest we ever got was 298. Of course, as you know, last fall we, like all other Government agencies, were affected by the general freeze in hiring and promotions.[44]

[41] P.L. 95–624, sec. 7, 92 Stat. 3463 (1978).

[42] Senate Report No. 95–911, 95th Congress, 2nd session, 1978, p. 15. For committee review of the reprogramming procedure, see U.S., Congress, House, Committee on Appropriations, *Departments of State, Justice, and Commerce, the Judiciary, and Related Agencies Appropriations for 1980: Hearings, Part 5,* 96th Congress, 1st session, 1979, pp. 581–586; U.S., Congress, Senate, Committee on Appropriations, *Departments of State, Justice, and Commerce, the Judiciary, and Related Agencies Appropriations for Fiscal Year 1980: Hearings, Part 1,* 96th Congress, 1st session, 1979, pp. 905–914; and Senate Report No. 96–173, 96th Congress, 1st session, 1979, pp. 6–7.

[43] P.L. 95–509, Title II, 92 Stat. 1777–78 (1978), and P.L. 95–601, sec. 1(c), 92 Stat. 2948 (1978).

[44] U.S., Congress, Senate, Committee on Appropriations, *Departments of State, Justice, and Commerce, the Judiciary, and Related Agencies Appropriations for Fiscal Year 1974: Hearings, Part 1,* 93rd Congress, 1st session, 1973, p. 689. Statement of Benjamin F. Holman, director of the Community Relations Service.

Since passage of the Congressional Budget Act in 1974, Congress has taken steps, both statutory and nonstatutory, to counteract OMB. In its effort to preserve legislative priorities, Congress finds itself increasingly involved in monitoring personnel levels.

Nonstatutory Warnings. In 1975, the House Appropriations Committee objected to personnel ceilings when they resulted in less efficient reliance on outside contracting or on temporary personnel. It directed its investigative staff to review operations of agencies where the problem seemed the most acute: the National Park Service, the Fish and Wildlife Service, the Bureau of Land Management, the Forest Service, and the Indian Health Service.[45] In that same year, the Senate Appropriations Committee did more than criticize personnel ceilings from an efficiency standpoint. It saw the nexus between those ceilings and congressional priorities. It had increased several programs of the National Park Service and the Fish and Wildlife Service "to correct glaring deficiencies in the budget requests," only to find its increases thwarted by personnel ceilings. It did not intend the filling of vacancies in one agency to be at the expense of another "simply to keep within an overall Departmental ceiling." Unless the Department of the Interior respected legislative priorities, the committee threatened to place controls in a future appropriation bill.[46]

The investigative report of the House Appropriations Committee, released in 1976, showed that personnel ceilings in the Interior Department were a breeding ground for waste and inefficiency. In the five bureaus studied, over 9,000 "temporary" employees were working substantially full-time schedules, although not counted toward the personnel ceiling. This contrivance led to recruitment difficulties, morale problems, wasteful turnover and retraining, "a watering down in the quality of the staff and the buildup of a caste system with two classes of employees." The study concluded that in many instances contracting was more expensive than in-house performance. Playing the "ceiling game," whereby agencies separated thousands of employees just before the end of the fiscal year and rehired them when the new fiscal year began, was criticized as "wasting manpower, generating volumes of unnecessary paperwork, impugning the credibility of Government employment figures, confusing employees, and accomplishing nothing."[47]

To discourage artificial personnel ceilings, the committee placed in its report the number of authorized permanent positions for each agency.

[45] House Report No. 94–374, 94th Congress, 1st session, 1975, p. 8.

[46] Senate Report No. 94–462, 94th Congress, 1st session, 1975, pp. 3–4.

[47] House Report No. 94–1218, 94th Congress, 1st session, 1976, pp. 4–5.

The numbers were taken from justification material submitted by the agencies (adjusting for committee changes). The committee expected that the numbers identified in the report would be the basis for establishing personnel ceilings. To the extent that adjustments were necessary as the fiscal year progressed, agencies were to inform the committee.[48]

The Senate Appropriations Committee continued to focus less on the inefficiency and waste of personnel ceilings than on the derangement of legislative priorities. In 1976, it added 683 positions to the Interior appropriation bill, expecting them to be filled without regard to department restrictions and OMB position ceilings. Although reluctant to write personnel provisions in the bill itself, the committee said that it was prepared to move in this direction if its policy was not followed.[49]

In reporting the Interior appropriation bill in 1977, the House Appropriations Committee repeated its concern about the impact on agency operations of employment ceilings. The ceilings were being used to constrain agency operations that Congress had favored through the appropriations process. The committee noted that Congress had provided the Forest Service with more positions than the administration requested. It considered establishing employment floors in the bill itself, to remove administrative restrictions, but concluded that statutory controls were too cumbersome. If the administration, however, continued to ignore the concerns of the committee and of Congress, "there may be no recourse other than legislation to insure that employment ceilings do not impede the progress of important congressional initiatives and the guardianship of this nation's great natural resources."[50] Throughout the report, the committee identified the number of authorized permanent positions for each agency. Then came this warning:

> If the Departments and agencies find that employment ceilings established contrary to those set forth in this report, impede their ability to administer the programs, they should place the money into a reserve and report it for deferral or rescission pursuant to Title X of the Congressional Budget Control Act of 1974.[51]

The Senate Appropriations Committee took a similar position. With regard to the Forest Service, the committee stressed the importance of personnel levels recommended by Congress:

> Any effort by the Department [of Agriculture] to thwart either the funding or personnel levels will be expected to [be] subject

[48] Ibid., p. 5.

[49] Senate Report No. 94–991, 94th Congress, 2nd session, 1976, pp. 13–14.

[50] House Report No. 95–392, 95th Congress, 1st session, 1977, p. 13.

[51] Ibid.

> to the Budget Impoundment and Control Act and thus require a specific deferral or rescission proposal that Congress can consider and act upon.[52]

Statutory Controls. This reliance on nonstatutory controls (committee report language) and good-faith agency efforts was abandoned in case of the agriculture appropriation bill. The House Appropriations Committee added section 609, which provided that end-of-year employment ceilings on permanent positions could not be less than certain specified levels for the Farmers Home Administration, the Agricultural Stabilization and Conservation Service, and the Soil Conservation Service. The committee believed that the statutory language was necessary "to prevent the Department from holding back programs provided for by Congress by restricting the number of personnel assigned to the program and, therefore, defeating the provisions of the Impoundment Control Act."[53]

The Senate Appropriations Committee resisted the adoption of statutory controls. Believing that the problem was govenment wide and not limited to the Department of Agriculture, it deleted section 609 and requested the comptroller general to rule on whether the failure to provide funds appropriated by Congress specifically to increase staff levels constituted a violation of the Impoundment Control Act.[54] The conference committee followed the plan proposed by the House Appropriations Committee. Consequently, section 609 became part of Public Law 95–97, 91 Stat. 828:

> Section 609. (A) None of the funds provided in this Act may be used to reduce programs by establishing an end-of-year employment ceiling on permanent positions below the level set herein for the following agencies: Farmers Home Administration, 7,440; Agricultural Stabilization and Conservation Service, 2,473; and Soil Conservation Service, 13,955.

The GAO Position. On July 21, 1977, Comptroller General Staats ruled on whether the executive branch's failure to use funds appropriated to increase staff levels constituted a violation of the Impoundment Control Act. He said that the act is "concerned with the rescission or deferral of budget authority, not the rescission or deferral of programs or authorized activities (such as increasing staffing levels)." If all of the budget

[52] Senate Report No. 95–276, 95th Congress, 1st session, 1977, p. 35.

[53] House Report No. 95–384, 95th Congress, 1st session, 1977, p. 106.

[54] Senate Report No. 95–296, 95th Congress, 1st session, 1977, p. 11.

authority is used, no impoundment would occur "even though the executive branch may be consciously limiting staffing levels and the consequent use of salary funds below those levels contemplated by the Congress." Only in cases where an appropriation act specified staffing levels and funded on a line-item basis and only when excess funds had not been reprogrammed or transferred to other uses, would the possibility of an impoundment arise. Employment limitations would have to be examined by GAO on a case-by-case basis to determine violations of the Impoundment Control Act.[55]

The July 21 letter covers GAO's general position on personnel ceilings. Turning from hypotheticals, a specific instance was reported on August 2, 1977, when Staats told Congress of a rescission and three deferrals of Forest Service budget authority "that should have been, but were not, reported to the Congress by the President pursuant to the Impoundment Control Act of 1974." GAO found that the Forest Service would not fully utilize all of the funds appropriated in the supplemental bill (Public Law 95–26) because of OMB's hiring restrictions. For the funds that were expected to lapse at the end of fiscal 1977, GAO reported an undisclosed executive proposal to rescind budget authority. For funds that would not lapse at the end of fiscal 1978, GAO reported an undisclosed deferral.[56]

This notice to Congress was consistent with past GAO holdings. Personnel restrictions, by themselves, were not impoundments unless they resulted in unused budget authority. OMB and the Forest Service subsequently determined that the excess funds resulted not because of OMB hiring limitations but because of normal spending patterns.

OMB and the Civil Service Reform Act. During 1977, the Carter administration took two steps to alter its policy on personnel ceilings. On May 12, in a memorandum to the heads of departments and agencies, Carter addressed the problem of federal reliance on consulting services. Included among his areas of concern were the use of consultants to perform work that should be retained by agency officials and the use of consultant arrangements as a device "to bypass or undermine personnel ceilings, pay limitations, or competitive employment procedures." The agencies

[55] Letter from Comptroller General Staats to Senator Thomas F. Eagleton (Democrat, Missouri), chairman, Subcommittee on Agriculture and Related Agencies, Senate Committee on Appropriations, July 21, 1977, p. B–115398. See also letter from Comptroller General Staats to Senator Warren G. Magnuson (Democrat, Washington), chairman, Subcommittee on Labor-HEW, Senate Committee on Appropriations, April 5, 1978, p. B–115398.

[56] Letter from Comptroller General Staats to Congress, August 2, 1977, p. B–115398.

were asked to study their consulting services and report the results to OMB by June 30, 1977.[57] While preliminary returns indicate some decrease in contracts, accurate data are not expected before February or March 1980. OMB officials are preparing to testify before Congress on this issue sometime in October 1979.

On September 16, 1977, Carter issued another memo to agency and department heads authorizing an experiment to shift from end-of-year employment ceilings to annual work-years. Part of the purpose was to avoid the various subterfuges invented by agencies to gain relief from employment ceilings. The test, being run during fiscal 1979, affects five agencies: the Veterans' Administration, General Services Administration, Environmental Protection Agency, Federal Trade Commission, and Export-Import Bank.[58] Thus far, the results seem promising. After study in 1980, the policy might be extended governmentwide.

Congressional efforts to end restrictive personnel ceilings have been unsuccessful, partly because of inconsistent legislative policy. When James T. McIntyre, Jr., appeared before the Senate Governmental Affairs Committee on March 16, 1978, for his nomination hearing as OMB director, Stevens objected to OMB's withholding positions from the National Gallery of Art. McIntyre responded:

> I can assure you that we do not use and will not use personnel ceilings to stop or delay carrying out any program established by the Congress. . . . There are times when it is important to institute some type of personnel ceilings to bring about efficiencies and greater productivity in agencies . . . . But we certainly do not use them to thwart or delay or stop anyone from carrying out the program of the Congress.[59]

To further clarify OMB's policy, Senator Edmund Muskie (Democrat, Maine) wrote to McIntyre about impoundments that result from limits on personnel. McIntyre gave this assurance:

> Limits on federal employment are intended not to restrain programs below authorized levels but to help assure that programs are implemented in the most efficient manner. . . . I assure you that we will not use personnel ceilings to stop or delay carrying out any program established by the Congress.[60]

[57] U.S. Weekly Compilation of Presidential Documents, vol. 13, no. 20, pp. 718–719. See OMB *Bulletin* no. 78–11, "Guidelines for the Use of Consulting Services," May 5, 1978, and OMB report, "Executive Departments and Agencies Use of Consulting Services," May 1979.

[58] House Report No. 95–932, 95th Congress, 2nd session, 1978, p. 5.

[59] U.S., Congress, Senate, Committee on Governmental Affairs, *Nomination of James T. McIntyre, Jr.: Hearing*, 95th Congress, 2nd session, 1978, pp. 76–77.

[60] Ibid., p. 7.

This agreement between OMB and Congress was short-lived. The Civil Service Reform Act, which became law on October 13, 1978, included a temporary employment limitation known as the Leach Amendment (section 311). The limitation states that the total number of civilian employees in the executive branch on September 30, 1979, on September 30, 1980, and on September 30, 1981 "shall not exceed the number of such employees on September 30, 1977." Although the language provides some latitude for the president, it also gives OMB a firm statutory foothold to impose personnel ceilings.

Agencies, for example, received from OMB ceilings on civilian employment for fiscal 1980. The president assigned the ceilings "in keeping with his commitment to reduce full-time permanent employment throughout the Executive Branch by 20,000 positions and also in conformance with the statutory requirements of section 311 of the Civil Service Reform Act of 1978." [61]

Agencies still resort to contracting as a means of seeking relief from restrictions on permanent full-time positions. They do so despite additional costs, and they do so with the knowledge and blessing of OMB. Consider the following dialogue in 1979 between John R. McGuire, chief of the Forest Service, and Congressmen Sidney Yates (Democrat, Illinois) and Robert Duncan (Democrat, Oregon):

> Mr. Yates. Does OMB know that you are going to do it by contract?
> Mr. McGuire. Oh, yes.
> Mr. Yates. And they say to go ahead and do it by contract?
> Mr. McGuire. Yes.
> Mr. Yates. Mr. Duncan?
> Mr. Duncan. Is that cheaper than in-house? It doesn't cost more?
> Mr. McGuire. It often costs more at least at the beginning.[62]

At almost the same time that Carter signed the Civil Service Reform Act, he signed another bill that promises more accurate statistics on personnel. The Federal Employees Part-Time Career Employment Act of 1978, passed by Congress to encourage part-time careers throughout the federal government, includes a section on personnel ceilings. In administering any personnel ceiling for an agency, an employee who works on a part-time basis shall be counted as a fraction "which is determined by dividing 40 hours into the average number of hours of

[61] U.S., Office of Management and Budget, form letter from OMB to the agencies, January 4, 1979.

[62] U.S., Congress, House, Committee on Appropriations, *Department of the Interior and Related Agencies Appropriation for 1980: Hearings, Part 9*, 96th Congress, 1st session, 1979, p. 708.

such employee's regularly scheduled workweek." This section became effective on October 1, 1980.[63]

Congressional Action in 1978–1979. Committees show continued concern about the imposition of personnel ceilings. In its report on the Labor–Health, Education and Welfare (HEW) appropriation bill in 1978, the House Appropriations Committee objected to year-end employment ceilings "which, in effect, contravene congressional directives and/or overturn decisions made by Congress in the course of the appropriations process." In some cases, the committee found that employment ceilings force work to be done through overtime or by contracting out, both of which might be more expensive and less effective than filling the positions intended by Congress. Employment ceilings might also mean that the work is not done at all. At various points in the report, the committee specifically stated its intent that a specific number of positions be filled for a given program. If the departments or agencies covered by the bill found it necessary to depart from the positions specified by Congress, "they will seek congressional approval through the submission of a request for rescission or a request for reprogramming." The committee hoped that this understanding would be followed by the agencies, rather than having to resort to statutory controls.[64]

The Senate Appropriations Committee stated in its report on the Labor-HEW bill that the executive branch had "repeatedly neglected the intent of Congress by not following the distribution of positions included in the reports—either Committee or conference." Over 1,100 positions that Congress had directed HEW to fill had been left vacant. To forestall this practice, the committee decided to provide for specific staffing levels for each of the health programs in the language of the bill. Still, it did not want to bind the executive branch to mandatory floors: "The establishment of these minimum ceilings is not to be construed as mandating that employment be maintained at these levels when efficient and effective program management would dictate a lower level."[65]

The conference report followed the Senate's recommendation, plac-

[63] P.L. No. 95–437, 92 Stat. 1057 (1978).

[64] House Report No. 95–1248, 95th Congress, 2nd session, 1978, p. 5. GAO studies have shown that personnel ceilings tend to be disruptive to management. Agencies resort to overtime labor, military personnel, and contracting out. Agency efficiency also declines because experienced employees are encouraged to retire early. U.S., General Accounting Office, "Implementation and Impact of Reductions in Civilian Employment, Fiscal Year 1972," July 2, 1974, p. B-180257.

[65] Senate Report No. 95–1119, 95th Congress, 2nd session, 1978, pp. 23–24.

ing in the bill specific numbers for full-time permanent positions in various health programs.[66] In each case, however, the language appeared to be permissive and discretionary for agency officials. The National Cancer Institute, for example, received a lump sum of $917 million, "including 2,062 full-time permanent positions."[67] Implementation was again left to good-faith administrative efforts.

The Senate Appropriations Committee expressed "alarm" in 1978 concerning OMB's practice of establishing unilateral ceilings on employment. Personnel ceilings were being used to frustrate congressional add-ons. To illustrate what it regarded as the wastefulness of OMB's policy, the committee noted that, because of personnel ceilings, the attorney general had hired GS-15 attorneys instead of GS-9 paralegals, who could have performed the particular tasks involved. The committee inserted personnel floors in the appropriations for fourteen different agencies, stipulating that ceilings or permanent positions shall not be established at less than the number indicated.[68] In deleting these minimum position ceilings, the conferees indicated that they did so not because they were unconcerned about the ceilings but rather to underscore the traditional policy of Congress that the number of personnel should be governed by the amount appropriated. Dollars should dictate personnel, not vice versa. The conference report continued:

> Over the last several years the Office of Management and Budget has broken this longstanding policy by establishing personnel ceilings at levels lower than the number that could be funded by the appropriation. There is no problem when the ceilings are established on the basis of good, prudent, and efficient management. However, there is substantial evidence that the ceilings, for example, in the case of the National Atmospheric and Oceanic Administration, have been employed in order to minimize Federal employment by contracting out functions at a higher cost to the government. The conferees expect the ceilings to be established in conformance with the amount appropriated and not in an arbitrary fashion.[69]

In reporting the agriculture appropriation bill in 1978, the House Appropriations Committee discussed the practice of the executive branch over the years in establishing arbitrary personnel ceilings "to slow down or stop various programs with resulting lack of proper handling of the

[66] House Report No. 95–1746, 95th Congress, 2nd session, 1978, pp. 11–16.

[67] P. L. No. 95–480, 92 Stat. 1572 (1978).

[68] Senate Report No. 95–1043, 95th Congress, 2nd session, 1978, pp. 10–11.

[69] House Report No. 95–1565, 95th Congress, 2nd session, 1978, p. 29.

program, and in violation of the spirit, if not the letter, of the Impoundment Control Act."[70] Funds that Congress had added for staff had been diverted to travel or equipment and supplies. To stop these "de facto impoundments" in the future, the committee recommended in several instances separate appropriations: one for "personnel compensation and benefits" and another for "other expenses." By resorting to this bill language, the committee said that any attempt to withhold funds for salaries would have to be reported to Congress for its consideration.[71]

The Senate Appropriations Committee recommended that the House provisions be deleted from the bill, even though it agreed that OMB personnel ceilings had resulted in program inefficiencies, use of funds for purposes not intended by Congress, and a failure to implement congressional mandates. The committee acknowledged uncertainty as to the proper division of legislative and executive duties:

> The Committee finds pursuasive [sic] the arguments advanced by the Administration that provisions in the bill which specify personnel numbers or total salary levels are legislative encroachments on the Executive power of program management. At the same time, however, the Committee is cognizant that Congress bears a significant responsibility in assuring sound management of programs and efficient use of taxpayer dollars in conjunction with the executive branch.[72]

As a compromise, the committee decided to delete specific salary costs and personnel numbers from the bill but included in its report a table showing the recommended salary and benefit levels for six agencies. It also directed the secretary of agriculture to report quarterly to the appropriations committees on any deviations from the table. Moreover, for "significant deviations" from the table, the administration should follow the procedures of the Impoundment Control Act.[73] The conferees agreed to provide a single appropriation amount for both salaries and expenses, instead of separate accounts.[74]

Congressional protests continued in 1979. The House Appropriations Committee, in its report on the Interior bill, conceded that seasonal workloads are reasonable circumstances for dictating the allocation of temporary personnel ceilings to agencies. However, it accused the administration of subterfuge in enforcing the ceilings. It said that thousands of personnel were working thirty-nine-hour weeks or fifty-one-

[70] House Report No. 95–1290, 95th Congress, 2nd session, 1978, p. 30.

[71] Ibid.

[72] Senate Report No. 95–1058, 95th Congress, 2nd session, 1978, p. 9.

[73] Ibid., p. 10.

[74] House Report No. 95–1579, 95th Congress, 2nd session, 1978, passim.

week years in "temporary" positions in order to keep permanent position ceilings artifically low. Such tactics, said the committee, have

> severe morale effects within the agencies involved, and are administratively burdensome. The net effect of such procedures is to reduce productivity and increase cost in the government under the guise of prudent management. The Committee recommends that the administration examine those positions classified as "temporary" and convert those that provide permanent services to permanent positions.[75]

During hearings in 1979, the chief of the Forest Service said that he had about 8,000 temporary employees who were substantially full-time. Many of them had been around for ten years, fulfilling the responsibilities of permanent staff.[76]

Absorption Policy

Each year OMB prepares instructions to cover pay raises for civilians, the military, and blue-collar workers. Agencies are urged to absorb such costs from available funds "to the maximum extent possible," as a means of avoiding requests to Congress for supplemental appropriations. As a result of overestimates by agencies of their ability to fill jobs or because of vacancies, there are usually extra funds in salaries and expenses (S&E) accounts to support this policy. The appropriations committees and GAO agree with OMB that funds withheld because of the absorption policy need not be reported to Congress as a Title X impoundment.

OMB Procedures. When funds are reapplied from one purpose to another within the same S&E account, the shift of funds follows reprogramming guidelines adopted by the executive and legislative branches. If agencies lack adequate resources within those accounts, OMB asks them to use existing transfer authority to shift surplus funds from other accounts. When that option is foreclosed, agencies are supposed to seek additional transfer authority for accounts within the agency. Pay supplementals should be proposed "*only* when the head of the agency has determined that full absorption is not possible."[77]

The policy of using absorption to cover pay increases (as well as the reliance on transfer authority) has been acceptable to the executive and legislative branches for a number of decades. In 1960, for example,

[75] House Report No. 96–374, 96th Congress, 1st session, 1979, pp. 7–8.

[76] U.S., Congress, House, Committee on Appropriations, *Department of the Interior and Related Agencies Appropriations for 1980: Hearings, Part 9*, 96th Congress, 1st session, 1979, pp. 708–709.

[77] U.S., Office of Management and Budget, Bulletin no. 79–3, November 6, 1978, p. 2.

a Budget Bureau bulletin stated that agencies "will make a continuous and progressive effort to absorb as much as possible of the increased costs within appropriations and funds available in the fiscal year 1961 and without increases in funds requested for 1962." Agencies were directed to take maximum advantage of existing transfer authority in order to increase the absorption of increased pay costs and to seek additional transfer authority when necessary.[78]

Aiming at Congressional Add-ons. Congress has complained about the absorption policy in the past few years because it appears that OMB is using it to discriminate against congressional add-ons. Instead of drawing from a large number of S&E accounts, OMB places an inordinate burden on S&E accounts that have been increased by Congress above the president's budget.

During hearings in 1979 before the Senate Committee on Appropriations, Senator Lawton Chiles (Democrat, Florida) asked the director of the Center for Disease Control about OMB's absorption policy. Congress had specifically earmarked in the previous year's conference report $2.5 million to increase the nutritional status program. In carrying out the absorption policy, the center cut from this program and others that had been increased by Congress, instead of cutting programs that were already spending at some fixed level. As with other types of impoundment, administration officials were using their powers of implementation to frustrate congressional priorities. As Chiles remarked: "From what you are saying, you have taken the pay raise absorption out of a few selected programs rather than through the cost of attrition; and that seems to contravene the intent of Congress, specifying increases in particular programs." Chiles noted that the center was not the only agency to behave this way. Other officials in HEW had picked programs that "they wanted to take the cuts out of and left a lot of their favorite programs untouched." He warned that continuation of this practice might prompt Congress to write into the appropriation bill the instruction that absorption cuts be made on a pro rata basis.[79]

Proportional cutbacks to absorb annual pay increases would be the least flexible of statutory remedies. Appropriation accounts differ widely as to controllability, mandatory language, annual savings, and unanticipated expenses. To protect legislative priorities, Congress might prohibit agencies from drawing in excess of a certain percentage from any

[78] U.S., Congress, House, Committee on Appropriations, *Third Supplemental Appropriation Bill, 1961: Hearings*, 87th Congress, 1st session, 1961, pp. 566–567.

[79] U.S., Congress, Senate, Committee on Appropriations, *Departments of Labor and Health, Education, and Welfare and Related Agencies Appropriations for Fiscal Year 1980: Hearings, Part 2*, 96th Congress, 1st session, 1979, pp. 175–176.

account for the purpose of absorbing annual pay raises. Congress might exempt programs and activities that it has increased above the president's budget request, unless the objectives established by Congress can be satisfied in full. The legislative history could make clear that the purpose of the statutory language is to prohibit the administration from using the absorption policy as a means of discriminating against congressional add-ons and initiatives.

Some committees object to the absorption policy to the point where they want total reliance on supplementals. In 1979, the Senate Committee on the Judiciary complained that congressional oversight had been made difficult "by the workyear manipulation effected as a result of OMB's requirement that the Department of Justice absorb $20 million of the $60 million associated with the October 1978, 5.5 percent pay increase." The committee added a section to the annual authorization bill that stated that the department shall not be required to absorb funds to cover salary increases, thus encouraging the department to seek a pay supplemental instead.[80]

Budget Resolutions. The budget committees assume that the administration will be able each year to absorb some of the pay increases. Thus, in reporting the first budget resolution for fiscal 1980, the House Budget Committee projected a 20 percent absorption for military and civilian pay raises.[81] The Senate Budget Committee recommended that the Pentagon and the civilian agencies be required to absorb, through savings in other activities, 25 percent of the cost of the October 1979 pay raise and each succeeding fiscal year's pay raise required by law from fiscal 1980 through fiscal 1984.[82] The conference report on the budget resolution is silent on a compromise between the House and Senate versions.[83]

Conclusions

Congressional participation in impoundment, reprogramming, personnel ceilings, and pay absorption may come as a shock to public administration experts who want administration (executive branch) separated from policy (legislative branch). Woodrow Wilson once advised Congress that its discretion and power operated only up to the point of granting or denying an appropriation or a law, "but once an appropri-

[80] Senate Report No. 96–173, 96th Congress, 1st session, 1979, p. 7.

[81] House Report No. 96–95, 96th Congress, 1st session, 1979, pp. 57, 158.

[82] Senate Report No. 96–68, 96th Congress, 1st session, 1979, pp. 78–79, 254.

[83] House Report No. 96–211, 96th Congress, 1st session, 1979.

ation is made or a law is passed the appropriation should be administered or the law executed by the executive branch of the Government."[84]

This theory of constitutional government has never made much headway. First, Congress can always indulge in "administrative details" by writing statutes with more specificity. One has only to recall line-item appropriations of earlier times, the detailed tariff acts, or statutes that took several pages to trace the specific route for post roads.[85] If administrators object to legislative activity in executive matters, Congress retains the power to tie the hands of agency officials with statutory restrictions.

Neither Congress nor the agencies want to encourage a return to government by statutory details. Neither branch has the knowledge, confidence, or clairvoyance to lock programs into statutory molds. No one wants the burden of rewriting statutes every year to take into account understandings that can come only from implementing a law. Whether by statute or not, members of Congress will maintain their interest in administrative details because they know too well that details are the building-blocks for policy. As President Taft once remarked: "Let anyone make the laws of the country, if I can construe them."[86]

Second, as I interpret constitutional and statutory powers, the final shape of the budget ought to depend on what Congress does to it, not on the budget's original condition as submitted by the president. Congress has never emulated the British model by totally surrendering to the executive the initiative in financial legislation.[87] The record here seems clear enough. Yet, over this past decade in particular, there has emerged the theory that what counts is the president's budget. Accordingly, funds that Congress adds to his budget can be safely ignored as mere surplus. Congress properly repudiates this doctrine. Whenever executive officials deny Congress the right to add to presidential estimates, and subsequently withhold funds or restrict programs by various devices, they provoke Congress to participate in the implementation of a statute.

Third, the growth of agency and congressional staff has placed a heavy strain on traditional notions of nonstatutory controls and good-faith agency efforts. As the distance between Congress and the agencies widens because of staff turnover, layering, and a confusing array of

[84] James D. Richardson, ed., *Messages and Papers of the Presidents*, vol. 17 (New York: Bureau of National Literature, 1920), p. 8846.

[85] 1 Stat. 232–23 (1792).

[86] William Howard Taft, *Our Chief Magistrate and His Powers* (New York: Columbia University Press, 1916), p. 78.

[87] Louis Fisher, *The Constitution between Friends* (New York: St. Martin's Press, 1978), pp. 176–183.

liaison teams, Congress is less able to rely on customary methods of control. From frustration, Congress is inclined to place restrictions in the public law. Members conclude that flexibility in a statute is used too often by agencies to thwart congressional policy. The message to legislators is to write statutes with less flexibility and less discretion. As Senator Muskie told one official in 1973, after discovering that a broad grant of discretionary authority had been used to cut in half a legislative commitment:

> Having in mind the devious motives that you pursued to undercut the purposes of Congress, I could now write better language and believe me, I will. Believe me, I will.
>
> The clear language and debate was what we were giving you, is what we understood to be legitimate administrative discretion to spend the money, not defeat the purposes. Then to have you twist it as you have, is a temptation to this Senator to really handcuff you the next time.[88]

The Nixon administration represented an abnormal failure in executive-legislative relationships. With the rapid increase in congressional staff, however, we cannot expect a return to "normalcy." Institutional resources are available to Congress to delve much more deeply into policy matters, sometimes prior to enactment of a law, sometimes afterwards. If administrators want to retain some independence in executing the law, they will have to do more than issue alarms about congressional "meddling" in agency details. They will have to demonstrate a willingness and capability of carrying out the laws as enacted, not as the executive branch wanted them enacted. Efforts to ignore or downgrade legislative objectives, in order to further administrative designs, will result in even greater legislative involvement in agency operations.

[88] U.S., Congress, Senate, Committees on Government Operations and on the Judiciary, *Impoundment of Appropriated Funds by the President: Joint Hearings*, 93rd Congress, 1st session, 1973, p. 411. The official was William D. Ruckelshaus, administrator of the Environmental Protection Agency.

The Congressional Budget Process and Tax Legislation

Joel Havemann

Without Watergate, a Republican might have been elected president in 1976. If a Russian army brigade had not been discovered in Cuba, the Senate might have speedily approved the strategic arms limitation treaty (SALT II) with the Soviet Union. If it were not for the congressional budget process, Congress might have enacted more tax cuts and tax expenditures during the last five years.

All of the above are true simply because there is no way to prove them false. Watergate happened; who knows who would be president now if it had not? SALT might have sailed through the Senate if the brigade in Cuba had not awakened old fears of Soviet untrustworthiness—and then again, it might have been delayed over the defense spending issue. Likewise, no one will ever know what kind of tax legislation Congress would have passed without the congressional budget process. All anyone can do is speculate.

Some of the speculation borders on certainty. It is safe to assume, for example, that without the congressional budget process, Senators Edmund Muskie (Democrat, Maine) and Russell Long (Democrat, Louisiana) would have been at each other's throat less often on the Senate floor. Members of Congress would be less aware than they are of tax expenditures and the impact they have on the federal budget. In fact, it can even be argued that some tax expenditures, such as the tuition tax credit, might have been enacted instead of defeated, and others, such as the deduction for state and local gasoline tax payments, might still be in the tax code.

The Value of the Budget Process

Drawing any such cause-and-effect relationship between the budget process and overall revenues is much more difficult. Even if the House and Senate Budget Committees had not been providing Congress with revenue targets each spring, total revenue for the 1979 fiscal year probably still would have been about $466 billion. Except at a smaller scale—the scale of the tuition tax credit and the gasoline tax deduction—there is no reason to think that the budget process has forced Congress to do anything that it would otherwise not have done. It has merely opened its eyes to the consequences of what it has done.

The importance of that educational function should not be underestimated. Thanks in large part to the budget process, Congress is beginning to understand the rough equivalence between tax expenditures and direct spending. It is growing unwilling to tinker with the tax code without looking at the fiscal policy impact of what it is doing. In short, it is making more enlightened public policy.

Enlightened public policy is not as impressive an achievement as actual impact on legislation. The budget process simply has not had the impact on the revenue side of the budget that it has had on the spending side. On at least a few occasions, the budget process has proved to be a valuable implement for accomplishing spending cuts or spending increases. In his first experiment with the powers of the budget process, Senate Budget Committee Chairman Muskie forced a reduction of $250 million—not large but large enough to upset the Armed Services Committee—in the 1975 defense authorization bill. In August 1979, the House used the budget process to knock an entitlement provision from a bill reauthorizing a child welfare program.

Sometimes the budget process has worked in the other direction. In early 1977, the House Democratic leadership, arguing that the third budget resolution for fiscal 1977 made room for considerable spending increases to boost the economy, forced the Appropriations Committee to approve some spending items that it probably otherwise would have killed. In 1979, the Senate used the second budget resolution for fiscal 1980 to express its desire for more defense spending than President Carter or its own Budget Committee wanted.

Why has the budget process had more impact on the spending side of the budget than on the revenue side? The budget committees argue that the 1974 Congressional Budget Act provides more controls on spending than on revenue. The authors of the act reply that the act is unbiased but the budget committees have failed to take as great an interest in the spending side of the budget as the revenue side. The truth is probably a little of each.

The Budget Act treats total spending and revenue identically (except that spending is treated in two of its manifestations, budget authority and outlays). The annual first budget resolution sets overall spending and revenue targets; the second resolution establishes an upper limit for spending and a lower limit for revenue.

The components of the two sides of the budget are not treated alike. The resolutions divide spending into eighteen functional categories—defense, health, and the like. The subtotals for functions in the second resolution are not binding—only the grand total has that force—but they provide strong guidance because any increase in one function requires a decrease somewhere else. On the revenue side, however, the resolution does not split the grand total into its components. The committee reports accompanying the resolution break the total into its sources—individual income tax receipts, corporate income tax revenue, social security tax proceeds, and so on—and they itemize the costs of tax expenditures. Thus, they provide the budget committees with an opportunity to recommend the kinds of general tax legislation and changes in tax expenditures that would enable Congress to reach the revenue total. As Muskie found when he unsuccessfully challenged a Senate Finance Committee tax bill in 1976, report language does not carry nearly as much weight with Congress as the resolution itself.

During the drafting of the Budget Act, the version reported by the Senate Government Operations Committee would have been much tougher on revenue. It would have placed the itemization of revenue by source in the resolution itself, along with a list of tax expenditures by function.[1] The Finance Committee objected, and it was this sort of objection that persuaded Senator Robert C. Byrd (Democrat, West Virginia), then the Senate Democratic whip and chairman of the Rules and Administration Subcommittee on the Standing Rules of the Senate, that the Government Operations Committee bill would not work. Byrd established a group of Senate staff members, representing every major committee in the Senate, to rewrite the Government Operations Committee bill. Most committee staff directors delegated the job of working on budget reform to assistants, but Michael Stern, the able staff director of the Finance Committee, participated personally. While he could hardly object to including a revenue total in budget resolutions, he made sure that the budget process would preserve the Finance Committee's jurisdiction over the details of tax legislation.

Stern succeeded well. When the Rules and Administration Committee sent the rewritten budget act to the Senate floor, it said, "It is clear that a sound congressional budget policy cannot be based on the assumption that control of spending levels is sufficient to achieve desirable economic results."[2] Perhaps it is not, but, on the revenue side of the budget, the Rules and Administration Committee bill was silent on sources of revenue. On the Senate floor, Senator Alan Cranston (Democrat, California), amended the bill without objection to include

[1] U.S., Congress, Senate, Committee on Government Operations, Senate Report No. 93–579, accompanying S 1541, November 20, 1973.

[2] U.S., Congress, Senate, Committee on Rules and Administration, Senate Report No. 93–688, February 21, 1974.

sources of revenue in the reports accompanying the first resolution.[3] As enacted, the Budget Reform Act included a provision similar to Cranston's, along with a clause requiring that the report estimate tax expenditures by function.[4] Even so, the act included nothing on the revenue side that was comparable to the division of spending into eighteen functions.

If the Budget Act did not treat revenue on a par with spending, the budget committees did not concern themselves as much with revenue as spending. Both budget committees hired specialists in various areas of the spending side of the budget, but neither recruited a tax expert. The Senate Budget Committee gained a tax specialist only when Ira Tannenbaum, who had worked with the Treasury Department, applied for a job. When Tannenbaum left, in spring 1979, for the Federal Home Loan Bank Board, no one took his place. The House Budget Committee staff has never had a tax specialist, relying instead on its chief economist to keep track of tax issues.

Tannenbaum's presence on the Senate Budget Committee staff helps explain why that committee proved much more aggressive than its House counterpart on revenue issues. Probably more significant is the fact that the Senate Budget Committee generally has asserted itself more readily than the House Budget Committee. A number of factors help account for this phenomenon. Senate Budget Committee members, with their permanent appointments, have used their positions to build institutional reputations for themselves, while members of the House Budget Committee, generally limited to four-year terms, have no opportunity to turn their committee assignment into a lasting power base. The Senate Budget Committee's ability to fashion substantial Senate majorities in favor of its budget resolutions has given the committee a sense of security during a period when the House Budget Committee, never able to move budget resolutions through the House with many votes to spare, has hesitated to take aggressive steps that might alienate other House committees.[5]

The nature of the two tax-writing committees—and their chairmen—also helps explain why confrontations have been confined to the Senate. Senate Finance Committee Chairman Long, one of the Senate's foremost wheelers and dealers, does not appreciate efforts to strip him of any of his control over tax legislation. Al Ullman (Democrat, Ore-

[3] U.S., Congress, Senate, *Congressional Record*, 93rd Congress, 2nd session, March 22, 1974, p. 4303.

[4] P.L. 93–344, 88 Stat 297, sections 301(d)(2) and 301(d)(4).

[5] See John W. Ellwood and James A. Thurber, "The New Congressional Budget Process: The Hows and Whys of House-Senate Differences," prepared for the *Praeger Reader on the U.S. House of Representatives* (1976).

gon), chairman of the House Ways and Means Committee until 1981, was a much less forceful legislative personality. Ullman, in fact, was a cochairman of the Joint Study Committee on Budget Control, which wrote the first version of budget reform legislation in 1973, and he served as the first chairman of the Budget Committee in 1974 before replacing Wilbur D. Mills (Democrat, Arkansas) at Ways and Means. He had a considerably greater stake than Long in the survival and the success of the congressional budget process.

Finally, House and Senate rules played a role in the less contentious nature of the relationship between the Budget Committee and the tax-writing committee in the House. The fact that the House must consider tax legislation before the Senate has meant that on some occasions, notably with the 1976 tax bill, revenue legislation has gone to the House floor before a budget resolution has been in place to guide it. More important, the House Rules Committee generally sends tax bills to the House floor with closed rules that block most or all floor amendments. The Senate, with its guarantee of unlimited debate, has no such procedure; all variety of amendments are in order when the Senate debates tax bills. Thus, there is considerably more opportunity for mischief on the Senate floor than on the House floor.

The Budget Process and Annual Revenue Totals

On first inspection, the budget process seems to have determined effectively the annual revenue total—and therefore the magnitude of tax legislation—ever since fiscal 1976, the first fiscal year for which the process was implemented. In every year, the Ways and Means and Finance Committees have striven mightily to meet the revenue target of the first budget resolution and to hold revenue at or above the floor set by the second resolution. To be sure, they have sometimes resorted to the subterfuge of delaying the effective dates of tax cuts far enough into the fiscal year so that their impact would not result in a violation of a budget resolution. They have regarded the resolution's revenue total as inviolable. Even in 1976, when Long and Muskie battled over the components of the $15.3-billion tax cut permitted by the second budget resolution for fiscal 1977, Long told the Senate, "We have no problem whatever . . . in living within this $15.3 billion figure."[6]

That might appear to be quite a concession from the chairman of the Finance Committee, who for years had manipulated tax legislation to his own liking. Long probably had not given up as much control over

[6] U.S., Congress, Senate, *Congressional Record,* 94th Congress, 2nd session, June 17, 1976, p. 9714.

the overall size of tax bills as he might seem to have. It is always important to keep in mind that the budget committees do not give final approval to budget resolutions: Congress does. In the five years that the budget process has been operating, the tax-writing committees have never complained that they could not live with the revenue total in a budget resolution.

There is good reason. When the budget committees prepare their resolutions, they have a good idea of what the Ways and Means and Finance Committees have in store for the tax code. For the first resolution, the budget committees have the revenue estimates supplied by the tax committees in their March 15 reports, as required by the 1974 Budget Act. If taxes are still an issue at the time of the second resolution, the tax committees convey their plans to the budget committees in less formal ways.

Table 1, comparing the Ways and Means and Finance Committees' March 15 recommendations with the revenue totals in the budget resolutions, is instructive. It might look as if the budget committees consistently try to prevent the tax committees from cutting taxes as much as they would like. Indeed, only in fiscal 1978 did a budget resolution permit a lower revenue target than the tax committees had recommended. The tax committees carefully include every conceivable tax cut in their March 15 recommendations, lest they be accused later in the year of proposing a revenue-losing measure without warning the budget committees. Both the Ways and Means Committee and the Finance Committee take their March 15 reports seriously, devoting several days in late February or early March to marking up their reports as if they were working on actual legislation. Both of them are careful to leave all their options open—not to foreclose action on measures that any of their members feel they might want to pursue. "If one thing closes an option and another leaves it open," Long told his committee in 1976, "I think we ought to leave it open."[7]

Although the first resolution as reported by the House and Senate Budget Committees has added as much as $18.2 billion to the Ways and Means Committee's March 15 recommendation and $15.1 billion to the Finance Committee's, the two tax-writing committees have never complained that the budget resolutions were too high. As the table shows, the difference betwen the March 15 recommendations and the first budget resolution has generally been shrinking over the five years of the budget process. This suggests not so much that the budget committees have become more responsive to the tax committees as that the tax committees have been preparing more realistic recommendations.

[7] U.S., Congress, Senate, Committee on Finance, meeting, February 24, 1976.

TABLE 1

BUDGET RESOLUTIONS COMPARED WITH THE MARCH 15 REPORTS OF THE WAYS AND MEANS AND FINANCE COMMITTEES, 1976 TO 1980
(in billions of dollars)

		First Resolution		*Second Resolution*	
Fiscal Year	*March 15 Report*	Budget Committee	Final	Budget Committee	Final
1976					
House	$280.0	$298.2	$298.2	$301.8	$300.8
Senate	284.2	297.8		300.8	
1977					
House	356.0	363.0	362.5	362.5	362.5[a]
Senate	355.1	362.4		362.0	
1978					
House	399.4	398.1	396.3	399.9	397.0
Senate	398.5	395.6		395.0	
1979					
House	437.0	443.0	447.9	450.0	448.7
Senate	428.2	443.3		447.2	
1980					
House	502.5	509.0	509.0	519.5	—
Senate	502.6	503.6		514.7	

[a] Two more resolutions were adopted for fiscal 1977, the first to accommodate President Carter's proposed tax cut and the second to acknowledge that most of it would not be enacted. The revenue totals were $347.7 billion in the third resolution and $356.6 billion in the fourth.
SOURCE: House Ways and Means Committee and Senate Finance Committee March 15, 1979, reports to the House and Senate Budget Committees.

1975. In the first year of operation for the congressional budget process, President Ford signed a tax-cut bill on March 29, largely dictating the revenue total in the first resolution.[8] The resolution assumed that the tax cut, enacted only through the end of calendar year 1975, would be maintained in the next year.

Technically, the second resolution employed the power of reconciliation to force an extension of the tax cut. Legislation extending the tax cut had not been passed at the time the resolution was adopted. The resolution assumed an extension and required the Ways and Means and Finance Committees to report such legislation. In fact, an extension of the tax cut through the first six months of 1976 had already moved well

[8] P.L. 94–12, 89 Stat 26.

along, and its enactment was a foregone conclusion. Ford signed the bill on December 23.[9]

1976. The big issue for this year—the issue that provoked the first in what became an annual series of donnybrooks between Muskie and Long—was tax reform. For purposes of total revenue, the only issue was extension of the "temporary" tax cut beyond June 30. While Ford asked for not only an extension of the tax cut but also an additional reduction to be accompanied by spending cuts, the Ways and Means and Finance Committees asked in their March 15 reports only for a simple extension. Both budget resolutions for fiscal 1977 accommodated that request, and the Tax Reform Act of 1976 extended the tax cuts for 18 months, through calendar 1977.[10]

Despite its battle with Muskie over tax reform, the Senate Finance Committee consistently treated the revenue totals of the first budget resolution for fiscal 1977 not only as a target but also as a floor below which it would not allow revenue to fall. To be sure, it did so by approving less revenue gain through tax reform than Muskie wanted and by providing for the extension of the temporary tax cut only through June 30, 1977, nine months into the fiscal year. For purposes of revenue totals and fiscal policy, there is no question that the budget resolution made itself felt. As Senator Lloyd Bentsen (Democrat, Texas), a member of the Finance Committee, said, "Nobody questions the responsibility of the Senate Budget Committee to establish an overall figure on federal revenues."[11]

1977. After two years of tax-cut legislation, the revenue total was not an issue in 1977. From first to last—from the tax committees' March 15 reports to the final version of the second budget resolution for fiscal 1978—revenue remained between $395 billion and $400 billion.

1978. Once again, the revenue total was not an issue, although the budget process may have worked to defeat some tax expenditure proposals that would have left the revenue total below the level actually reached. During debate of the Revenue Act of 1978 on the Senate floor, the Senate upheld points of order aimed by Muskie at two revenue-cutting amendments that would have forced revenue below the floor set by the second budget resolution for fiscal 1979.[12] The two amendments,

[9] P.L. 94–164, 89 Stat 970.

[10] P.L. 94–455, 90 Stat 1520.

[11] U.S., Congress, Senate, *Congressional Record,* 94th Congress, 2nd session, June 16, 1976, p. 9574.

[12] P.L. 95–600, 92 Stat 2763.

to be discussed more fully in the next section, would have granted a $75 energy tax credit to the elderly poor and restored the federal tax deduction for state and local gasoline tax payments. The former proposal would have cost an estimated $212 million in fiscal 1979 and $1.2 billion annually when it reached complete effectiveness, while the cost of the latter was estimated at $471 million in fiscal 1979 and $2 billion by fiscal 1983.

1979. The budget committees helped to counteract the pressure for a recession-fighting tax cut, which the Carter administration and many economists regarded as premature. During debate of the second budget resolution on the Senate floor, Senator William V. Roth, Jr. (Republican, Delaware) proposed tax cuts of $24 billion in 1980, $35 billion in 1981, and $75 billion in 1982, coupled with spending cuts large enough to allow a balanced budget in fiscal 1981. After an extensive discussion of the economic effects of his proposal and the likelihood of achieving the necessary spending cuts, the Senate rejected his amendment, 36 to 61.[13]

In the House, Republicans proposed a 1980 tax cut of $20 billion, combined with about $20 billion less spending than the Budget Committee recommended in the second budget resolution for fiscal 1980. They too were defeated, 187 to 230.[14] In both chambers, the debate on the budget resolution provided an opportunity to weigh the pros and cons of a tax cut and to consider the effects of a combination of tax cuts and spending cuts. Without the budget process, Congress would have had no forum for such a debate.

The Budget Process and Tax Expenditures

Tax expenditures can be regarded as the tax code's equivalent of direct federal spending. They are special provisions of the code that allow tax relief to encourage certain kinds of economic activity or to benefit taxpayers in particular circumstances. The investment tax credit, for example, was designed to encourage business expansion; the exclusion of social security benefits from taxable income provides aid for the elderly. The government could accomplish the same outcome with direct aid for businesses that expand and with additional social security benefits.

[13] U.S., Congress, Senate, *Congressional Record,* 96th Congress, 1st session, September 19, 1979, pp. 12912–12934.

[14] U.S., Congress, House, *Congressional Record,* 96th Congress, 1st session, September 19, 1979, pp. 8143–8172.

The 1974 Budget Act does not treat tax expenditures as equivalent to direct spending. The act could have required that tax expenditures be categorized by function in the budget resolutions, as spending is. That is, the tax deduction for home mortgage payments could be classified in the same function as federal spending for Federal Housing Administration mortgages. The exclusion from taxable income of employer contributions to group health insurance policies could be grouped right alongside of direct Medicare and Medicaid payments. Thanks in part to the efforts of Michael Stern, Senate Finance Committee staff director, the Budget Act requires that tax expenditures be listed by function only in Budget Committee reports accompanying budget resolutions.

The Budget Act did not clarify whether report language would carry as much weight as the resolution itself. Congress would have to answer that question as it put the new budget process into effect. The effort to resolve this ambiguity has led to some of the budget process's most heated debates.

1975. The first resolution for fiscal 1976, adopted after the year's major tax bill had been adopted, set a target of $1 billion in new revenue to be raised through tax reform, that is, the elimination of tax expenditures. When no tax reform legislation had materialized by the time of the second resolution, the Senate Budget Committee struck that item from its version of the resolution, but the House kept the $1 billion. The Senate committee, arguing that tax reform seemed unlikely that year, prevailed in conference.

1976. This year it was the Senate Budget Committee's turn to insist on tax reform, an approach that touched off the first major confrontation of the budget process. The first resolution for fiscal 1977 made room for a tax cut of $15.3 billion from current law. The conference report accompanying the resolution said that the $15.3 billion should be the product of a $17.3 billion tax cut and $2 billion in new revenue through tax reform. The House could do little about this directive, since it had already passed its tax-cut bill, which included about $1.6 billion in tax reform, the previous December. The Senate did not take up the tax bill until June.

In its version of the bill, the Finance Committee included only $1 billion worth of tax reform. Although it kept total revenue above the budget resolution's target by extending the temporary tax cut for only nine months of the fiscal year, meeting the target was not enough to satisfy Muskie. In floor debate with Long, Muskie said, "He refuses to see that underlying those numbers is a rational economic policy and fiscal policy, which cannot be expressed on the face of the resolution, but which by law is required to be stated in the committee report."[15]

Muskie insisted that "this is not a contest between the Budget and Finance Committees. . . . The question before the Senate is whether to sustain the congressional budget." [16] The Finance Committee felt otherwise; it regarded Muskie's effort as an attack on its authority over tax legislation. Bentsen warned other committees that their jurisdiction might be next:

> If the Budget Committee prevails in this extension of its powers to what will ultimately result in denying any useful role for the Finance Committee or the Appropriations Committee and, finally, all the other committees, then the Budget Committee in turn will have sown the seeds for the failure of the new budget reform act.[17]

Muskie was slaughtered on the Senate floor. First he failed, by votes of 55 to 39 and 49 to 42, to get the Senate to endorse his approach to the revenue side of the budget—$2 billion in tax reform plus extension of the temporary tax cut for the full fiscal year. Then the Senate adopted a series of new tax breaks, including a tuition tax credit, that would have turned the $1 billion in tax reform in the Finance Committee bill into a $300 million loss. Muskie made his feelings clear: "It is quite clear to me that as far as the internal revenue code is concerned, the Senate has indicated the budget process is meaningless. . . . You kicked the biggest hole in the budget process that you could conceivably kick. . . . I am going to sit down. I am tired of wasting my voice."[18]

Muskie's voice had not been entirely wasted. When the House tax bill, with its $1.6 billion in new revenue through the elimination of tax expenditures, went to conference with the Senate bill, with its $300 million in new tax expenditures, a compromise emerged that included $1.6 billion in tax reform. The Senate prevailed on many of the issues dearest to Long, who said the final bill contained none of the "meat-ax" tax reform provisions that would have "seriously harmed the economy."[19] It gave away more than it gained; the tuition tax credit and most of the amendments tacked onto the bill on the Senate floor did

[15] U.S., Congress, Senate, *Congressional Record,* 94th Congress, 2nd session, June 17, 1976, p. 9713.

[16] U.S., Congress, Senate, letter from Senators Edmund Muskie and Henry Bellmon to all other senators, dated June 15, 1976.

[17] U.S., Congress, Senate, *Congressional Record,* 94th Congress, 2nd session, June 16, 1976, p. 9574.

[18] U.S., Congress, Senate, *Congressional Record,* 94th Congress, 2nd session, August 5, 1976, pp. 13568–13569.

[19] U.S., Congress, Senate, *Congressional Record,* 94th Congress, 2nd session, September 16, 1976, p. 16013.

not survive the conference with the House. Most of them probably would not have survived even without the budget process; Long traded away Senate floor amendments to tax bills in return for provisions that were important to him personally. As he bargained, the maximum of $15.3 billion in net tax cuts was prominent in his mind. He may have been merely using the budget process as an excuse when he told the Senate, "In several cases, we had to recede on Senate amendments in order to meet our revenue targets."[20] Muskie said that the final version of the tax bill "reflects the substantial impact of the new budget process."[21]

1977. Tax expenditures were at issue in the energy tax bill reported by the Senate Finance Committee as part of the congressional response to President Carter's energy program. The Finance Committee's version of the bill included so many tax incentives for energy production and conservation—$1.9 billion worth—that it would have left total revenue $300 million below the floor set by the second budget resolution for fiscal 1978. To avoid leaving the bill vulnerable to a point of order, the committee included a clause directing the Treasury secretary to postpone the effective dates of the revenue-losing provisions long enough so that the second resolution's floor would not be breached.

That "artifice," as Muskie called it, opened the way for further revenue-losing amendments, which could be offered without fear of violating the budget resolution. The Senate voted, 88 to 2, for a provision offered by Senator Pete V. Domenici (Republican, New Mexico) to provide the elderly poor with a seventy-five dollar tax credit. When Senator Charles H. Percy (Republican, Illinois) proposed eliminating the tax deduction for state and local gasoline tax payments, the Senate tabled his amendment, 65–12. Long had succeeded in making the budget resolution irrelevant to the provisions of the tax bill.

1978. In the following year, the Senate merged the energy tax bill into a general tax-cut bill. With the help of the budget process, which had once again become relevant to tax legislation, the Senate killed the energy tax credit for the elderly poor and voted to abolish the tax deduction for state and local gasoline tax payments.

As sent to the Senate floor in October, the tax bill would have left total fiscal 1979 revenue comfortably above the total set by the second budget resolution for fiscal 1979. The Senate quickly used up the breathing room by voting on October 6 alone for a tuition tax credit and other tax expenditures that would have cost $5.8 billion. By October 7, Muskie

[20] Ibid., p. 16014.

[21] Ibid., p. 16019.

warned the Senate that only $16 million remained between the Senate bill and the revenue floor.

Two days later, Senator John Heinz (Republican, Pennsylvania) offered as an amendment the Domenici proposal for an energy tax credit, which the Senate had accepted so easily a year before. Muskie raised a point of order, arguing that its $212 million cost in fiscal 1979 would send revenue below the second resolution's floor. The Senate upheld his point of order, 65 to 22.

The Finance Committee bill eliminated the tax deduction for state and local gasoline tax payments, despite the previous year's Senate vote to keep the deduction. Senator Jesse A. Helms (Republican, North Carolina) moved to restore it. This time his motion was ruled out of order because of the revenue floor, and the Senate sustained the ruling, 49 to 42. The Revenue Act of 1978 ultimately upheld the Senate on both tax expenditure issues. Even without the budget process, Congress might have voted down the energy tax credit for the elderly poor and killed the deduction for state and local gasoline tax payments. The difference between 1977 and 1978 in Senate floor votes on these issues suggests that the budget process made the Senate's ultimate course of action a lot easier.

1979. The House—over the objections of Budget Committee Chairman Robert N. Giaimo (Democrat, Connecticut)—made one of its infrequent attempts to use the budget process to force repeal of a tax expenditure, but it was unsuccessful. The House voted, 355 to 66, to attach an amendment to the first budget resolution for fiscal 1980 calling for $1.2 billion in new revenue through repeal of the tax credit for oil companies for foreign earnings. Representative Elizabeth Holtzman (Democrat, New York), the amendment's sponsor, called the tax expenditure a loophole that should be closed. Ways and Means Committee Chairman Ullman responded that the budget resolution was not an appropriate vehicle to debate the merits of individual provisions of the tax code. He added that the Holtzman amendment would raise only about $300 million.

Ullman lost the debate, but he had the last laugh, for the Ways and Means Committee ignored the Holtzman amendment and failed to act on the foreign tax credit for oil companies.

Timing

As the energy tax credit for the elderly and the gasoline tax deduction demonstrate, the budget process has made timing a crucial factor in the success or failure of tax proposals. To avoid the fate that befell these two tax expenditures, a number of senators have resorted to manipulation of the effective dates of their tax proposals to escape the strictures of the budget process. This technique has been used more frequently on the revenue side of the budget than on the spending side, perhaps because the effective dates of tax provisions can be manipulated more easily than those of spending programs. It was a practice restricted almost entirely to the Senate, and its leading practitioner was Russell Long.

Muskie, always on the receiving end of the tricks that Long and other senators tried to play, regarded the budget process as "a vehicle for making economic policy." When Long inaugurated the practice of manipulating effective dates in 1976, Muskie told him, "The Senator keeps looking at the budget process as simply a budget game."[22] In practice, the Senate seemed to regard the budget process as a game at least as often as a vehicle for policy making.

1976. This was the year when the Finance Committee sought to circumvent the recommendation in the report accompanying the first resolution for $2 billion in new revenue through tax reform, coupled with a $17.3 billion tax cut, for a net cut of $15.3 billion. The Finance Committee included only $1 billion in tax reform revenue in its tax bill; to keep the total tax cut under $15.3 billion, it extended the temporary tax cut for only nine months of fiscal 1977. Muskie regarded the nine-month extension as nothing more than a ploy to hit the budget resolution's target; he fully expected Congress to extend the tax cuts through all of fiscal 1977. After Muskie failed in his initial attempts to shape the tax bill according to the budget resolution, the Senate ultimately chose to extend the tax cut through fiscal 1977. At the same time, it decided that it would rather miss the revenue target of the budget resolution than approve enough tax reform to hit the target.

1977. The energy tax bill, the major tax legislation of 1977, moved through the Senate after Congress had adopted the second budget resolution for fiscal 1973, placing a binding $397 billion floor on revenue. The resolution left room for $1.1 billion in revenue losses. The Finance Committee, which included $1.9 billion worth of revenue-losing features in the bill, added a provision requiring the Treasury secretary to postpone the effective dates of the revenue losers long enough to keep the bill within the bounds of the budget resolution. Long told the Senate that the final version of the bill, after conference with the House, would

[22] U.S., Congress, Senate, *Congressional Record,* 94th Congress, 2nd session, July 20, 1976, p. 11987.

not require such a provision. "The bill will not break the budget resolution limits," he promised. "We will take care of it."[23]

Muskie, hospitalized with a pinched nerve in his back, was unable to lead the opposition in person on the Senate floor. Senator Ernest F. Hollings (Democrat, South Carolina), a Budget Committee member and tax reformer, read on the floor a statement in which Muskie called the bill a 'Thanksgiving turkey" that would have Congress yield to the executive branch the power to determine when tax provisions should take effect. "Whatever the merits of this bill as energy legislation, it is irresponsible as fiscal action," Muskie said.[24]

Senator James Abourezk (Democrat, South Dakota) challenged Long's ploy, which would have allowed the Treasury secretary to postpone the effective dates of new tax expenditures all the way to October 1, 1978. Abourezk pointed out that October 1 was the first day of fiscal 1979. That made Long's trick out of order, he argued, because the Budget Act prohibits revenue legislation that takes effect in years for which Congress has not yet adopted a budget resolution. Long neatly resolved that challenge by amending the date from October 1 to September 30, the last day of fiscal 1978, a year for which a budget resolution was already in place.

1978. A year later, the Senate again became embroiled in a dispute over the Budget Act provision that requires adoption of a budget resolution before the consideration of tax (and spending) legislation. Section 303(a) of the act forbids floor debate of tax legislation for any fiscal year "until the first concurrent resolution on the budget for such year has been agreed to." There is an exception in section 303(b): Section 303(a) does not apply to tax bills that "first become effective in a fiscal year following the fiscal year to which the concurrent resolution applies."

The purpose of the exception was to permit tax legislation that would take effect in distant fiscal years. As far as the Senate was concerned, it was ambiguous as it applied to the fiscal year immediately after the fiscal year covered by the most recent budget resolution. No one in the Senate argued that the exception in section 303(b) applied to tax legislation effective in the coming fiscal year that reached the Senate floor between January 1 and May 15, when the first budget resolution for the coming year would be adopted. During these four and a half months, it was agreed, tax bills had to wait until the budget resolution was in place to help shape them. What if, as was the case

[23] U.S., Congress, Senate, *Congressional Record,* 95th Congress, 1st session, October 25, 1977, p. 17692.

[24] U.S., Congress, Senate, Committee on the Budget, meeting, October 25, 1977.

when the Kemp-Roth tax cut was proposed in 1978, the tax legislation went to the floor before January 1?

There was precedent both ways. No one objected in December 1975, when the House passed a major tax bill that was not to take effect until the following fiscal year, 1977. On the other hand, Abourezk objected in the Senate in October 1977 to the feature in the Finance Committee tax bill allowing for the postponement of new tax expenditures until the first day of fiscal 1979. Rather than challenge Abourezk's objection, Long merely changed the date to the last day of fiscal 1978, a year for which the second budget resolution was already in place.

When the Senate debated taxes in 1978, Roth advanced the proposal that he and Congressman Jack Kemp (Republican, New York) had been promoting: a 33 percent cut in federal income taxes, phased in over three years. The Kemp-Roth proposal included tax cuts both in fiscal 1979 (for which a budget resolution was in effect) and in fiscal 1980 and 1981 (for which there was no budget resolution). Muskie agreed that the exception provided in section 303(b) of the Budget Act, which allows tax cuts in future fiscal years, permitted the 1981 tax cut. He maintained that the 1980 tax cut was out of order because it would come in the first year for which there was no budget resolution.

Long, although he opposed Kemp-Roth on its merits, supported Roth's right to propose it. Only after January 1, 1979, when the Budget Committee would begin writing a budget resolution for fiscal 1980, would the prohibition against tax cuts in fiscal 1980 take hold, he said. "Otherwise," he said, "Senators would not be able to offer a tax cut affecting their people after the end of the budget year without the consent of the Budget Committee, unless it went into effect way up in 1981. That is a long time before it could take effect."[25]

Muskie responded that Long's interpretation of the Budget Reform Act would allow the Finance Committee to push all variety of tax legislation for fiscal 1980 through the Senate floor before January 1 without worrying about the discipline of the budget process. "I see no point in trying to protect the budget from January 1 to May 15 if, prior to that time, Congress is free to enact any tax cuts for any fiscal year that it chooses," he said.[26]

Roth pointed out that he could avoid Muskie's objection merely by making the second-year tax cut effective on September 30, 1979, instead of October 1— the tactic that Long had used the previous year to short-circuit Abourezk's objection. Roth chose to accept Muskie's

[25] U.S., Congress, Senate, *Congressional Record,* 95th Congress, 2nd session, October 5, 1978, p. 17238.

[26] Ibid., p. 17240.

challenge. The Senate parliamentarian ruled in Muskie's favor, but the Senate voted, 38–48, to overturn that ruling. (The Senate proceeded to defeat the Kemp-Roth tax cut, 36–60.)

Later in the debate of the 1978 tax bill, the Senate had to postpone the effective dates of two revenue-losing measures to avoid violating the revenue floor established by the second budget resolution for fiscal 1979. On October 6, the Senate adopted a tax credit effective the following July 1 for families who pay college tuition. The next day, Muskie reported that a recalculation of the revenue impact of the tuition tax credit showed that, even if it were in effect for only three months of fiscal 1979, it would cost more than the budget resolution allowed. The Senate passed a revised tuition tax credit that would not take effect until August 1.

Even after that revision, only $16 million remained between the revenue floor and the estimated revenue impact of the Senate's version of the tax bill. That was not enough room for a proposal of Senator Howard M. Metzenbaum (Democrat, Ohio), for a 10 percent investment tax credit for modernizing buildings. To keep his proposal from violating the revenue floor, Metzenbaum made it effective on September 1, 1979, for only one month of fiscal 1979. He could have accomplished the same result by postponing the effective date to October 1—assuming that the Senate would have voted the same exception for his proposal that it had permitted for Kemp-Roth.

After five years of experience with its new budgeting procedures, it is clear that Congress can use them when it suits its purposes and circumvent them when it does not. The exception granted for Kemp-Roth may have been justified; the legislative history is ambiguous. Even in cases in which the budget process unequivocally dictates one course of action, Congress can waive the process and follow another. When it does, however, it can act only with a clear awareness that it is circumventing what it deems to be fiscally responsible procedures. It can act only with an explicit understanding of the implications of what it is doing for the overall federal budget. That, more than the impact on any particular spending or tax decision, is the real contribution of the congressional budget process.

Commentary

William Lilley III

Both the Havemann and Fisher papers raise the fundamental issue of power. Implicitly, they start from the fundamental assumption underlying the Budget Act: that, given our separation of powers and system of checks and balances, the enormous power that the executive branch had gained through its control over the budgetary process was not appropriate for our form of government. Hence, the Budget Act and the budget process developed.

Louis Fisher's paper is one of the most impeccably researched papers about the budget process that I have read. All experts on this should review it. The bottom line in the Fisher paper is that the budget process, from the legislative side, is working extremely well. The kinds of techniques that the Carter administration has been forced to use to bewilder and bully Congress are so complicated and sophisticated that they offer testimony to how tough the congressional committees and CBO have become. For an executive, for example, to control spendout rates for different programs, he must engage in complicated kinds of subterfuges. The Fisher paper presents these executive branch techniques.

I would like to explore some of the points that Congressman Tim Wirth raised and also stress some simple-minded kinds of things often done by Professor James Barber and others who do psychopolitical profiles of individuals and the kinds of environment in which they operate. In this instance, I want to discuss how the budget process creates a kind of political environment that changes people's attitudes and then begins to change their behavior. From this perspective, the budget process gets a good report card, at least from the two years I spent there and the one year I have spent on the outside working as much with Democrats as with Republicans.

Tim Wirth was correct to focus on the extremely important, near-term changes on the House side. One of the problems on the House side has been that the House initially did not take this process as seriously as the Senate did, even though the Constitution gives much of the power over the purse to the House. That is being changed because of institutional patterns flowing from the budget process that in turn are modifying House behavior patterns on many fronts, not just fiscal ones.

The first of these—simple but important—is that the House budget process is setting the House's calendar. Speaker O'Neill goes to the Budget Committee staffs, and they plan the calendar for each session, based on what will have to be done with the budget, because the budget is the only thing that must happen in the House at certain times every year.

A New Calendar

Flowing from that innovation is not only a kind of simple calendar, which the House never had before, but also specific time frames for authorizing and appropriating and taxing measures. The calendar shows when those things have to happen to achieve rational budgeting, not just to satisfy someone's inclination that there should be subsidies for elderly bus riders in New York City, for example, because of some local transit emergency.

The budget process is forcing congressmen to make fiscal decisions with the kind of trade-off mentality that drives the executive branch and Office of Management and Budget (OMB). When we were in the executive branch, we were always irritated by senior OMB officials saying, "Well, if you want that, then you have to give up something else." We were always irritated—when justifying our budget requests before Congress—that Congress never had to face that kind of trade-off mentality. This calendar is beginning to push the authorizing and taxing committees to recognize that, if they are going to give so much to *X*, there might be less left for *Y*.

The setting of five-day voting periods for considering the two budget resolutions is becoming extremely important in terms of the politics of the House. Voting on the resolutions is becoming an increasingly important psychological and political act, which in turn is adding a new element of drama to the House and therefore elevating the budget process in the eyes of House members. This element of drama has, in turn, further modified House behavior in fiscal matters. Most important, the endless roll calls over cuts and increases for this or that function (and usually this or that discrete program) have built an element of dread into the members. Those roll calls force members to make public trade-offs and give future local opponents potentially damaging campaign ammunition.

The voting also gives the members something that makes macroeconomic fiscal policy a merit in political terms, something it never was before. Members vote for the deficit. Before the budget process, they voted only for smaller bills that spent increments of money. They now can vote for a lower deficit, or lower taxes, or less spending, and they can go back home and say, "I did that." Congress never had that before; that is an important thing psychologically for the members.

Those of us originally interested in the Budget Act wanted two things from it. We wanted a stronger legislature, and we hoped for a short-run conservative influence on the attitudes of the members of Congress. Just as the budget process is strengthening Congress, the process has had enormous conservative influences. When the process began in the House, members were reluctant to serve; the Budget Committee was considered a "second" committee. Now assignment to the committee is avidly sought by aggressive, articulate members, who see the committee as a potential power base in a coming political era, when voters expect their members to be fiscally conservative. Tim Wirth—new to the committee, able, and articulate—reflects those attitudes.

Three Serious Problems

In turning from the positive to the negative, I believe that the budget process has three relatively serious problems. Perhaps "problem" is too strong a word; perhaps "unrealized potential" would be better. The first area where there has not been sufficient congressional awareness is the area of budget authority.

When Tim Wirth was talking about entitlements, he was really talking about budget authority. Because of the hypersensitivity in the House over the current year's deficit and outlays, which in any one-year range cannot be moved that much, there is less attention paid to the future years' "bow wave" of budget authority. Accordingly, there are a lot of trade-offs in markup or conference, where people say, "Oh well, you know, we'll start the program this year, but we'll only have so many outlays, one-dollar outlays, but we'll really build in big budget authority for the next three years." The budget authority bow wave is getting steadily bigger but is still relately unnoticed.

A second and related weakness involves the failure of the committees to come up with five-year budget plans, as required by the Budget Act. The president has taken this task seriously, but the budget committees have not done so as yet.

The third, and possibly the most irritating, problem reducing the success of the process to date—and Tim Wirth has noted it—is the semantically misleading and politically damaging rhetoric about "budget cutting." Those of us in the underground budget intelligentsia—whatever our political persuasion—should try to get members to think more in terms of slowing the rates of increases in spending, rather than in terms of absolute cutting. If politicians talked in those terms, and hence alleviated interest groups' unfounded fears about absolute losses, we could save everyone problems in getting things done.

Finally, I would like to add a word about how experts in other countries see our budget process. I spent last week in Ottawa helping the new Conservative government, which is trying to graft our budget process onto their parliamentary process. I have no idea how far they will get; my real point is how highly they regarded our accomplishment—all to my amazement.

I asked the Canadians, "What do you see so good in the process? You know, for starters, our rate of inflation is 13 percent and yours is 8 percent, and there are lots of problems with this budget process." They said, "Well, maybe so, but look at what you have that we don't have. And the best way to look at it is by the fiscal state that we have gotten ourselves into. Our deficit now is $12 billion, and our outlays are only $52 billion; your deficit is in the $20 billion and your outlays are around $550 billion."

Innocently, I asked, "How did you get in that situation?" The Canadian fiscal advisor said, "Well, we have this weird system whereby the programmatic bureaucrats prepare their own budgets. They come before the cabinet, and approve each one seriatim in the cabinet. Then we ram each one through with the parliamentary majority, seriatim, all during the year at different times during the year. At the end of the year, we dust our hands off and say, 'Well, the budget for this year is *x* amount and the deficit will be *y* amount,' and we did that for every year in the Trudeau administration, and now we are in a deep hole. You Americans with your budget process have turned that completely around, at least you have the parliamentary members voting on a macroeconomic package." This is the first time in years that I have heard people seeking to emulate something we are doing.

Bruce Davie

Joel Havemann has put the right focus on the implications of the Budget Act for tax legislation; the important part is setting a floor under budget receipts. He has reviewed history over recent years and shown how that process has, indeed, worked.

There are some additional ways in which the budget process has affected tax legislation. That is not the legislation that one sees; it is the legislation that one does not see. The members of the tax-writing committees have become more disciplined than they were a few years ago in what items they will put on their agenda for serious consideration.

There are fewer so-called member's bills of special interest that might have affected receipts in only a small way.

There was the interesting example, in spring 1979, of the Ways and Means Committee reacting to the administration's proposal for real wage insurance. Here was a new tax expenditure designed to create an incentive for compliance with wage and price guidelines. The committee looked at that, looked askance, and looked for a way out. It found it through the budget process by discovering that it could not include that item in the March 15 recommendation to the Budget Committee. The committee had a way of giving a nice, decent burial to a proposal that, had it been considered on its legislative merits, would have resulted in a great deal of acrimonious debate among the committee members and with the administration.

In setting the tax-writing committees' agendas, particularly on the House side, it is much easier with the budget resolution for the chairman to tell a member of the committee or a member of the House, "Yes, indeed, that is an interesting proposal; we might want to look at it some day, but, under the terms of the budget resolution, we cannot take it up this year." It is a nice excuse for not considering a wide range of proposals.

There is an additional example, not mentioned in the paper, of the way in which setting the floor under budget receipts affects tax legislation. This happened a year ago when the final version of the Revenue Act of 1978 was before the conference committee in that famous all-night session.

While that conference was in session, there was another conference going on, regarding the tax treatment of Americans working abroad. Had it not been for the constraint of the budget resolution, those conferees would have adopted a much more generous proposal than, in fact, they did. What constrained their appetites and forced a consensus around a particular proposal was identifying a specific amount of money and saying that was all that will fit into the budget resolution, now go to conference, and return with something that will fit.

Joel Havemann's paper brought out an interesting question of timing. Members will try to postpone the effective dates of tax measures that would erode receipts, in order to avoid violating the terms of the budget resolution. This timing problem works the other way, too. It tends to undervalue reform provisions that may have a small effect on budget receipts this year but a large effect in the future. This is certainly happening at the moment with the carryover basis repeal controversy. If the carryover basis provision is repealed, it can easily fit into the budget resolution because the impact is small on budget receipts for the coming fiscal year, even though it has more significant effects on receipts in the outyears.

Tax Expenditures

Another aspect of the Budget Act was designed to have an effect on tax legislation; this has had a rather minimal effect. This is the set of provisions in the budget act dealing with tax expenditures.

Several of the authors of that act seemed to have been looking forward to a day when the level of tax expenditures would be specified by functional category in the budget resolution, as outlays are. There has not been any movement in that direction for several fundamental reasons. The conceptual foundation underlying the tax expenditure notion seems to be quietly eroding. The concept was formed with the norm of a pure income tax in mind. Any deviation from this normative income tax was identified as a tax expenditure.

On closer analysis, it appears that many controversial items in the tax code do not fall under the rubric of a tax expenditure. In determining what is taxable income, for example, the Internal Revenue Service must deal with the problem of fringe benefits. The IRS attempted, a few years ago, to take a stronger line in the identification of fringe benefits that should be treated as taxable income. Congress said, "No, you should postpone those regulations until we legislatively deal with the issue." Congress has not done that yet. One can look down the list of tax expenditure items and never see an item for the failure to include fringe benefits in taxable income. The tax expenditure concept merely accepts whatever line is drawn by the Internal Revenue Service between nontaxable and taxable fringe benefits.

A similar argument can be made with respect to independent contractors. There is no tax expenditure item for the failure to treat as employees individuals who declare themselves to be independent contractors, who ought to be treated as employees for tax purposes.

Another item referred to in this paper is the foreign tax credit for the international oil companies. The House Budget Committee did address this item in 1979 and indicate that some money should be raised in that area of the code, but that is not a tax expenditure item. The basic concept of tax expenditures accepts the notion that tax credits should be given for foreign income taxes paid and ignores the critically important question of what specific foreign taxes will be creditable.

The conceptual foundation is also eroding because the old consensus notion of tax reform has broken down. The old consensus was that tax reform means broadening the income tax base so that income tax rates can be reduced.

There is a great deal of academic interest these days in progressive expenditure tax. Many tax code provisions that are categorized as tax expenditures under our current set of definitions would be part and parcel of an expenditure tax.

More important than this erosion of the conceptual foundation behind tax expenditures is the desire, at both ends of Pennsylvania Avenue, to use the tax code for a growing variety of nonrevenue purposes. Look through the current list of tax expenditures and put a plus sign behind those that have been either added or substantially expanded since the Budget Act was enacted. My count of pluses equaled twenty-one. Put a minus sign behind those that were either repealed or substantially reduced. I count four minus signs. We have introduced a whole range of new tax expenditures in the energy area; it looks like we may introduce some more before the year is out. A number of items were substantially expanded when the treatment of capital gains was liberalized in the Revenue Act of 1978.

On the other side of the coin, let me give an example of the way in which the tax expenditure provisions of the Budget Act have been helpful. For several years, the tax expenditure listing carried a single item for the revenue loss associated with tax-exempt state and local government bonds. A few years ago, it was broken into two separate categories: tax-exempt bonds for general purposes and another category for industrial revenue bonds. A specific item for tax-exempt bonds to support housing has recently been added.

In this year's budget, the administration indicated that it would make a proposal for restricting the use of tax-exempt bonds to finance owner-occupied housing and included a rough estimate of the effect of such a proposal on receipts. When the Ways and Means Committee did take up that issue, the fact that a specific item for tax-exempt housing bonds had been specifically identified in the list of tax expenditures permitted the Budget Committee to include a revenue pickup from restrictions on that use of tax-exempt bonds as they developed their floor for receipts in this year's budget resolution.

While some of the conceptual foundations behind the tax expenditure provisions in the Budget Act have eroded, there is still some utility in those provisions.

Summary of Discussion

Robert Hartman asked whether Mr. Havemann thought that it was practical for the budget process to specify targets for various categories of tax receipts just as it now does for individual spending functions. Mr. Havemann replied that it might serve some purpose in developing longer-run strategies, but taxes were often less flexible than spending in the short run. For example, any change in social security payroll taxes must be made effective January 1.

Stephen Entin noted that the budget process deals with tax receipts and not with tax rates. The relationship between these depends on the economic response to tax rate changes. While Congress is getting more interested in this issue, there is little consensus on the importance of "reflows." This problem makes it difficult to apply the budget process to tax policy.

Mr. Entin also said that he did not share Mr. Davies's concern about the inability of the process to alter tax expenditures. He felt that the special tax incentives in the law may, given the disincentives inherent in regular tax rates, be essential in bringing forth savings and investment.

Rudolph Penner noted that one should carefully differentiate complaints about the results of the budget process from complaints about the process itself. He also asked whether Mr. Fisher believed that President Ford overloaded and therefore damaged the budget process by requesting a very large number of deferrals and rescissions. Mr. Fisher replied that the deferrals and rescissions imposed an enormous load on OMB staff who might otherwise have been able to use their time for more productive work, but that the 1975 Ford request for dollar-for-dollar cuts in spending and taxes was much more damaging to the budget process in that it completely ignored the schedule set down by the Budget Act.

Mrs. Olsen wanted it to be clear that she was not enthusiastic about either the process or its results and that the conference discussion had generally been too favorable toward the process. Although people will judge the results by their own values, inflation and the tax burden have risen since the process was installed and it has not worked well even according to Keynesian criteria. For example, as fiscal 1979 evolved, unemployment turned out to be about what was anticipated in the second resolution, but inflation was higher. Yet the second resolution was eventually revised to allow more spending, even though less spending was clearly called for in the new economic circumstances.

Mr. Lilley noted that two points could be made in favor of the process. First, many believed that the executive branch became too powerful in the early 1970s and the budget process has been a factor in restoring the relative power of the Congress. Second, though it is hard to argue that the process has slowed spending growth—except by making the very weak argument that things would have been even worse without it—the Congress has become more conservative, especially those Democratic members who were elected from suburban districts in 1974. The budget process—though it has produced much subterfuge—has played an educational role by forcing votes on aggregate spending, receipts, and deficits. It may thus have made Congress more aware of conservative views and this may have important policy implications in the future.

Mrs. Olsen replied that this reverses the true causality. The voters swung right and forced members of Congress to move in the same direction. Mr. Lilley responded that, in either case, the budget process is a new institutional mechanism which can be used to implement policies reflecting changing attitudes.

Edward Clarke of OMB noted the lack of any mention of the executive budget process during the conference. Was this because the Congress was increasing its power over the budget and the executive branch was playing a less important role?

Mr. Fisher felt that the immense amount of paperwork required by the process was preventing the staff of both the executive branch and the Congress from doing the kind of thoughtful analysis necessary for the development of sensible budget policies.

Mr. Hartman said that there was an important role for the executive branch. The Congress is not organized in a way that facilitates instituting broad budgetary strategies. The Congress can only react to themes created by the executive branch. Admittedly recent presidential budgets have lacked any theme, with the possible exception of President Ford's last lameduck budget, but that does not mean that a theme cannot be developed that suggests a coherent strategy for the long run.

A NOTE ON THE BOOK

The typeface used for the text of this book is
Times-Roman, designed by Stanley Morison.
The type was set by
FotoTypesetters Incorporated, of Baltimore.
Braun-Brumfield, Inc., of Ann Arbor, Michigan
printed and bound the book, using paper manufactured
by the S.D. Warren Company.
The cover and format were designed by Pat Taylor,
and the figures were drawn by Hördur Karlsson.
The manuscript was edited by Ann Petty and
by Anne Gurian, of the AEI Publications staff.

SELECTED AEI PUBLICATIONS

The AEI Economist, Herbert Stein, ed., published monthly (one year, $10; single copy, $1)

Food and Agricultural Policy for the 1980s, D. Gale Johnson, ed. (229 pp., paper $7.25, cloth $15.25)

Health and Air Quality: Evaluating the Effects of Policy, Philip E. Graves and Ronald J. Krumm (156 pp., paper $6.25, cloth $14.25)

The Consumer Price Index: Issues and Alternatives, Phillip Cagan and Geoffrey H. Moore (69 pp., $4.25)

The Economy: Is This a Change in Direction? John Charles Daly, mod. (31 pp., $3.75)

Reforming the Income Tax System, William E. Simon (53 pp., $4.25)

The Economics of Legal Minimum Wages, Simon Rottenberg, ed. (534 pp., paper $10.25, cloth $18.25)

Minimum Wages and On-the-Job Training, Masanori Hashimoto (72 pp., $4.25)

The Federal Income Tax Burden on Households: The Effects of Tax Law Changes, Attiat F. Ott and Ludwig O. Dittrich (43 pp., $3.25)

Prices subject to change without notice.

AEI ASSOCIATES PROGRAM

The American Enterprise Institute invites your participation in the competition of ideas through its AEI Associates Program. This program has two objectives:

The first is to broaden the distribution of AEI studies, conferences, forums, and reviews, and thereby to extend public familiarity with the issues. AEI Associates receive regular information on AEI research and programs, and they can order publications and cassettes at a savings.

The second objective is to increase the research activity of the American Enterprise Institute and the dissemination of its published materials to policy makers, the academic community, journalists, and others who help shape public attitudes. Your contribution, which in most cases is partly tax deductible, will help ensure that decision makers have the benefit of scholarly research on the practical options to be considered before programs are formulated. The issues studied by AEI include:

- Defense Policy
- Economic Policy
- Energy Policy
- Foreign Policy
- Government Regulation
- Health Policy
- Legal Policy
- Political and Social Processes
- Social Security and Retirement Policy
- Tax Policy

For more information, write to:

AMERICAN ENTERPRISE INSTITUTE
1150 Seventeenth Street, N.W.
Washington, D.C. 20036